The New SBC

Fundamentalism's Impact on the Southern Baptist Convention

Grady C. Cothen

Smyth & Helwys Publishing, Inc.®
Macon, Georgia

ISBN 1-57312-025-1

The New SBC
Fundamentalism's Impact on the Southern Baptist Convention

Grady C. Cothen

Copyright © 1995
Smyth & Helwys Publishing, Inc.®
6316 Peake Road
Macon, Georgia 31210-3960
1-800-568-1248

All royalties from this book will be contributed to Baptist causes.

Library of Congress Cataloging-in-Publication Data

Cothen, Grady C.
    The New SBC: fundamentalism's impact on the Southern Baptist
    Convention / Grady C. Cothen
    vi + 226 pp.   6" x 9" (15 x 23 cm.)
    Sequel to: What happened to the Southern Baptist Convention, 1993.
    Includes bibliographical references.
    ISBN 1-5731-025-1   (alk. paper)
    1. Southern Baptist Convention—History—20th century.
    2. Baptists—United States—History—20th century.
    3. Fundamentalism—History. 4. Cothen, Grady C. I. Title.
    BX6462.3.C66   1995
    286'.132—dc20   95-2441
                                                              CIP

Contents

Preface

In one sense, this book is a sequel to *What Happened to the Southern Baptist Convention?* It is a continuing look at one of the century's greatest religious upheavals. In this volume, I discuss the nature of the aberration called fundamentalism and how it has changed the nature of the denomination. I examine some events, but more importantly give a critique of their results over the last sixteen years.

This book contains some limited reiteration of material I used earlier so as to properly contextualize passages and for the benefit of those who did not read the former volume. It is a personal witness account of the revolution. The limitations of perspective are mine and, generally, the evaluations are mine. The staggering losses in fellowship, commitment, cooperation, and brotherhood belong to all persons who were touched by the tragedy.

I have attempted to eliminate the anger and frustration that many of us have felt, although I fear that I have not succeeded to the degree I would have wished. If any person or event has been misrepresented, I apologize in advance. My purpose has been to tell what has happened to the Southern Baptist Convention and how it has appeared to me.

The incidents used in this book are not intended to "prove" anything but to illustrate the impact of fundamentalism. I have not tried to use the methodology of the historian. Rather, I have used materials that will give the reader an understanding of result as much as cause.

My thanks to Bettye for her patience and constant support and to the staff of Smyth & Helwys for its encouragement and assistance in the preparation of this work.

To
Don, Nicole, and DC III
Anne and Ronnie, Katy and Jacob
Elizabeth
Will
Matt and Cristy
Steve
Andy
Ralph and Debbie
Grady and Debbie, Kirsten and Kathleen

Introduction

A Sketch of the Problem

When Christian fundamentalists took a hard look at the world of the 1960s and 1970s, there was substantial cause for concern. The society was in turmoil with virulent pluralism. The moral and ethical convictions of the biblically oriented were under violent assault. While this opposition had always been present to a degree, it had now assumed proportions that were not only unmanageable but menaced a whole way of life.

The frightening onslaught was particularly threatening to conservative Bible-believers. The biblical principles of morality were not only neglected by a large proportion of society, but were being laughed out of court. The sexual revolution, rapid change in the nature of the family, lack of respect for law and order, malfeasance in public office, and sometimes violent citizen response to ills real or imagined were enough to give pause to anyone.

The school systems had been used as instruments of social adjustment, and serious problems were exacerbated. The Protestant control was lost, and many of society's problems invaded the classrooms. Various forms of naturalism were emphasized in opposition to creationism. Interest in the organized church declined following the historic highs of the 1950s. Generally, both conservative and fundamentalist Christians were concerned for themselves and the future of the society.

In trying to determine the causes of the problems and sources of blame, grave errors were easy. The "perpetrators" of this opposition to the Christian understanding inevitably and conveniently were seen as enemies. Any ordered Christian response would have required a proper attitude, method, and carefully designed course of conduct. Some appropriate questions would have been: What does the church do about its enemies? What does the Bible say about this kind of situation? What is the place of the individual in corporate Christian response? What does history teach us about the conflict between the world and the church? Does the Holy Spirit still guide the body of Christ? Do ancient biblical principles apply to modern problems? What methods can the church use and yet remain Christian? What attitudes should control the dialogue?

A new form of fundamentalism began to prosper. The 1920s definition of fundamentalists as "a people preoccupied with the salvation of
souls through Jesus Christ"[1] was only a part of the new understanding of
the disciples of the old-time religion. The study of the present forms of
fundamentalism seems to dictate that we have a "Gestalt" phenomenon.
The Gestalt (a German word that can be translated "configuration") psy-
chologists developed the idea that human consciousness is greater than
the sum of the parts of the brain, or a mass firing of neutrons.[2] These
researchers believed that the perceptions of the human mind were determined by context, configuration, and meaning rather than the simple
accumulation of sensory elements. Certainly the present configuration of
fundamentalism is more than a simple reaction to an accumulation of elements of the current predicament of society.

Fundamentalism as now expressed is enlarged and configured by a
context as big as the "culture war." In the Christian church and civil society, the movement has taken on crusades and tasks not formerly a part
of its concerns. As a part of a much larger set of causes, it has been
molded by forces and influences outside the usual pursuits of evangelical
Christians. It has created in the American society an atmosphere, an attitude, a climate in which "permission" is given to protectors of the faith
to think, say, and do anything necessary to achieve whatever goal is seen
as desirable.

In other words, this new brand of fundamentalism has taken on a
character all its own. Among Southern Baptists, there is now room in the
Christian psyche for many activities other than the traditional and biblical, for example: the old biblical theology, organizing the church for
political activism, a new ecumenism that includes former enemies and
excludes former colleagues whose sin is dissent, and "new age" appurtenances that were formerly rejected.

New styles of worship are common, and entertainment in worship is
prominent. The wisdom of the Baptist heritage is now sacrificed on the
altar of modern experience. The business of the denominational body is

---

[1]George Marsden, *Fundamentalism and American Culture* (New York: Oxford University Press, 1980) 3.

[2]For further information see the work of Kurt Koffka, Wolfgang Kohler, and Max
Wertheimer.

now often decided in closed meetings of both caucuses and business sessions. Former participants in all of the affairs of the denomination are excluded from participation because they exercise their freedom to give to good causes as their consciences dictate. Reasons for actions to inform the constituency are no longer necessary. Those who do not agree with the leadership can be excluded. Use of political power for religious purposes is permitted.

Present-day fundamentalism is more than the sum of its parts and the cadre of its leaders. For Southern Baptists, it is an aberration that has taken on a character, an atmosphere, a mindset, and method of operation that is at home in the milieu of this generation. The objective of the group and its guiding philosophy is control. The method is power and coercion. The spirit is critical and censorious of all who disagree. The attitude toward other Christians is disdain and judgment. The ethic is established by vote of the majority. The mantra is inerrancy and anti-abortion. The consuming passion is domination. In short, the movement now has room for all kinds of causes and people except those who disagree with the leadership.

The movement among Southern Baptists claimed that it began its organized crusade because of departure by some leaders from biblical truth. This was a faith issue that was transformed into an endless stream of "believe about" issues that are foreign to Baptist polity. As a result, the emphasis on a vital personal relationship to Christ has shifted to intellectual assent to a body of theological and social propositions and acceptable actions.

With great emphasis on the nature of scripture, modern fundamentalism ignores many of its teachings. For example, SBC leaders feel the necessity for separating the "sheep from the goats." On one occasion, the disciples sought to do precisely that by stopping a man who was driving out demons. Jesus said:

> Do not stop him; no one who does a miracle in my name can in the next moment say anything bad about me, for whoever is not against us is for us. (Mark 9:39, 40 NIV)

These self-chosen ones feel that they have the right to reward the sheep, punish the goats, and determine which is which. This radical departure from the Baptist way is felt to be their responsibility, right, and privilege. To press the point a bit further, modern fundamentalism has adopted the methodology of the world it professes to hate. It is now far more than simple resistance to modernism. It has generated and unleashed all sorts of demons. Animosity and hatred loom large.

Out of the pain and struggle of the denominational conflict and my years of study of it, I recall the words of Thomas Merton:

> It is the rankling, tormenting sense of unworthiness that lies at the root of all hate. The man who is able to hate strongly and with a quiet conscience is one who is complacently blind to all unworthiness in himself and serenely capable of seeing all his own wrongs in someone else. But the man who is aware of his own unworthiness and the unworthiness of his brother is tempted with a subtler and more tormenting kind of hate: the general, searing, nauseating hate of everything and everyone, because everything is tainted with unworthiness, everything is unclean, everything is foul with sin. . . . He who loves feels unworthy, and at the same time feels that somehow no one is worthy. . . .[3]
>
> In our refusal to accept the partially good intentions of others and work with them (of course prudently and with resignation to the inevitable imperfection of the result), we are unconsciously proclaiming our own malice, our own intolerance, our own lack of realism, our own ethical and political quackery.[4]

I have been unable to turn loose of this unholy conflict. It has involved my own identity and my perhaps extremism in loving a group of people and admiring a truly unique organization devised to achieve what was conceived to be God's purposes. In retrospect, life would have been far easier and the nights not so long and dark if—like so many others—I had not gotten involved. To follow that course would have meant avoiding the defining event in the history of that which I served and loved. So, for better or worse, this volume is a last look at the anatomy of one expression of religious fundamentalism.

---

[3]Thomas P. McDonnell, ed., *New Seeds of Contemplation, A Thomas Merton Reader* (New York: Image Books, 1989) 321.

[4]Ibid., 278.

Chapter 1

Overwhelmed by Ideology and Religion

When James Draper was elected president of the Southern Baptist Convention (SBC) in June 1982, I was president of the Baptist Sunday School Board. He gave an address to the August meeting of the trustees of that institution. Before the dinner, he said to me, "You and I are usually on the same side of the fence." He was speaking of the fact that he and I did not agree on what was happening in the convention. We had been friends, and he had invited me to speak to the national pastor's conference two years before. We had never had any disagreements or theological arguments. Now we were on "different sides of the fence."

I could not refrain from replying, "Jimmy, what is the fence?" He did not answer, and the fence is still there. My theology had not taken a bend toward the left. I was still the same person with essentially the same convictions and attitudes that had developed over the years. My theology was conservative, and so was his. The fence was a point of view and an attitude, a mindset.

Draper had just been elected by people who believed that they had the correct theology and any variance from their norm was unacceptable. They had a different understanding of polity. Further, they were convinced that all incumbents in national offices should give way to their choices. They believed their viewpoint must prevail and that to differ from it placed the dissenter on the wrong side of the fence. No labor was too strenuous, no goal too far, and no price too high. The manifest intent was to take control of the SBC. Organized fundamentalism had come to the Southern Baptist Convention.

The Meaning of Fundamentalism

The generally accepted definition of fundamentalists in the 1920s was, as George Marsden expressed it, "People professing complete confidence in the Bible and preoccupied with the message of God's salvation of sinners through the death of Jesus Christ."[1] According to this definition, most Southern Baptists would qualify.

The SBC was not preoccupied with salvation through Jesus Christ, however. In fact, the new orthodoxy often seemed to deny the teachings of the gentle Lord. The Southern Baptist brand of the old fundamentalism included a great deal more than conservative theology. All the virulent strains of fundamentalism that had plagued other bodies were included, and some new ones were added.

In discussing the modern outbreak of fundamentalism, George Marsden noted several troublesome features:

- depicts advocates as a faithful remnant
- persistent militance
- inerrancy of scripture an important battlefield
- bitter attacks on modernism (called "secular humanism")
- involvement in partisan politics abandoning strict separatism
- renewal of the idea of a "Christian America"
- opposition to biological evolution
- attacks on the public school system
- opposition to the women's movement and abortion
- the gospel of personal success.[2]

Edward Carnell, a former fundamentalist, acknowledged these traits:

- expects conformity
- highly ideological
- dismisses non-fundamentalist efforts as empty, futile, and apostate
- distinctiveness from its attempt to maintain status by negation
- a religious attitude rather than a religious movement
- intransigent, inflexible, and demands conformity
- fears academic (and religious) liberty.[3]

---

[1]*Fundamentalism and American Culture*, 3.
[2]*Fundamentalism and American Culture.*
[3]*A Handbook of Christian Theology* (New York: Meridian Books, n.d.)

Albert McClellan added that fundamentalism is a temperament that includes negativism, exclusiveness, and criticism of those who differ. "Fundamentalism's chief characteristics are legalism, exclusiveness, rancor, arrogance, and pride."[4]

My friend Draper wrote some years before: "The fundamentalist tactic is simple: hatred, bitterness, and condemnation of all whom they despise."[5] He characterized fundamentalism as doing everything in the name of the Lord, condemning all who disagree, and proclaiming to have a corner on the truth. It is a divisive spirit and is unfair.

In *What Happened to the Southern Baptist Convention?* I listed some of the distinctives of the Southern Baptist brand of fundamentalism. They still seem to characterize the movement:

- doctrinal rigidity
- religious exclusiveness
- militant attitude
- defense of the faith posture
- negativism
- legalism
- literalism in interpreting scripture
- ideological
- authoritarianism
- inerrancy
- overtly political
- premillenial.[6]

The preceeding descriptions are suggestive but not exhaustive concerning the nature of what has become a religious "cause" in the Southern Baptist Convention. These attributes had appeared in individuals in our denomination from time to time, but there had never been an organized effort to control it with these attitudes. Certainly not all persons who support this cause have these characteristics. Thus, I am not

---

[4]"Theses Concerning the Great SBC Takeover Controversy of the 1980s, a Traditional Baptist View" (1991) 2.

[5]James T. Draper, Jr. *The Church Christ Approves* (Nashville: Broadman, 1973).

[6](Macon GA: Smyth & Helwys, 1993) 92-93.

describing individuals as much I am the movement, the cause, and the aberration.

Fundamentalism and the SBC

The controlling mindset of the SBC for the last fifteen years has produced a remarkable and disturbing set of actions and pronouncements surrounding secular politics as well as denominational agencies, institutions, and organizations. In very recent years, the indictments often have been aimed against the Cooperative Baptist Fellowship (CBF) and its supporters. A random and non-inclusive set of illustrations taken from 1993–1994 alone will be helpful in understanding fundamentalism and its impact on the public.

Secular Politics

—At the 1993 meeting of the Southern Baptist Convention, a motion was made to expel the Immanuel Baptist Church in Little Rock, Arkansas, because it did not censure its most prominent member: President Bill Clinton. The motion did not pass but invaded new territory. It was unheard of for a democratic body to attempt to censure a church for the conduct of an individual member. In the same meeting about twenty anti-Clinton resolutions were introduced. The measure that denounced his stand on abortion and homosexuality passed. [7]

Foreign Mission Board

—After a major shakeup in the administration and the resignation of his supervisor, Tom Warrington, associate area director for Europe, was abruptly fired. His new supervisor, recently hired from a non-denominational seminary, denied that the move was political. Other highly-placed officers said Warrington was singled out for his close association with his

---

[7]Associated Baptist Press, 24 June 1993.

former supervisor. Another administrator said that the firing was "strictly a power play."[8]

—Because the board was unhappy about Keith Parks' working for the Cooperative Baptist Fellowship, it reversed a decision to dedicate its new history to Parks and his wife, Helen Jean. Instead, the board dedicated the book to the ten men who had served as board president over 150 years.[9]

—The board asked the trustee chairman to "investigate reports that Woman's Missionary Union is promoting a (Cooperative Baptist) Fellowship book on missions."[10]

Home Mission Board

—The board employed a new female missionary but refused to appoint her husband because he was a member of the coordinating council of the Cooperative Baptist Fellowship. The board violated its own policy since it requires that both the missionary and his/her spouse be appointed.[11]

—The assistant director of the Interfaith Witness Department, Gary Leazer, was fired after he made a speech to a regional Masonic convention. He had led a study of Freemasonry that drew the ire of Texas physician Larry Holly. Holly had demanded that such a study be made, and it was ordered by the SBC. Holly did not like the study nor the speech that Leazer made to the Masons.[12] (Incidentally, Holly was also a leader in the Sunday School Board's forced retirement of its president, Lloyd Elder.)

Seminaries

—**Southeastern.** At its display booth at the 1993 Southern Baptist Convention, a paper by President Paige Patterson was distributed that outlined what he considered to be the differences between orthodox, neo-

---

[8]Ibid., 25 June 1993.
[9]Baptist Press, 11 February 1994.
[10]Associated Baptist Press, 11 November 1994.
[11]Baptist Press, 14 October 1993.
[12]Ibid., 26 October 1993.

orthodox, and liberal Christian beliefs. The paper labeled several prominent Baptist leaders as "neo-orthodox (really neo-liberalism)."[13]

He included in this category Roy Honeycutt, then president of Southern Seminary; Glenn Hinson, a long-time professor at Southern; Russell
Dilday, president of Southwestern Seminary; Cecil Sherman, coordinator
of the Cooperative Baptist Fellowship; Randall Lolley, former president
of Southeastern Seminary; Milton Ferguson, president of Midwestern
Seminary; and "most Baptist state paper editors."

He listed Baylor University, Gardner-Webb University, Cumberland
College, Carson-Newman College, and Midwestern Seminary as advocating the views of the "neo-orthodox (really neo-liberalism)." An uproar
ensued, and Patterson immediately said that the paper's distribution was
unauthorized and intended for classroom use only!

—**Southern.** The trustees moved to encourage the faculty to support the
Cooperative Program and to "encourage those churches of which they are
a member to focus their giving through the Cooperative Program." Previously, some trustees had expressed their concern regarding faculty
members who held membership in churches that channeled some of their
missions giving through the Cooperative Baptist Fellowship.[14] The action
was not binding on the faculty, but there are widespread rumors that the
faculty members are no longer permitted to hold membership in churches
that cooperate with the CBF.

—**Southwestern.** The trustees were interested in whether the proposed
recipients of the B. H. Carroll Award were involved with the Cooperative
Baptist Fellowship. The award had been voted for conspicuous service to
the seminary by C. J. and Ophelia Humphrey. A motion was made to rescind the award pending an investigation. After discussion during a two-
day meeting, the motion was withdrawn.[15] The hurt and confusion could
not be withdrawn, however.

In the same meeting, the trustees considered a motion from the last
meeting of the SBC. It asked that "alumni associations of our seminaries
which have exhibited at the Cooperative Baptist Fellowship gatherings be
discouraged from doing so." The motion asked that Cooperative Program

---

[13]Ibid., 29 June 1993.
[14]Ibid., 15 October 1993.
[15]Ibid.

funds be withheld from seminaries whose alumni associations continue to exhibit at the CBF.[16]

In considering this instruction labeled "alumni associations . . . be discouraged," a trustee made a motion that gives the reaction of many fundamentalists to fellow Christians who disagree with the party line. It said in part,

> The CBF exists for the purpose of maliciously creating a chilling and adversarial relationship within the Southern Baptist Convention for the purpose of depriving the SBC of the needed funds to finance the Cooperative Program missionary endeavors.[17]

His substitute motion was tabled pending a study committee report.

In other actions, the trustees postponed the election of a dean for the school of music after questions were raised about his membership in Broadway Baptist Church, a Fort Worth congregation that supports the Fellowship.[18]

The editor of the *Biblical Recorder* of North Carolina, R. G. Puckett, expressed the sentiments of many Southern Baptists at their dismay over the firing of Southwestern president Russell Dilday. In an editorial he titled, "Have We Reached the Pits?" he expressed concern over the "brutal and vicious" action of the trustees. Puckett said,

> The time is long past that millions of good and decent, Bible-believing, God-fearing, Southern Baptist Christians should rise up in outrage against the ruthless and wanton destruction wrought by the fundamentalist horde which has descended upon the Southern Baptist Convention. God will not hold us guiltless any longer.[19]

---

[16]Ibid.
[17]Ibid.
[18]Associated Baptist Press, as reported in *Baptists Today*, 11 November 1993, 5.
[19]4 February 1994.

State Conventions and Local Associations

—**California.** The messengers at the convention refused to seat representatives from a San Francisco church that had a woman pastor. Later, the executive board refused to return the church's mission contributions.[20]

—**Kentucky.** When Keith Parks retired from the Foreign Mission Board and went to work for the Cooperative Baptist Fellowship, Long Run Baptist Association in Louisville rescinded its invitation to him to speak at its annual meeting. (He received numerous other cancellations, as well.)[21]

Fundamentalists overturned a previous action that would have funded the Baptist Joint Committee, an organization largely founded by the SBC and that it supported for half a century.[22]

The South District Association split when the Lexington Avenue church in Danville ordained a woman as deacon. Subsequently, a woman was ordained to the ministry. It appeared that as many as eleven churches would withdraw over the action.[23]

—**Mississippi.** Guy Henderson, editor of the *Baptist Record*, protested outside interference with Mississippi Baptist business. The politically active chairman of the SBC executive committee, Fred Wolfe of Alabama, called a Mississippi pastor asking him to nominate a certain pastor for president of the Mississippi convention. Henderson said,

> For a decade he has called pastor search committees in Mississippi with recommendations. These pastors usually were in the fundamental-conservative camp. Wolfe maintains he only does this when requested and there is no political nor ulterior motive. . . . Other big name pastors have joined Fred until Mississippi search committees are recipients of many such recommendations. It is as if the Holy Spirit's leadership must come through Mobile, Memphis, or Nashville.[24]

—**North Carolina.** An effort to reduce funding for the state paper, the *Biblical Recorder*, was defeated.[25]

---

[20]Baptist Press, 2 February 1994.
[21]Baptist Press.
[22]Ibid., 22 November 1993.
[23]Associated Baptist Press, 21 September 1993.
[24]14 October 1993.
[25]Baptist Press, 22 November 1993.

First Baptist Church of West Jefferson was expelled from the Ashe Baptist Association for ordaining a woman as deacon.[26]

—**Ohio.** The Cincinnati Baptist Association requested that Mount Carmel Baptist Church report to the association its reasons for electing a woman as deacon.[27]

—**Oklahoma.** During the meeting of the Baptist General Convention, the president took dead aim at the CBF. He said in part,

> I feel like I've been the victim of a drive-by shooting. My heart breaks that there are those who are Southern Baptists that would seek to do missions in a way other than the Cooperative Program. . . . (The CBF issue) is like a lighted stick of dynamite thrown on our doorstep. . . . . (The Cooperative Baptist Fellowship) is not cooperative, it's uncooperative. . . . It's not Baptist, at least it's not Southern Baptist. . . . It is not a fellowship, but a division. . . . It seems to me that the Cooperative Baptist Fellowship would be more accurately named the Uncooperative Non-Southern Baptist Division.[28]

With only a few negative votes, the Oklahoma convention passed a motion targeting a key CBF supporter, Joe Ingram, the convention's retired executive director. The motion called for the president and four other men to meet with Ingram, who later told the newspaper reporters he would not meet with them. A few months later, Ingram died. One source close to him said that he was deeply wounded by the convention's action.[29]

—**Texas.** Efforts were defeated to defund Baylor University and the state contributions to the Baptist Joint Committee.[30]

O. S. Hawkins, the new pastor of First Baptist Church in Dallas, called for a comparative examination of the theology of the SBC and the Cooperative Baptist Fellowship leadership and "then let our individual churches choose this day with whom they will serve." He did not call for a comparison of their mission gifts, however![31]

---

[26]*Baptists Today*, 17 February 1994, 11.

[27]Ibid.

[28]Baptist Press, 22 November 1993.

[29]Ibid.

[30]Ibid.

[31]Ibid., 15 April 1994.

SBC Committees

—After attending the spring meeting of the executive committee, Guy Henderson commented in the *Baptist Record* that the committee had "slapped the hands" of the Annuity Board and decided to study whether to allow agencies to accept money from Cooperative Baptist Fellowship churches. He wrote,

> The penalty flag was thrown on the Baptist World Alliance for inviting Keith Parks, former Foreign Mission Board leader, to address a BWA-sponsored conference in Cyprus, and the motion was made to deduct $20,000 from BWA budget allocation as a protest. Never mind the autonomy of other Baptist bodies, nor that the convention and pastors conference have invited former President Bush and Jerry Falwell in the past. Keith Parks is as sound biblically as any Southern Baptist. Gratefully, the motion was defeated, but even in defeat it cast a long shadow.[32]

—Joe Atchison, who chaired the 1993 committee on nominations, confessed what had long been charged by moderates. Baptist Press quoted him as saying,

> Biblical beliefs and commitment to the SBC were two key factors the committee used (in naming trustees). . . . And we did not feel that those who support the CBF should serve on a board.[33]

(Curiously, the people who promoted this idea had led their churches to participate in non-denominational mission giving for years. Various ones of them had supported Mid-America Seminary, a privately owned and operated institution, from its inception. One of the chiefs of the fundamentalist movement had started a non-denominational mission effort in Mexico. At least two of the movement's SBC presidents supported non-denominational mission efforts of various kinds. The leadership

---

[32]3 March 1994.
[33]Reported in *Baptists Today*.

publicly endorsed and promoted a private psychiatric therapy company. In addition, there are publicly promoted luncheons annually at the SBC.

These independent activities were not unusual in Baptist life since every Baptist was considered a priest with the right to determine his/her own spiritual decisions. Every church is considered independent and autonomous, thus not subject to any ecclesiastical control. (All of these activities were kosher until the CBF was organized to do a similar thing.)

*****

This litany of authoritarianism and exclusivism is cited to give the reader something of the impact the controversy has had on the public for years. Like popcorn jumping in every direction, incidents that are un-baptistic and unscriptural have sprung up around the Baptist world.

Fundamentalist leaders did not cause nor sanction all of these actions or opinions. They are too politically shrewd to air some of these incidents. Yet they have created an atmosphere, attitude, and climate that nourishes authoritarianism and exclusiveness instead of fellowship. Their mindset of judgment and criticism has loosed all the "loose cannons" that fire at will at anything they do not like.

Fundamentalism as a Religion

For fifteen years the fundamentalists have insisted that the SBC controversy has been theological, whereas the moderates have contended it has a political nature. It is undoubtedly both, as I have noted elsewhere. The movement is not about biblical theology, but now is at the point of preserving and promoting the values of fundamentalism. As we shall see, these are attitudes and strictures that go beyond biblical theology and in a number of issues run counter to that standard.

In his provocative and controversial book *Why People Do Bad Things in the Name of Religion*, Richard E. Wentz describes the characteristics of a religion:

> We express our religiousness in ideas, in beliefs or values. The soul cannot celebrate alone. . . . Therefore, in addition to ideas and beliefs, our religiousness expresses itself in actions, in practices. . . . We are related to other persons and places. . . . Our religiousness expresses

itself socially as well as in ritual, special practices, or in stories and teachings. . . . When all *three* expressions of our religiousness are present in some coherent fashion, it is possible to recognize a particular way, an identifiable arrangement or scheme. . . . Religions are walls erected based on our quest for order and meaning. And building walls is inevitable and good as long as people are more important than walls. When it is the other way around, bad things may be done in the name of religion.[34]

The discrete entity of fundamentalism has its own distinct walls, and it seems to have the characteristics of a religion in its own right. In the SBC it has its own confessions of faith and orthodoxy usually summed up in the phrase "the conservative resurgence." It certainly has had its actions that carry out its ideals and has related socially to many facets of the society. Fundamentalism has the three characteristics of a religion. Also, the public perception of the movement is that it often serves fundamentalism as its guiding spirit rather than the spirit of the scriptures. The little-noticed fact of its true nature contributes to the confusion surrounding the movement.

Note that this religion of "conservatism" bears little resemblance to conservative biblical theology, though it claims to be at one with it. If the superimposed clutter of fundamentalism as an attitude and a religion were divorced from the present movement in the SBC, the conflict might be resolved around the biblical ideal of love.

Fundamentalism as an Ideology

The fierce determination of many people in the SBC to defend their ideas of marginal reality has been disconcerting to persons who have been preoccupied with proclamation and education. The ideas of fundamentalism have always existed and have usually had some advocates, but not in the history of our denomination has there been an organized holy crusade to foster these ideas that as often as not diverge from New Testament practices. The mood, atmosphere, and determination of the designers of the movement have smacked more of ideology than theology.

---

[34](Macon GA: Mercer University Press, 1993) 28, 29.

As Richard Wentz wrote,

> Professor Bruce Lawrence, in a study of what he calls "fundamenta-lism" among Jews, Christians, and Muslims, demonstrates that these *Defenders of God* are uncompromising supporters of ideologies, not of theologies. That is a very important distinction to make. . . . So they take these ideas, . . . and they make them into a manifesto, an instrument of protest. An ideology is a manifesto of ideas to be defended against all odds. It has been our experience in the Western world that a favorite place to locate ideas that may become part of a manifesto is in a text that is considered "sacred." If a text is the fundamental source, the unchallenged authority, for truth about human destiny, then obviously it is a good place to go hunting for an ideology. . . . Ideology arises in order to defend. . . . Theology is not ideology, although many people have used it for ideological purposes."[35]

Wentz also suggests that much of the violence that occurs in the name of religion is an ideological response to change.

The appearance is that the leaders of the "resurgence" began with some assumptions, such as the reliability of scripture, and built a system of ideology. It purports to defend the scripture and God, the church and the family, and in addition will defend the nation. The wall built around its set of ideals must be defended at all costs, regardless of what happens to persons or organizations.

This ideology will defend God and the Bible from those who ask questions or arrive at different conclusions from the ideologues. It will defend the family against abortion and homosexuality. These are popular causes that ideologues from many camps can join. At this juncture, the ideology ignores more serious threats to the family coming from adultery, divorce, poverty, illegitimacy, and the disintegration of moral values.

This ideology defends the seminaries, colleges, and other enterprises from the invasion of the unbelievers by capturing the mechanisms of power and refusing to seat a trustee who does not agree with the ideological assumptions. This ideology defends the church and society from women by refusing them the rights of participation in the responsibilities of leadership. It defends the nation by endlessly insisting that one minute

---

[35]Ibid., 84.

of mandatory prayer in school and prayer at commencements will "get God back in the nation and its affairs."

I certainly do not denigrate prayer in any setting. At the same time, I reject the idea that an action of Congress or the Supreme Court can get God out of or into anything. I also reject the idea that legal manipulations can establish a legitimate religious experience or act. To be genuine, prayer or any other religious act must be voluntary and represent a relationship to God, not to the school or state.

Is Modern Fundamentalism a Cult?

In discussing the matter of authority for the Christian and the church, Bernard Ramm penned this description of a cult:

> A cult is a religious group which places a secondary need in the position of a primary need. Any group which puts its emphasis on health, or mental hygiene, or some religio-political program is cultic. The chief enemies of man are sin and death (1 Cor 15), and the divine remedy is Jesus Christ crucified and risen from the dead. This is the first witness of the Bible (2 Tim 3:15). If the cultists heard the Holy Spirit they would hear this message. The fact that they do not so speak indicates that they do not hear the voice of the Spirit, which in turn means that they have an improper principle of religious authority.[36]

Webster's Dictionary defines a cult as "great devotion of some person, idea, or thing, especially such devotion viewed as an intellectual fad."

Various segments of the SBC pronouncements sound cultic: the preoccupation of the Christian Life Commission with the issues of abortion and homosexuality, especially in the light of other problems facing society; the long-running determination to impose school prayer in spite of widespread belief that the end may be worse than the beginning; the frequent opposition to persons nominated to high office based on the foregoing reasons; and the fervent support of the political right for the same reasons. The devotion to these important but peripheral matters fits the pattern of cultism if Ramm's definition is followed. Incidentally,

---

[36]*The Pattern of Authority* (Grand Rapids MI: Eerdmans, 1957) 35.

these apparently partisan efforts flirt with big problems with the Internal Revenue Service.

This is not to say that the denomination should not speak to such issues, but that putting secondary matters to the public as the principal emphases of the denomination has serious problems. As Ramm summed up the problem of cultism, "The cultic fails to keep the person and work of Jesus Christ central. He substitutes some alien gospel for the biblical gospel."[37]

Fundamentalism and Conservative Theology

During the last fifteen years, the public and particularly Christians have perceived in error that conservative theology and fundamentalism are identical, a misrepresentation of the true nature of New Testament Christianity. Conservative theology based on scripture holds to the truths of the love of God, the sacrifice and resurrection of Christ, the nature of the church, and the necessity to live out the biblical mandates. It forbids judgment by a fellow Christian, admonishes forgiveness, gives careful consideration to the feelings of others, and condemns hypocrisy.

Fundamentalism may theoretically begin with the premises of conservative theology but departs to condemnation of all who disagree. It refuses dialogue with anyone who suggests a relaxation of its rigidity, dominates by power, and punishes those who disagree. It is willing to decimate institutions and discard highly skilled professionals who refuse to submit to its authority. Authority is a key element of fundamentalism.

For the public, Christian or not, to see fundamentalism operating in the name of conservative Christianity results in confusion. Perception is truly reality for those who do not recognize the difference between fundamentalism and conservatism. In these times, the furious conflict between right-wing politicians and the remainder of the population has created a climate in which all political and religious fundamentalism are categorized together. Society has a difficult task of separating the fundamentalist Christians from the right-wing politicians. Indeed, many of the fundamentalists seem to have joined the political movement without any distinction between politics and religion.

---

[37]Ibid., 37.

Fundamentalism, whether deliberately or ignorantly, has created the false perception in the public mind that fundamentalism and conservative Christianity are one and the same. This travesty has done great damage to conservative Christianity and given to fundamentalism the unwitting or unknowing support of many persons who do not recognize the difference.

For half a generation, the "conservative resurgence" has in effect said to Southern Baptists and the world:

- We have/know the truth.
- We are responsible for defending/propagating it.
- Those who do not agree with us are wrong.
- They are the enemy; they must be attacked and defeated (unless they come to our point of view).
- They must be excluded from leadership and fellowship.
- We are in control by divine decree; you should not resist.
- The power of government should be used to accomplish our purposes; political action is warranted or demanded.
- The denomination should be used to gain our political objectives.
- Our understanding of truth is so solid that the end justifies the means.
- Individuals are not important if they get in the way; women must not be admitted to leadership or power.

These basic propositions seem to apply to the fundamentalist movement. They spell authoritarianism, exclusiveness, aggressive sponsorship of its ideals, ideological narrowness, religious fervor for its cause, and free exercise of religion only for fundamentalists.

Chapter 2

Fundamentalism and the Bible

My father was a small town, country preacher for forty years. As I grew up, he taught me that the Bible was the inspired Word of God. He was not concerned with how God inspired it nor with any tortured explanations of any of its so-called problems. His knowledge of it was based on the King James Version, enlightened by a few commentaries of conservative bent that sometimes raised questions about problematic passages. He could not read Greek or Hebrew and adopted the stance attributed to B. H. Carroll, who believed that his inability to reconcile or understand certain passages was due to his own limitations.

These answers were good enough for me as I became involved in college and seminary. I studied the opinions of the scholars and critics, which raised interesting questions. Some of the ideas made sense, while others seemed absurd. I wanted to know the problems and deal with the issues.

The crucible for testing conservative theology and belief in an inspired Bible came early and lasted long for me. Two months after graduating from seminary, I entered the Navy at the height of World War II. Liberal theology made little sense to me, since during the first months I met plane after plane loaded with casualties of the Pacific war. Casualty sounds so innocuous until you remember that it meant a soldier, sailor, or marine was missing half a face, an arm, a leg, an eye, or a mind, or all of these. The stench of burned and rotting human flesh is a legacy that does not fade quickly.

What does a green, young chaplain do when he discovers a plot to heave the executive officer over the side of his new ship on a dark night? What answers does he give to soldiers and sailors on their way to the invasion of Japan where casualties are expected to exceed a half-million men? What is an adequate belief when the general alarm blasts one out of deep sleep at 3:00 A.M.? Are philosophical speculations sufficient in the midst of a typhoon with winds so high the naval instruments cannot measure them? When you sit all night listening to the radio pleas for help from nineteen ships that are dying and their men with them—and there is nothing you can do—where do you turn? Forty years later, you go to a cemetery outside Manila and search for the graves of men you left there and try to remember what you said to their families long ago. Was it good enough or honest enough, and did it make sense?

Add to those experiences as a military chaplain years in the pastorate and leadership of a state convention in an enormous mission field. Then there was a university torn with hatred, false issues, confusion, divisions, and distortions. A seminary that was rapidly declining with divisions among the faculty, trustees, and alumni was next on the agenda. Then came the nation's largest religious publishing house with half-a-dozen publics clamoring for attention and guidance.

Such variety in a ministerial career is inclined to help a man make up his mind about whether the Bible is true and adequate for human trust. I long ago came to the conclusion that while I could not reconcile some parts of the Bible or did not understand some of it, and recognized the so-called problems, it was good enough to live and die by. So after a lifetime of labor and hazards, joy and sorrow, wonder and conviction, I came to the conclusion of my father before me.

I believe the Bible came from God and is more than a counselor, guide, comforter, and disciplinarian. It is God's way of communicating to us from the written page made alive by the Holy Spirit. A person cannot understand it without some understanding of Jesus, the Christ by whom one measures and interprets it.

My beliefs about the Bible explain something of why I was startled with the sudden onslaught of fundamentalism. Certainly, I had extensive experience with the spirit of fundamentalism in my work across the years, but now some people had devised an intricate network to enforce their understanding of religious truth. I term it so because I did not then nor do I now believe that the argument was about the Bible. When we adhered to the text of the scriptures, there were differences about interpretation but no tyranny. In my fundamentalism, the Bible was a central factor, but I thought no one could believe that a particular set of precepts should be standardized by force.

Certainly, the idea of freedom under God to exercise one's own understanding of faith was central to my belief. The idea that someone should interpret scripture for everyone else, with penalties for those who did not subscribe, was totally foreign to everything I believed about the Bible. The idea of churches being intimidated by actions of a larger body was anathema. The concept of the pastor ruling the church was laughable —given the deacons and church members I had known and loved and with whom I had served.

The fundamentalist capture of the Southern Baptist Convention set the stage for a most difficult period in my life. It introduced a personal nightmare that would last for the rest of my life. These people who were so efficient and ruthless were not in the tradition of Baptists as I knew them.

The Conservative Resurgence

In the preparation of her doctoral dissertation, sociologist Nancy Ammerman spent about a year as a participant in a fundamentalist church she called Southside Gospel Church. Her purpose was to study fundamentalism as expressed in a local congregation. In the book that resulted from her dissertation, she begins with a quotation from Jerry Falwell.

> The Bible is absolutely infallible, without error in all matters pertaining to faith and practice, as well as in areas such as geography, science, history, etc. The disintegration of our social order can be easily explained. Men and women are disobeying the clear instructions God gave in His Word.[1]

Ammerman deals at length with her analysis of the place of the Bible in the church. For these people, the Bible is literally true and is interpreted literally. It has absolute authority over their lives. The pastor is the official interpreter of what this literal interpretation means. At one point she comments that the Bible is the "very presence of God in their midst."[2]

These observations about a local congregation are strangely similar to the litany of the "conservative resurgence." Followers of this crusade

---

[1]*Listen America* (Garden City NJ: Doubleday, 1980) 63.

[2]Nancy Tatom Ammerman, *Bible Believers* (New Brunswick and London: Rutgers University Press, 1987) 132.

charged that the leadership of the SBC and particularly the seminaries did not believe the Bible. The fundamentalist mantra became "inerrancy." While fundamentalists referred to the "autographs," they argued the King James Version of the scriptures. They argued that the Bible was absolutely accurate in every matter including history, science, and chronology. The better educated ones listed the "errors" of the scholars as exceptions, scribal inadvertencies, miscopying, rounded numbers, and a variety of other reasons for seeming inconsistencies.

Widespread charges were made against many professors, writers, and administrators. These people were accused of not being inerrantists and not believing in the Bible. If they did not use the word "inerrancy" in their speeches or writing, they were considered to be unworthy to serve the denomination. Some critics even denounced the seminaries for allowing the use of the historical-critical method of biblical study in the institutions. For the fundamentalists, the method soon became a principal son of Satan and was to be exterminated at all costs.

This sudden orthodoxy and the virulent attacks on SBC leadership presented several problems. First, there was widespread ignorance about the meaning of inerrancy. (One leader could not spell it.) Some persons were unaware of the several, if not many, opinions concerning it. In arguing the inerrancy of the King James Version, some individuals were not even cognizant of its problems with translation and text.

A second problem was the gross inconsistency—sometimes called hypocrisy—of some of the leaders of the resurgence. *The Criswell Study Bible*[3] was published in 1979, the year of the emergence of the fundamentalist movement. The study helps used the terminology, methodology, and conclusions of modern biblical scholarship. These comments were clearly based on the historical-critical methodology. A sample conclusion of the comments was that the Nile River could not have turned to blood as the King James Version and most other translations clearly state. Numerous other such conclusions were given, particularly the comments on the textual problems of the KJV.

The volume bore the name of W. A. Criswell, who is believed by many to be the godfather of the fundamentalist movement in the SBC. The managing editor was Paige Patterson, one of the principal authors of the movement, and an assistant editor was his wife. A consulting editor

---

[3](Nashville: Thomas Nelson).

was L. Russ Bush, soon to be elected dean at Southeastern Seminary and lauded for his belief in inerrancy. Another consulting editor was Richard D. Land, who would become head of the Christian Life Commission.

All of these noted inerrantists had signed on to a volume full of commentary that frequently departed from inerrancy, at least as far as the KJV was concerned. Some of the conclusions of the study helps were more radical than the materials used by Paul Pressler as accusations against SBC scholars. As the reactionary heat grew, the book was withdrawn from the market.

Early in the controversy, the fundamentalists used literal readings and interpretations of several New Testament passages to prooftext their contention about women in leadership positions and pastors as rulers of the church. These interpretations ran counter to other passages on the same subject. The hermeneutic (determining of the meaning and method of interpretation of a written passage) of the fundamentalists did violence to the scriptures.

Hermeneutics 101

A quick look at elementary and usually accepted methods of biblical interpretation will highlight the problem. Though the criteria may be stated in different ways, depending on the objective of the writer, these general principles for determining the meaning of a given passage apply:

- What does the text actually say?
- What was the message God was trying to give to the people?
- What did the passage mean to those to whom it was written?
- Was the passage given for a particular situation in a given time frame and social context?
- What does the text say to us in our situation? Do the same conditions exist, and are the problems the same or similar?
- Is the message universally applicable?
- Obscure passages should be interpreted in the light of the passages on the same subject that are clear.
- One passage on a subject should be interpreted in the light of many other passages on the same subject.
- A passage should be interpreted in the light of the context as well as the whole teaching of scripture.

- The Old Testament is enlightened and expounded by the New Testament. The New Testament is enriched and sometimes explained by the Old Testament.
- Seemingly contradictory passages should be measured by the teachings of Christ.
- Use the most accurate information available such as the best rendering of the text, the cultural circumstances in which it was written, and the intended result of the passage.
- Seek the guidance of the Holy Spirit in interpretation.
- Christ is the final authority in interpretation.

Another formulation of the methods of hermeneutics is included in Sheri Adams' treatise on *What the Bible Really Says about Women.* Her more sophisticated model is formulated by listing important questions that are vital in scriptural interpretation.

> (1) Does the passage in question speak to us of divine initiative or human response?
> (2) If it is divine initiative, is it prescriptive or descriptive?
> (3) If it is prescriptive, is it universal or particular?
> The principles for applying them are:
> (1) The rules and goals for the Christian life should be understood in light of our relationship with God through faith in Jesus Christ.
> (2) We should read the Bible in the light of Jesus Christ.[4]

Other formulations for the same purposes exist, but these give a beginning point for biblical interpretation. The application of any one of them would have been helpful in the beginning of the SBC conflict. Of course, fundamentalists would acknowledge that not all scripture should be interpreted literally, only that necessary to bolster a preconceived position or that which obviously should be considered literally.

---

[4](Macon GA: Smyth & Helwys, 1994) 18-19.

Fundamentalism and Biblical Interpretation

The observance of the principles of hermeneutics would have avoided much conflict and heartache. The movement of fundamentalism came on the scene of the SBC proclaiming its faith in a perfect Bible and insisting on its own method of interpretation. Certain religious tenets of the movement needed the support of biblical authority.

The new religion and ideology came equipped with certain assumptions foreign to Baptist life. One was particularly important to the success of the fundamentalists. Inerrancy was essential to the basic understanding of their approach. Without a precise and unchanging text of scripture, fundamentalism could not survive. One of its favorite dicta was the idea of dispensational premillennialism. Without an inerrant text, this idea could not be successfully supported.

An attempt would be made to establish an official interpretation of certain biblical passages. To establish the authority to interpret, control of the democratic mechanisms was necessary. Then official interpretations could come from the democratic vote of the convention in session. Probably very few people understood this complex process. That all of this was utterly foreign to Southern Baptists apparently was of no concern.

The fundamentalists quickly moved to quoting scripture, primarily from the King James Version (KJV), to throttle the women's movement among Southern Baptists. They gave a rather interesting literal meaning to Paul's instruction in 1 Timothy that "a bishop then must be blameless, the husband of one wife, vigilant, sober, of good behavior, given to hospitality, apt to teach" (3:2). This passage alluding to the marital status of the bishop has been interpreted widely to forbid the ordination of women. Fundamentalists point out that a woman cannot be the husband of one wife and thus cannot be a pastor. The remaining requirements binding on the men are irrelevant to the argument.

A second passage is used to forbid women leadership in the church.

Let the woman learn in silence with all subjection. But I suffer not a woman to teach, nor to usurp authority over the man, but to be in silence. (1 Tim 2:11, 12)

In 1 Corinthians 14, Paul forbids women to speak in church "as the Law says." In chapter 11, he seems to say that a woman can prophesy and pray if her head is covered. The passage that follows sounds as if Paul had returned to the Law.

Interestingly, in the 1 Timothy passage quoted above and in the same chapter, the following admonition occurs.

> In like manner also, that women adorn themselves in modest apparel, with shamefacedness and sobriety; not with broided hair, or gold, or pearls, or costly array. (2:9)

The present SBC leadership does not discuss this passage. Using this same hermeneutic, the men with long hair shame themselves (1 Cor 11: 14).

Concerning women in ministry, the fundamentalist interpretation runs counter to Galatians 3:27, 28.

> For as many of you as have been baptized into Christ have put on Christ. There is neither Jew nor Greek, there is neither bond nor free, there is neither male nor female; for ye are all one in Christ Jesus.

Another illustration of the fundamentalist approach to scriptural interpretation has to do with ministry as well. Baptists historically have insisted on the idea that all believers are priests, responsible to God for their own spiritual pilgrimage. Fundamentalism came to the SBC insisting on the authority of the pastor over the affairs of the church. The biblical basis for this claim is found in Hebrews 13:17:

> Obey them that have the rule over you, and submit yourselves: for they watch for your souls, as they that must give account, that they may do it with joy, and not with grief: for that is unprofitable for you.

Many Greek scholars believe the passage is better rendered with the word "follow" rather than "obey" and "lead" rather than "rule." This understanding is in keeping with Peter's instruction in 1 Peter 5:3: "Neither as being lords over God's heritage, but being ensamples to the flock." Today's English Version puts the matter in perfect clarity: "Do not try to rule over those who have been put to your care, but be examples to the flock."

In 1 Timothy 5:23, Paul instructs Timothy to "drink no longer water, but use a little wine for thy stomach's sake and thine often infirmities." If fundamentalists read this passage literally in the spirit of the other interpretations of this book, wine becomes a treatment from the Word for stomach problems. Yet most of them would reject that interpretation.

1 Timothy 6:1-5 gives instructions to slaves and condemns anyone who does not subscribe to the admonitions. The passage was surely given to another generation as a solution to a problem that no longer exists in the Western world.

A portion of 1 Peter 3:21 says, "Even baptism doth also now save us." Obviously, Baptists do not subscribe to salvation by baptism. This fragment obviously must be taken in the context given and in the light of a host of other passages that indicate that salvation is by grace, through faith.

The Bible is full of passages that sound strange if taken in simplistic literalism. Solomon is recorded in Ecclesiastes 10:15 as saying, "Only someone too stupid to find his way home would wear himself out with work" (TEV). In 9:9ff. he says,

> Enjoy life with the woman you love, as long as you live the useless life that God has given you in this world. Enjoy every useless day of it, because that is all you will get for all your trouble. Work hard at whatever you do, because there will be no action, no thought, no knowledge, no wisdom in the world of the dead—and that is where you are going. (TEV)

The fundamentalist leadership would insist that the intent and context of each of these passages must be considered to arrive at an understanding of the true meaning. These examples give sufficient illustration to a principle of extreme importance. If enough skewed preconceptions are brought to the interpretation of scripture, it can be used to prove almost anything. Fundamentalism brings to interpretation a set of assumptions seeking validation. The spiritual prism through which it looks causes one to see the biblical world in a distorted way.

Fundamentalism, as practiced in the post-traditional Southern Baptist Convention, sees a religious world ideal made in its own image. It sees a Christian world in which the Bible is to be interpreted literally in support of its opinions. It sees a world in which religious decisions are made by a college of cardinals and handed down to the common people. It sees a hierarchy of high priests practicing in behalf of others who are not to be trusted with the burden of biblical interpretation. This reinvented world sees the pastor as the ruler of the church with the constituency obligated to receive his decisions and programs as though they came from God. The rule of the cardinals and priest-pastors is to be enforced by granting favors, position, and power to obedient followers and punishment to dissenters.

Since the Gospel is often slow to achieve God's purposes, the power of government and politics is to be used to achieve spiritual ends. The government should support schools that teach religion, and religion should be considered an integral part of the official functions of government. Any politician who deviates from the dicta of the fundamentalist leaders must learn to fear for his/her political life.

Fundamentalism also teaches that the place of a woman is in the home. Submission is the biblical ideal for her. (The biblical admonition for husbandly conduct toward the wife is often omitted.) She must not challenge the decisions of men and shall not teach, preach, nor lead in the church. If the modern practices are a part of the ideal, however, the wives of leaders may make a career of teaching submission to other women.

All of these fundamentalist interpretations are supposedly based on passages in the Bible. If one follows the previously listed criteria for interpretation, however, it seems that some of these passages were given to a different world for different reasons.

The words of Provost William E. Hull of Samford University should help us to make sense of the matter.

> Finally, therefore, he (Christ) is the supreme criterion of interpretation. Our study of the Bible leads to a grasp of its message when we seek to understand scripture through the intentionality of his historical ministry, the potentiality of his guiding spirit, and the centrality of his cosmic Lordship.[5]

The fundamentalist argument about scripture thus introduces several problems. It often requires interpretations that cannot stand careful

---

[5]Robert U. Ferguson Jr., ed., *Amidst Babel, Speak the Truth* (Macon GA: Smyth & Helwys, 1993) 82.

examination according to usually accepted criteria. The emotional and organizational violence wrought in the denomination cannot be justified if the words and ministry of Jesus are to be believed. For example, the spirit of Christ seems to be missing almost completely as the leadership discards highly skilled and dedicated servants of God in order to "complete the transition."

The Larger Issue

The way the inerrant Bible often is used in support of fundamentalist dogma is a grave injustice to the scripture. The spirit of truth is compromised by ideology. Interpretations are adapted to fit the presuppositions. Small gains in support of the creed create large losses in truth.

Whatever the hermeneutic, obedience is the proof of biblical faith. Words about the Bible are not very important if the spirit of the Bible does not saturate the doctrine of the Bible, the spirit of its interpreters, and the actions of its supposed believers. The aggressive modern movement to defend the Bible by its so-called friends has done more damage than all of its enemies.

Results of the Controversy over the Bible

The modern controversy about the nature of the Bible has had some other disturbing, far-reaching results. The fundamentalist uproar created in the heart of the nation's largest organized body of Bible believers not only has confused the members, but the unbelieving world as well. Studies show a serious decline in the number of Americans who believe that the Bible is the Word of God. Faith in scripture has declined in most areas of modern living. One ponders the effect of the conflict over the Bible on those who need it most.

Pollster George Barna spent three years gathering research on what American persons believe. His results are startling:

• Two out of three reject the notion of absolute truth.
• Four of ten believe Jesus made mistakes.

- One out of three believes God is something or someone other than the perfect, all-powerful, omniscient creator of the universe who lives and rules the world today.
- Three out of five do not believe in Satan.
- About half believe all religious faiths are basically the same.
- Three out of five say all people pray to the same god, regardless of the name or character of that god.
- Bible knowledge is very limited. Most Americans cannot name half of the Ten Commandments or who preached the Sermon on the Mount.[6]

Some of Barna's comments are very disturbing. He contends that most church members today do not know the basics of the faith they hold. In real life, Christians make decisions off-the-cuff, without a reasonable sense of a holistic, biblical worldview. He proposes some changes that could make a difference, however.

The church should live love, thus setting itself apart from the society drastically. He relates this suggestion to pursuing interracial harmony. (Baptists could afford a little pursuit of intradenominational harmony.) He also adovcates that Christians should live differently. Despite the Bible's admonition for Christians to be in the world but not of it, surveys find little difference in attitudes and actions between Christians and non-Christians in most areas.

The attention of the unbelieving world and non-Baptist Christians has been directed to the nature of the Bible by the conflict in the SBC. The assertions of the fundamentalists have caused me to ask questions that I have not considered since seminary days. I find myself, inadvertently, checking various passages to see if they harmonize with others and reviewing the pronouncements of the rabid right to see if they fit their understanding of scripture. If someone with my age and background faces such doubt, I wonder what it must be like for persons who search for truth and the way to follow in ministry.

The conflict has caused great uncertainty among many individuals who have not been grounded in biblical truth. Others, hearing the extreme statements of the fundamentalists, have abandoned serious study of the Bible. Still others have reacted to extremism with extremism and sought to prove the Bible errant.

---

[6]*Absolute Confusion*, as quoted by Associated Baptist Press, 20 May 1994.

One of my own reactions to the problems has been to wonder who can defend the Bible. It has survived for centuries despite the best efforts of many people to destroy it. It has been abandoned for tradition and still survives. It has been badly abused by those who used it for their own purposes, and it survives. It has been twisted and distorted, neglected and misrepresented, challenged and abbreviated. Yet, the eternal truth of the Book has not changed. The fundamentalists (and I) seem to be ill-equipped to defend something so much more durable than they.

Chapter 3

Fundamentalism and the Christian Witness

One day some friends, whom we have known for many years, confided that their son had AIDS. For the years of his life, the son had been unable to cope with a confusing and kaleidoscopic world. He drifted from crisis to crisis, and the best efforts of his parents seemed to make little difference. Drugs shadowed reality from him, and nothing seemed to break the cycle. Finally came the fatal diagnosis. The wanderer returned home to find the help and comfort he had rejected for so long.

From time to time, I checked with our friends on their son's progress or lack of it. Because we lived a long distance apart, I was able to see them only once during their trials. Their dignity and Christian faith were evident in the darkest times as they struggled with his physical care, repeated hospitalizations, ineffective treatments, pain, and disappointments. The son was civil to me but almost past anything other than the barest amenities. His misery was almost palpable, and the parents' hurt and concern were almost equal to his own.

Mary (not her name) tended to the needs of her son, George (not his name), as best she could as she watched him slowly die. Frustration does not describe a fraction of the hurt, disappointment, and misery this much loved son brought to these godly people. Counseling, medicine, love, tender care, and tough love had all been tried and failed. He died, and a part of his parents went with him.

In the midst of this situation, in one of the now-famous demonstrations against AIDS and homosexuality (not his problem), there was the sign, "Thank God for AIDS!" Christian theology? Biblical religion?

I thought of Jesus.

The teenage girl was terrified. She was pregnant by a family member who had raped her. She was afraid to talk to anyone in the family about it for fear of violence once again. She was rejected by the perpetrator and warned never to tell what had happened. What would she do with a baby? How could she pay the medical bills? What would her friends say? She was not a promiscuous girl, but no one would ever believe her.

In her desperation, the abortion clinic seemed the only answer. Ashamed, feeling guilty, and cut off from family and friends, she went to the clinic. Outside, a howling mob blocked the sidewalk and entrance. The accusations "Whore, harlot, slut" came at her from every side. As she tried to make her way through the seething crowd, she was pushed back and knocked down. "Murderer," the middle-aged woman screamed down at her. When she finally was allowed to get up, she ran with the screams of the "good people" from the churches scarring her soul. She did the only thing she could think of to solve the problem: she shot herself.

I thought of Jesus.

Political and religious fundamentalism—not conservative Christianity —have launched prolonged and vociferous attacks on several social fronts in the last few years. The attacks have been directed principally at abortion and homosexuality. As sharks have feeding frenzies, and the media has reporting frenzies, fundamentalism has its moral frenzies.

Political fundamentalists have launched furious attacks on the right to abortion and homosexuality. These efforts have taken many forms in many places. A principal target has been President Clinton and his administration. The right wing of the Republican Party has been the political leader in the secular aspects of the movement. Its success is being felt throughout our country.

In Virginia, Oliver North gained the Republican nomination for the United States Senate, the body he lied to during the Iran-Contra hearings in the 1980s. Though he lost the election, his views received worldwide attention.

The *Miami Herald* reported that fundamentalist Christians now hold one in five Republican votes nationally and dominate GOP organizations in twenty states.[1] Fundamentalist Christians are said by political observers to have been a major factor in the Republican landslide in the 1994 fall elections.

---

[1]October 1994.

In Texas, evangelicals now dominate the state Republican Party and forced out long-time chairman Fred Meyer. The religious right is expected to be the major force in electing new leaders. In the gubernatorial election, this prediction came true as Republican George Bush beat the Democratic incumbent. A Baptist minister in Austin led a campaign that repealed a city ordinance offering insurance benefits to the unmarried partners, including homosexuals, of government workers.

Party leaders in Iowa admit that a "civil war" is dividing the state GOP. The war is between religious fundamentalists and the more moderate faction of the party.

In Minnesota, the state's moderate Republican governor all but conceded defeat in his bid for renomination. Fundamentalist supporters of a corn farmer mounted an effort to control the GOP convention because the governor has favored abortion and gay rights.

No Sense of Sin

Some years ago, a famous psychiatrist asked an important question: "Whatever happened to sin?" He was commenting on the fact that the American public had lost any sense of sin. Increasingly in the last quarter-century, moral relativism has dominated the ethical and moral scene. Much of the public, and especially some segments of the intellectual and entertainment elite, has abandoned the idea of absolutes of any kind. Television and movies have distributed endless scenes of dozens of murders, rapes, armed robberies, and illicit/explicit sex with no consequent accountability. Little national conscience seems to exist among many young people about the right or wrong of taking human life or property.

This secular stream of consciousness has been accompanied by a religion of success and financial prosperity. Little seems to be heard from the pulpit or religious literature about the consequences of wrong-doing. Accountability for conduct seems to be passed on to society, parents, or inadequate finances. Repentance for and confession of sin in evangelism often has been abandoned as an emphasis. A cheap brand of intellectual acquiescence to a body of theological propositions often has been substituted for the idea of taking up a cross and following the suffering Christ.

The combination of these elements and others has produced a society that seems to believe that little is wrong if one does not get caught. With the psychology of the day decrying guilt and urging a high level of "self-

esteem," it is no wonder that the attacks of fundamentalism on the secular society are met with violent resistance.

The National Psyche

Numerous studies indicate the decline of American society. The Princeton
Religion Research Center Index recently released some interesting findings from a 1993 Gallup poll. The key index of religious beliefs hit an
all-time low in 1993. The following is a summary of some of the individual components.

- Confidence in the organized church fell in 1993 to just 53 percent of
  the population.
- Confidence in the clergy dropped again to 52 percent of the population.
- Belief in God remains high, from 94 to 99 percent in keeping with
  such belief in the last five decades.
- Opinions about the relevance of religion to answer today's problems
  remained steady, at 60 percent of the population.
- Church membership dropped one percentage point.
- Church attendance dropped one percentage point to 40 percent of the
  adult population.
- Yet, religion was deemed very important to 59 percent of Americans,
  the highest number since 1970.

William Bennett, former U.S. Secretary of Education and current co-
director of Empower America, a new conservative political organization,
compiled "The Index of Leading Cultural Indicators." In it he attempted
to focus on various cultural indicators to evaluate the social condition of
the nation. He concluded that there has been "substantial social regres-
sion," "serious social and behavioral problems," and a "marked shift in
the public's beliefs, attitudes, and priorities." He summarized that society
has shifted from self-responsibility and self-control to self-expression.
The Yankelovich organization concluded substantially the same findings
in its studies in the 1980s.

The Bennett report called attention to the increase in the number of
crimes committed from 1960 (288,000) to 1991 (1.9 million). The fastest
growing segment of the criminal population is juveniles. The teenage
pregnancy rate has doubled, going from 49 of every 1,000 juvenile girls

in 1970 to 99 of every 1,000 in 1990. The illegitimate birth rate has increased from 224,300 births in 1960 to 1.2 million in 1990. Comparable figures are cited for the number of abortions, problems in the family, poverty, and divorce. In 1960, 9 percent of all families in the country were single-parent households. In 1991 the percentage was 28.6, and nine of ten such families were headed by the mother.

The litany of decay continues. The lack of religion is highlighted by Yale professor Stephen Carter in a book, *A Culture of Disbelief.* He suggests that it has become embarrassing to mention any religious affiliation in public, much less profess one's faith. He and others argue that evidences of religious faith are disappearing from American mainstream culture.

According to Carter, prime-time T.V. shows contain practically no references to religion. Public school textbooks "tiptoe" around the subject of religion in discussing the Puritans or Martin Luther King, Jr. The news media—when it covers religion at all—focuses primarily on the scandals, infighting, and excesses of religious figures or denominations. The very presence of discussion indicates that at least the vestiges of religion remain. The vigorous attacks of fundamentalists on various segments of society and their equally vigorous counterattacks denote concern with religous feeling, if not much biblical faith.

The studies in the field are sufficiently alarming to stimulate conservative and fundamentalist reaction to existing conditions. Consider this quote from a *Newsweek* study of religion in society: "Provocative new surveys reveal a nation where most claim to be religious but few take their faith seriously." The study goes on to report that while 45 percent of Protestants and 51 percent of Roman Catholics report that they attend services weekly, "half the people who tell pollsters that they spend Sundays in church aren't telling the truth." A study by the United Church of Christ finds that only 20 percent of Protestants and 28 percent of Catholics show up in church on Sundays.[2]

The Apprehensions of a (Conservative) Moderate

From the data available on the condition of the society and from personal experience in the last two decades, the fundamentalists have reason to be

---

[2]Kenneth L. Woodward, "The Rites of Americans" (29 November 1993): 80-82.

alarmed at the state of America. The problems of the public school system alone are sufficient to arouse thoughtful people to action. In the society in general, the problems cited above are enough to require some kind of forceful and effective action plan.

But what is a Christian reaction to spiritual decay? Hereby hangs one of the most serious dilemmas of our time. The politicization of the church and denomination has added to the confusion. The methodology of politics has its place in some societal conflicts that involve the welfare of society at large. Politics can and should be used to protect the innocent and minorities. Individual citizens—perhaps Christians more than others —are responsible for citizenship.

In spite of the oft-repeated pronouncements of the SBC Christian Life Commission (CLC) that morality can be legislated, the fact is that in the main it cannot. In the limited areas where legislated morality is effective, it relates to that which is acceptable to the unbeliever or protects the citizenry at large. In such matters as personal morality, however, government effort fails.

The problems are exacerbated by the complex pluralism of the American society. Actions to force compliance with ethical and moral standards are ineffective except in those limited areas necessary to the protection of the public welfare. Even there, compliance is often limited to those who have some sense of social or religious responsibility.

The methodology of fundamentalism involves the use of intimidation, or power and coercion. The adoption of political methodology to gain religious goals, at best, is questionable. It means that the majority Christian community puts the minorities at risk in all kinds of ways. The end result implies that "might makes right" and that power gains religious privilege.

American Christians should remember that the country was founded by people seeking religious as well as political freedom. Also, nowhere in the New Testament is the use of political power for spiritual ends even suggested. Religious privilege must be surrendered to religious freedom. There must be freedom *from* religion for those who choose it, or there will not be freedom *for* religion for the rest of us.

Confrontation + Reaction = War

As to methodology, serious questions arise with every new fundamentalist assault. I previously mentioned the SBC resolutions against President Clinton for his views on abortion and homosexuals in the military and attempts at exclusion of his home church from the convention. The Christian Life Commission has also issued a stream of criticisms of the President and his program, including portions of his health care plan.

Personally, I do not agree with the President on these matters. Whether to use the methods of the Christian Life Commission is a matter of serious question, however. Methodology, spirit, and attitude are at least a major part of the problems. Increasingly, the religious and political right, while they have won some contests, have aroused equally serious opposition that carries over to all conservative Christian efforts.

In a meeting called to "build bridges" between fundamentalist Southern Baptist leaders with independent fundamentalists, the fireworks included the following words by Jerry Falwell.

> We have never had a White House that endorses wrongdoing, but we have one now. . . . Apparently the president wanted fifty perverts in key places, so he wanted Roberta Actenberg and he wanted Donna Shalala. If I had been president and somebody said, "we've got to have fifty perverts" I wouldn't know where to look. My soul, who would I check on to get that? But Hillary knew . . . all of these are her old friends.[3]

That diatribe won no friends for the cause of Christ.

An anti-abortion coalition that "includes the national right-to-life committee and the Southern Baptist Convention" (Christian Life Commission) announced a boycott of Hoechst AG and France's Roussel Uclaf, the developers of the so-called abortion pill RU-486. A test of the drug will be made in the U.S. Its potential treatment of cancer and other deadly diseases is buried beneath the anti-abortion hysteria.[4]

---

[3]*Church-State.*
[4]Associated Baptist Press, 16 June 1994.

David Broder commented at length about a recent meeting of the same Christian coalition. He acknowledged that religion-based movements are not new, but was critical of the self-righteous tone of the meeting. Citing the fundamentalist flip-flop on the NAFTA agreement, Broder commented:

> Frankly, I don't know what the "Christian position" on NAFTA should be—or the "Jewish," "Muslim," or "Hindu" position, for that matter. But it's pretty obvious that the Christian Coalition doesn't know either. . . . A lot of Republicans would welcome Christian Coalition if it would concede that on many vexing issues, the religious right may not have a monopoly on truth.[5]

Broder's sub-headline was "Christian Coalition Delegates Tolerate No Opposition."

In Tavares, Florida, near Orlando, the school board has a majority of fundamentalist Christians. In May 1994, this group decreed that students should be taught that

> our republican form of government, capitalism, a free enterprise system, patriotism, strong family values, freedom of religion, and other basic values are superior to other foreign or historic cultures.[6]

A group of teachers and parents sued the school board, arguing that pupils should not be taught that American culture is superior to all others. The litigants said that

> like other Americans, teachers are proud of the country in which we live. We also believe that America's democratic system of government is the best in the world. And we want students to come out of school sharing that belief. . . . The question is whether they reach that conclusion through education or indoctrination. We do not need to censor history or hide our flaws. Our approach is mainstream. The board majority's approach is extreme.[7]

---

[5]*Miami Herald*, 17 September 1993.
[6]Ibid., 25 May 1994.
[7]Ibid.

The hard-line approach of religious fundamentalism probably has done much more harm than good to the Christian faith. Society's response is growing and assuming more ominous positions. Recent events indicate problems with the present approach of fundamentalist methods.

A recent study by the Barna Research Group on American religion is alarming. Associated Baptist Press reported that while three-fourths of Americans desire a close relationship with God, only half find the prospect of belonging to a local church desirable. Consider these statistics:

- Sixty-nine percent of divorced people want to be close to God, but only 28 percent want to be in a church.
- Sixty-one percent of persons whose beliefs do not classify them as "born-again" want to be close to God, but only 34 percent want to be in a church.
- Fifty-six percent of the "unchurched" desire God, but only 19 percent desire the church.
- Persons who want to be part of a local church usually already are involved in one.
- "Churches that want to grow 'should realize that most growth is going to have to come from the very people who do not see local church involvement as a very desirable thing.' "[8]

To be sure, fundamentalism is not responsible for all of these statistics. Read on.

A startling result came out of a survey as to who was more believable. The Times Mirror Center for the People & the Press surveyed 10,000 Europeans and North Americans. Of the Americans, 60 percent find "the church" to be believable, while 68 percent rated newspapers believable, and 73 percent said T.V. news was credible.[9] We have a problem.

As if that were not enough, look at the status of the clergy. Gallup poll, working for the Princeton Religion Research Center, found what Religious News Service (RNS) called good news and bad news for preachers. The good news: Americans believe clergy are more honest and ethical than members of Congress, television talk show hosts, and car

---

[8]Associated Baptist Press, 12 October 1993.
[9]Reported by the *Baptist Messenger*.

salesmen. The bad news: Confidence in the honesty and ethical standards of clergy reached a new low.

• Eleven percent of Americans believe the honesty and ethical standards of clergy are "very high."
• Adding the 41 percent who see those standards as "high" brings the total positive rating to 52 percent—a bare majority.
• Clergy rank fourth in a list of professions—below pharmacists, college teachers, and engineers.
• Today 34 percent of Americans believe clergy have just "average" standards of ethics and honesty, while 11 percent rank clergy ethics and honesty as low.[10] Add to these statistics the *Newsweek* opinion that "Few Americans take their faith seriously."[11]

Consequences of Confrontation

Not only has extremism produced serious reactions in the society at large; it has aroused organized response by groups interested in the free exercise of religion and civil rights.

The American Civil Liberties Union is mounting a national campaign to counter what it calls "misleading assertions by the far right" about religion in public schools. The ACLU distributed a new legal bulletin to more than 16,000 school superintendents around the nation. It also released its first-ever video titled "America's Constitutional Heritage: Religion in Our Public Schools." The new products are described in a press release as part of a continuing effort to "combat misleading information being distributed by Pat Robertson's American Center for Law and Justice." The video is a direct response to "America's Godly Heritage," a video distributed by several religious right groups.[12]

The People for the American Way maintain that the religious right has won a string of quiet but important victories in the past year.

---

[10]*Biblical Recorder*, 12 October 1993.
[11]Woodward.
[12]Associated Baptist Press, reported in *Baptists Today*, 6 January 1994.

As city council and county commissions and Republican leadership positions fall under right-wing control, communities have been thrust into divisive battles centering on the most contentious issues in the public arena today.

The report cites what it calls anti-gay activity in forty-one states and the District of Columbia totaling 132 battles at both the state and local level.[13]

The Anti-Defamation League is equally upset at the religious right. In his book *The Religious Right: The Assault on Tolerance and Pluralism in America*, Art Teitelbaum blasts the "murderously mean" tactics of the Right in pursuing an "exclusionist" and "dangerous" political agenda, particularly in Florida. The book is the result of a year-long national research project to document what its authors call a

> bitter push to replace the wall of separation (of church and state) with a citadel of Christianity—while suggesting that those who defend the wall are "enemies of God."[14]

It warns that the religious right is seeking to Christianize public school curricula and gain control of the Republican Party.

Raul Molina, director of Dade County Christian Coalition, says such claims are inaccurate and mean-spirited.

> The 1.2 million members of the Christian Coalition are people of faith who have felt disenfranchised and under-represented and want to have a voice in our country's government. We are a political movement based on issues, not on religious doctrines. . . . It's the liberals . . . that are attempting to censor us and take away our voice in government. They are the ones who are intolerant and exclusionary.[15]

The lines are drawn for the launching of a new kind of crusade. The issues are being contested vociferously and with every new blast, the contestants prepare equally pungent responses.

Because of its own aggressive acts that appear to be more political than religious, the Southern Baptist Convention in the public mind now

---

[13]*Western Recorder*, 25 January 1994.
[14]*Miami Herald*, 29 June 1994.
[15]Ibid.

is lumped together with the political and other religious right. On the political front the Christian Life Commission's criticisms of the president, his cabinet, and his supporters have tended to arouse opposition to the convention and thus to the spiritual mission of the denomination.

The tactics of the anti-abortion forces at clinics became so violent that a law was passed by Congress and upheld by the Supreme Court protecting the clinics and patients. Some abortion-foe activists vow to violate the law and continue blocking clinics. Early on, the CLC seemed to encourage the idea of the demonstrations that resulted in the blocking of the entrances to clinics. While the director insists that the commission abhors the violence, the sponsorship has advocated participation by Baptists and likely intensified the hysteria surrounding the incidents. Whether this is true or not, the public now places Baptists in the category of violators of the law and infringing the legal rights of others.

The unrelenting vocal opposition to abortion and homosexuality on the part of the political and religious right has produced widespread reaction on the part of ordinary people. More than half of the American population defends the rights of women to have abortions. The backlash against the tactics of the activists has grown exponentially. One of the serious consequences for the SBC is that it has aroused the ire of multitudes and seriously affected our ability to witness to unbelievers.

The nature of the fierce struggle is illustrated by the plight of a Florida church. The members participated in a blockade of a doctor's office where abortions were performed. The National Organization for Women (NOW) sued the New Covenant Church in Pompano Beach and dozens of abortion protesters and won a judgment against the church for legal fees of $234,478. The church could not pay, so the lawyer is threatening to seize bank accounts and property to satisfy the judgment. The judge thought the problem was so serious that he awarded double legal fees to the plaintiff's lawyer.[16]

The precipitation of unnecessary conflict in schools, churches, and communities has produced a state of siege in some places. The creation and dramatizations of these problems have imperiled the ability to dialogue, adapt, or compromise on political solutions. The gridlock in Congress on numerous issues carries over to many churches and communities. The atmosphere has been so contaminated with ill-will and

---

[16]Ibid., 15 July 1994.

animosity that now many persons feel that the battles must be fought and won or all is lost.

One other illustration is in order showing the nature of the backlash that is produced by aggressive attacks on one segment of society. The problems of homosexuality now receive daily news coverage. The media is full of proponents and opponents and their vitriolic opinions of each other. The church has not escaped the fray. Conservative Christians generally believe that the practice of homosexuality is wrong, as are many other practices such as adultery and hating your neighbors. The extreme attacks on homosexuality by various organizations, including the CLC, has produced a rigid and encompassing reaction by the victims and a broad support base by sympathizers.

The "culture war" is on and growing in intensity. The religious right has vowed to take over the Republican Party in the name of religion. The cultural left is busy organizing to defend not only the party but the society. The vast middle without spiritual or psychic anchors is pushed left and right like the surging and ebbing tide, feeling used and abused.

As a result of the social conflict, Marv Knox of the *Western Recorder* titled an editorial, "Conspiracy Theories Hurt Conservatives' Cause." He said in part that the credibility of conservative Christians has taken a bruising lately, and a couple of their heroes have provided the cause. He discussed the accusations of Jerry Falwell and Pat Robertson against the President. Falwell's Liberty Alliance distributed a video called "Clinton's Circle of Power" that claims Bill Clinton has had his political enemies killed.

E. J. Dionne, a syndicated Washington columnist, cited the video's quote of long-time Clinton adversary Larry Nichols of Arkansas:

> You may also wonder what it's been like fighting Bill Clinton. People are dead in Arkansas. There are people that are dead. . . . There were countless and countless people that mysteriously died that, as it turned out, had some connection to Bill Clinton. I believe this is going on today.[17]

Robertson focused on the death of Vincent Foster, a Clinton aid and former law partner of Hillary Clinton. Erik Eckholm, a *New York Times*

---

[17]*Western Recorder*, 16 August 1994.

writer, quoted Robertson: "Was there murder of a White House counsel? It looks more and more like that."[18] Knox went on to discuss the culture war and urged readers to separate the issues from the tactics. Do you wonder if the future of America holds the promise of another India or Ireland torn with religious strife that depends on violence to gain the edge? Do you wonder if these kinds of excesses have an effect on the Christian witness? Consider what a new church in Lexington, Kentucky found.

The church organizers left the word "Baptist" out of the name. When residents of the target community were surveyed in preparation for the church start, about 70 percent of those interviewed said they had a negative association with the word. The youth minister said the decision to downplay the Baptist label has paid off in reaching people who otherwise might not have been approachable. The minister explained:

> Recently, one woman who had been attending about eight weeks asked a member if the church was affiliated with any larger denomination. . . . When the reply came back that they were Southern Baptists, the woman said she never would have walked in the door had she known the church was Baptist. If someone has a negative experience they can link to the name, those are people you may never reach.[19]

Perhaps this kind of problem caused Richard Mouw, president of Fuller Theological Seminary, to say that too often the

> fundamental posture is chip-on-our-shoulder, we're right and everybody else is wrong, triumphalist and arrogant. . . . Now, he cringes when aggressive anti-abortion advocates are motivated by murder. They are not really excited about murdering babies. There are other motivations out there. Christians should take uncompromising stands at times, but Christians also should heed Hebrews 12:14 which urges followers of Jesus to "pursue peace with everyone" and Titus 3:2 which recommends that believers "be gentle and show every courtesy to everyone." Evangelicals have entered into the public arena with the same kind of

---

[18]Ibid.
[19]Ibid., 11 October 1994.

oversimplification, the same cliches and sloganeering kind of mentality that had characterized our dealing with other issues.[20]

Even the much maligned president of the U. S. felt it necessary to appeal to a group of religious leaders, including some from the SBC and the CBF, to help slow the strident voices involved in the culture war. "Why can't people who disagree sit down together and say, 'What does the Bible say about this really?' Why can't we find some areas of agreement?"[21]

*****

The tools of Christian faith are not power and coercion. Strident voices beget strident reactions. Stridency discourages dialogue and arouses defense mechanisms. Fundamentalism, wherever found, often does not enter the world of ideas and dialogue. Emotional confrontation is often the *modus operandi*. A battle must be fought and won by cunning or power and a territory conquered and defended. To dialogue seems to threaten "truth," and compromise or accommodation is impossible.

The Southern Baptist Convention seems to be lost in the middle of this confrontation. One gets the impression that something has been misplaced. The emphasis is on doing without first being. Southern Baptists have become known for their "thou shalt nots." Condemnation of evil is proper; but, to be effective or Christian, it must be accompanied by a redeeming concern. A prophetic ministry and power plays aimed at control and coercion are remarkably different.

The unbelieving world should expect love from the church. Condemnation of wrong is more effective if love of the sinner is evident. The anger of the righteous often confirms the ungodly in their ways. The fundamentalist propensity to ignore the weightier matters of the law—love, mercy, compassion—widens the chasm between believers and unbelievers.

The testimony of the early church is a lesson for us. "We know that we have passed from death to life, because we love the brethren" (1 John

---

[20]Ibid., 16 August 1994.
[21]Associated Baptist Press, 9 September 1994.

3:14). God's plaintive protest should haunt us. "The scripture says 'Because of you Jews, the Gentiles speak evil of God' " (Rom 2:24 TEV).

Jesus reserved his most scathing criticism for religious leaders whom he called hypocrites. He held out his compassionate hand and heart to ordinary folk who had simply lost their way.

How like the inerrant scripture is the conduct of those who are responsible for the leadership of the SBC? How like it is the reaction of us all? How like the attitude of Jesus is our own toward religious or secular sinners? Why are we here? Is the religious war irreparably damaging the witness of the folk called Baptist?

Edward Schillebeeck commented that the church for centuries "focused on orthodoxy and left orthopraxis in the hands of nonmembers and unbelievers." Thomas H. Graves commented, "The sin of fundamentalism, whether from the right or the left, is to confuse our human interpretation with divine truth. Christ alone is Lord"[22] My nomination for one of the great sins of fundamentalism is that, in the mind of the public, it has confused fundamentalism with conservative Christianity.

One of my friends who is a former Roman Catholic priest and still a practicing Catholic is in a position to receive a constant flow of information and opinion about the world of religion. Sometimes we get together to talk about issues that interest us. We talk about education, particularly theological education, and the state of the religious world, among other things. He has been keenly interested in the problems of the Southern Baptist Convention and knows personally many individuals involved in education.

The last time we were together, I asked him about the opinion of non-Baptists about the SBC and its troubles. He told me that the way other Christians were characterizing our fundamentalism was "self-righteousness." He then gave me his evaluation of the situation. "Southern Baptists are the laughing stock of the religious world." No wonder baptisms and mission giving are down and state bodies are considering different arrangements for carrying out the Great Commission!

---

[22]*Amidst Babel, Speak the Truth*, 110.

Chapter 4

A New Ecumenism

When I was a child growing up in Mississippi, about as far south as you could get without falling into the Gulf of Mexico, our town was made up primarily of evangelicals. The Baptist church was the largest, followed by the Methodist, and trailing far behind numerically was the Presbyterian church. These were the only churches in town. The Baptists held worship services on the first and third Sundays and the Methodists on the second and fourth Sundays. The Presbyterians held services on the fourth Sunday.

My father was the Baptist pastor. He and the Methodist parson were friends and friendly rivals. They engaged in a good deal of brotherly banter but held little if any anger or personal rancor. We attended the semi-monthly services and revivals at the Methodist church, and some of the Methodists attended the Baptist services. During the Depression when tax money ran out and the school term was to be cut short, the two congregations jointly raised enough money to finish the year.

The congregations competed some, and the kids conversed a good deal about the differences between the churches. My neighbor Sy Wilson and I engaged in a running battle, mostly friendly, about various doctrines. His mother, a pillar of the Methodist church, and my mother were good friends. If they ever had difficulty about religion, I did not know it.

Such was the ecumenicity of our town until the Imbrogulios, Italian Catholics, moved to town. They opened a market in an already over-marketed town during the deep depression years. So far as I knew, they were the first and only practicing Catholics who ever lived in our town. In the following days and weeks, there was much conversation about them and their religion. They were harmless and good citizens, but the market struggled—as did everything else in town. The talk and animosity gradually died, but the fact remained: they were Catholics.

The Old Days

Traditionally, Baptists have not been very ecumenical. Our vision has been sharply limited by a combination of factors, some of which I am not very proud. In the 1930s and for nearly a hundred years before then, Southern Baptists were largely a rural and small town constituency. With very limited forms of communication, our horizons were narrow and our interests provincial.

I can remember the first radio I saw. It belonged to a friend. The newspapers were small weekly circulars and a daily edition from New Orleans. We were limited, as were most of those who went before us, by the circumstances of our lives. Needless to say, anything outside the perimeter of our narrow lives was suspect.

The culture of southernness did not lend itself to ecumenism. In college I began (but never finished) a study to illustrate that our culture was not inferior to the Yankees in New York! In those ancient times the epithet "damn Yankee" held meaning for us. Even the educational systems were still controlled by "Southern" ideals and ideologies. Religion of the Protestant and/or Baptist variety permeated the culture and sometimes the politics of the area. In short, culture and religion were mixed, and sometimes it was difficult to distinguish one from the other.

Another deterrent to any world vision among Baptists was the relatively large number of uneducated ministers. They were men with no formal or little theological education. Many of them did not attend college; some had not even completed high school. This is not to say that they were ineffective in the church, but rather that many of them had little knowledge of the outside world and how it related to our lives. Their theological knowledge was limited to what they could dig out of the Bible for themselves or what they heard in a Baptist meeting. Some of them were good students of the English Bible, and the attitudes they formed from that basic resource often exceeded their learning.

Too often, the narrow provincialism of the uneducated, untraveled, and unsophisticated ministry reigned in the churches. Because of their Bible study, the ministers of that tradition knew what God required of individuals, but they did not know how to connect it with the modern world that frightened the uninitiated. Needless to say, they added to the lack of ecumenism among Christians.

The Roman Catholic Church was to many Christians, particularly Baptists, the anti-Christ or at best the instrument of Satan. Many people knew little about it, which tended to enhance their prejudice or animosity. Most of them had heard about the Church, and many had developed a fear or hatred of what they thought it represented. Persons living along the wide sweep of the Gulf coast from Florida to Brownsville were acquainted with various manifestations of the reciprocal animosity of the Catholics as well.

While I was in seminary in New Orleans, a part of our practical training was to preach on the street corners, parks, and wherever we could attract an audience. The memory is still vivid of trying to speak while a group of kids under the visible supervision of the priest banged on a drum and tin pans. They successfully suppressed that gem of a sermon. Many students reported active opposition of the Catholic Church in one form or another. The Catholic Church in the towns of Cajun Louisiana strongly opposed the attempts at evangelization by the students.

To this day there are relatively few strong evangelical churches along that part of the Gulf coast. The Catholic and evangelical interaction were strong deterrents to mutual understanding and ecumenical relationships. The adamant insistence of the church in those years that one had to be a member of the Catholic Church to be saved did not help the matter. This situation did not change much until after Vatican Council II.

When considering ecumenism, one must add the struggle against "modernism." This problem had existed in the North for generations. The arguments ran from the nature of scripture and the church to the meaning of eschatology. Evolution and the Genesis record created more than their share of controversy. Many persons held that they were mutually exclusive. Interpretation of scripture varied according to many factors. Fundamentalism sparred with theological education. Lack of mutual knowledge of each other kept many Christians from having fellowship with each other.

The difference in the emphases of the various bodies contributed to the isolationism. The Catholic Church emphasized the liturgy and conducted the mass in Latin. Episcopalians used a so-called "high church" form of worship. Baptists and Methodists were evangelistic and pietistic but had other differences. Baptists were not supposed to drink or dance; Methodists did both (as did a lot of Baptists).

Of perhaps more long-range significance to the exclusiveness of Southern Baptists were the seminaries and sometimes the colleges. The vast majority of the seminary professors had a Southern Baptist background, were southerners, and had a Southern Baptist education. As time passed, however, a substantial number of professors pursued further educational opportunities in the North and in Europe. Still others had some variation in their preparation.

Another tendency toward isolationism was the nature of the "closed denomination." For doctrinal and financial reasons, materials from the Sunday School Board and other agencies had a virtual monopoly with the churches. These materials not only provided biblical instruction, but "denominationalized" the churches. Promotional emphases, mission endeavors, and cooperative ventures were featured in a wide variety of materials available to the churches. Only denominational materials were sold at state and national meetings. Other vendors were usually barred from the meetings.

At the state and national meetings, usually the speakers and leaders came from the denomination. Rarely was a major program spot filled by a non-Southern Baptist, with the exception of representatives from the Baptist World Alliance and the American Bible Society. The Baptist Joint Committee on Public Affairs, composed of delegates from the major Baptist bodies in the United States, usually made a report to the national convention. Still the ecumenical forces lacked a proper platform for espousing their ideas. Thus, ecumenism was not on the agenda of many people. To others, it was a dirty word. Southern Baptists actively opposed many forms of ecumenism such as the National and World Council of Churches. Even other Baptists were often held at distance or ignored altogether.

By the end of World War II, the situation began to change slowly. The Baptist World Alliance opened the doors of inter-Baptist cooperation to many. I attended my first World Congress in Atlanta in 1939. There I was exposed to many fellow Baptists from the rest of the world—of varied colors, costumes, and languages. It was an interesting experience that initiated my education into the larger world. Of course, the meeting would have been more enlightening if I had not been more interested in the girl my parents invited to accompany us. (She later became my wife.)

My first broad exposure to ecumenical issues came during my service in the Navy during World War II. There I met many chaplains and religious dignitaries from a wide variety of faiths. My Lutheran chaplain friend was as earnest about the faith as I was. My Episcopalian friend was more concerned about the nature of worship than I was. One day at an air station, I preached an evangelistic sermon and gave an invitation to receive Christ. Seven sailors, including a chief petty officer, came forward. I expected a strong reprimand from my Catholic supervising chaplain for my Baptist behavior, but after the service he held out his hand and congratulated me on the sermon and fine response. During the military service, I never had anyone interfere with my work or theology.

In 1955, I was immersed in the larger fellowship in London and saw first-hand the religions and their work in Egypt, Israel, Italy, and several other countries. My experiences were sobering and often deeply disturbing as I saw the needs following the war, the concentration camps, the destroyed cities, and the hunger of the people for something better.

Shortly before, I had led an effort in Oklahoma City to gather used clothing for the European refugees. We, along with Baptists from all over the South, secured and shipped thousands of pounds of clothing. As I preached in other countries and other sections of America, my eyes gradually opened to the faith and practices of other Baptists and finally other Christians.

The generation of leaders in the denomination with whom I worked seemed to work through about the same processes of enlightenment that I did. Some were much more sophisticated and had better opportunities than I, but most of us were rather limited in our understanding of the larger issues and practices of the faith.

Many efforts were made across the years to introduce into the denominational milieu a broader view of other Christians. The Woman's Missionary Union with its missionary education programs was instrumental in acquainting many Baptists with the work of the mission boards both in the United States and abroad. The Foreign Mission Board was very active in promoting its work, resulting in widespread information about missions. Increasingly, the leadership made various contacts with other Christian bodies. Gradually, more of them were invited to meetings as participants.

The population shift during and after World War II contributed to a more heterogeneous constituency, so as the denomination spread to other areas of the country, ecumenical activities began as a matter of necessity.

As the educational level of the people rose, particularly among ministers, the denomination gradually emerged from its isolation.

The work of the Baptist World Alliance, North American Baptist Fellowship, Baptist Joint Committee on Public Affairs, and other consultative groups contributed especially to the leadership opportunities to know and cooperate with other Baptists. From time to time, one of these organizations or the Home Mission Board would sponsor "conversations" with other religious groups. These were usually conducted through academics in closed meetings with little publicity.

Despite some joint efforts among religious groups, not even in 1979 could Southern Baptists be called truly ecumenical. The denomination generally refused organizational ties with non-Baptist bodies and refused cooperation with many Christian enterprises not directly related to its own purposes.

Interestingly, there was considerable grassroots cooperation in many causes. Social issues such as alcohol and gambling would cause cooperative efforts with almost anyone who held the same views as the local Baptists. Sometimes evangelistic or charitable causes drew cooperation from the faithful. Typically, the churches did what they wanted to do in the fashion they wanted. The denomination as such was considerably less flexible. This inflexibility usually was caused by the votes of the very folks who at home were cooperating in some effort with their fellow Christians. As a usual policy, Southern Baptists rarely supported that which they could not control.

One exception was the gradually increasing pattern of cooperation with other evangelicals on the mission fields. For years cordial relationships had existed with various groups in a variety of locations. As the home constituency became more heterogeneous and old strictures were eliminated, those efforts grew. As the Foreign Mission Board gradually was freed from the problems of public criticism of cooperative ventures, its endeavors multiplied. These undertakings most frequently were on a local and personal level rather than with organizational entanglements.

A New Day

With the takeover of the convention by the fundamentalist forces, new and different forms of ecumenism began to appear. Many of these new leaders had long been involved with other groups than Southern Baptists.

They had supported independent seminaries, colleges, and a variety of mission movements. Very often their support of denominational causes was from limited to nil, often resulting in the lack of prior leadership positions in the denomination.

As the new leaders began to control SBC enterprises, they brought with them their relationships to other groups, particularly to independent fundamentalists. Their ties to main-line denominations were not visible, if they existed at all. The principal nature of their ecumenism, if it truly can be called that, was that it related to causes and personalities similar to themselves. Soon an unusual series of events occurred that was both confusing and disturbing to old-line Southern Baptists. Almost simultaneously with the coming of the Ronald Reagan candidacy and the rapid rise of the right wing of the Republican Party, the new Southern Baptist leadership became identified with partisan political activity.

At a meeting in Dallas of fundamentalist Christians (and perhaps some others), Reagan commented, "You can't endorse me, but I can endorse you." The new-style SBC leaders sat on the platform, some of whom spoke. They obviously endorsed Reagan and he them; no one was fooled. Outsiders could not tell if the gathering was a religious meeting or a political rally. That incident posed the classical dilemma for years to come. Traditionally, the SBC had been politically neutral. Now it was being politicized. This seemed fuzzy thinking to many, but it actually represented a basic understanding of the fundamentalism of the times.

The philosophy dated back to the Puritan idea that government involvement in religion was desirable if the religion was mine. The political right-wing adherents made sure that the religion was theirs. The fundamentalist leadership of the SBC quickly joined that effort. From time to time, the fog would roll back enough to see the ties between the leadership and the various prominent figures and causes of the political right.

For thoughtful and knowledgeable people in the SBC, the politicization of the denomination could only lead to conflict and division. Many of them thought they could envision a public departure from our traditional idea of church-state separation. They did not imagine enough conflict and division, however. From the beginning, it was difficult to determine whether these new cooperative efforts were ecumenical religion or organized partisan politics. If ecumenical, they did not deal with mainstream Christianity. If political, they did depart drastically from our historic positions.

At first the efforts at organized cooperation with other Christian forces, other than in politics, were relatively unspectacular. For example, John Bisagno of First Baptist Church in Houston, Texas, urged the Foreign Mission Board to discover new ways to cross political-theological barriers to cooperate in missions and evangelism. He asked the interim president, Don Kammerdiener, to meet with other evangelical denominations and para-church organizations to find ways to work together in missions. Kammerdiener told Baptist Press that for the past ten years the FMB has made extraordinary efforts toward

> partnering kinds of activities with everybody committed to the great commission. The FMB also has a close working relationship with such para-church groups as Campus Crusade for Christ and Wycliffe Bible Translators.[1]

By the fall of 1993, some fundamentalist leaders began to hope for mergers between independent Baptists and the Southern Baptist Convention. A group of ministers from Maryland, Virginia, and Pennsylvania organized a meeting stressing "reconciliation on the right." They considered it something "of a coup" to get Jerry Falwell on the same platform with Ed Young, SBC president and pastor of Second Baptist Church in Houston. Falwell had already appeared at the SBC Pastors Conference. Falwell exulted: "I don't think there's any question that we're heading toward some . . . mergers that will probably surprise a lot of people."[2] In reporting on the meeting, a reporter for the *Washington Post* commented,

> Until recently, Southern Baptists were seen as too liberal by many independent Baptist groups. But conservatives are now firmly in control of the Southern Baptist Convention.[3]

When Southern Baptists met in Orlando in June 1994, Falwell was on the scene. When Ike Reighard, president of the Pastor's Conference, was

---

[1]Baptist Press, 4 April 1993.
[2]Associated Baptist Press, 13 June 1994.
[3]16 November 1993.

asked if Falwell would bring his church to the SBC, Reighard replied, "I would be shocked if he would; he's so much bigger than the SBC." In his address, Falwell commented that 40 forty percent of the student body at Liberty University came from Southern Baptist churches. The college publication *Flame* indicated in May 1994, that at least seven of thirty-five trustees at Liberty are prominent Southern Baptist leaders.[4]

In another example of fundamentalist-independent cooperation, the Frank Norris Church in Fort Worth had been courted by the fundamentalist leadership for a number of years. Norris had been a thorn in the side of the SBC for nearly a generation before his death. Now there was little enough difference between the ideology of the SBC and the dissident church that it should feel at home in the organization Norris hated.

Another forum of ecumenicity and politics showed up in the "Real Evangelism 1994 Bible Conference." Bailey Smith, a former president of the SBC and part of the "conservative resurgence," invited some interesting guest speakers to his annual event. Featured by photo in his advertisement were D. James Kennedy of Fort Lauderdale Presbyterian fame, former U.S. Vice-President Dan Quayle, and former SBC president Adrian Rogers. Whether this represented the new ecumenism or political acumen is not clear.

The most startling development in the new direction was yet to come. Frank Ruff has long been a representative of the National Conference of Catholic Bishops in the meetings of Southern Baptists. He has become a fixture at the meetings of the SBC executive committee. A friendly and knowledgeable man, he has mingled and conversed with Baptist leaders for years.

In March 1994, Ruff spoke with the press about relationships between Baptists and Catholics. He commented that a

> major convergence is taking place between us on social issue after social issue such as abortion, pornography, education and many other things. . . . We are working together in ways that we have never worked together before.[5]

---

[4]Associated Baptist Press, 13 June 1994.
[5]Baptist Press, 4 March 1994.

He listed as major signs of change: (1) The National Federation of Catholic Youth Ministry joined the SBC "True Love Waits" effort against premarital sex, and (2) SBC and Catholic activists stood together on the Religious Freedom Restoration Act insisting it should not be used to promote abortion rights.

For decades, Catholics and Baptists clashed over government support for parochial schools. The current generation of Southern Baptist leaders is becoming more and more critical of public education trends, however, and many are advocating a school voucher system that would put public money into Baptist schools.

The Catholic church and the SBC Home Mission Board are jointly publishing a series of tracts on issues of common interest including racism, poverty, health, and pro-life issues. The tracts will be called "A Southern Baptist and Roman Catholic Perspective" on the various issues.

In March 1994, the Home Mission Board heard a former missionary to Ghana urge dialogue with people of other faiths. Almost simultaneously, the board sponsored a meeting of interfaith witness coordinators. A Southwestern Seminary professor suggested to the group that Baptists can witness better to Catholics by developing friendships than by winning arguments. He urged a positive message in contrast to argumentative disputes about some point of doctrine.

On 29 March 1994, Larry Lewis of the Home Mission Board and Richard Land of the Christian Life Commission signed an unprecedented pledge of cooperation with Catholics and others groups. They included statements of agreement on these central areas of faith:

• Jesus Christ is Lord
• justification by grace through faith "because" of Christ
• authority of the "divinely inspired" and "infallible Bible"
• a hope that all people will come to faith in Jesus Christ as Lord and Savior.[6]

The agreement centers on social issues related to the "culture war." The signers declared their united opposition to abortion and pornography, their desire for "parental choice" in education of their children, and their belief that Christian perspectives often are trampled by too-strict

---

[6]Ibid., 30 March 1994.

interpretations of the First Amendment. The statement asserts that "politics, law, and culture must be secured by moral truth."[7]

The pledge also acknowledged differences between Catholics and Baptists such as

- whether the church is a visible communion or invisible fellowship of true believers
- whether scripture is authoritative on its own or only as interpreted by the church
- whether Christians have soul freedom or must submit to the teaching authority of the church
- whether the sacraments and ordinances of the church are merely symbols of grace or a means of grace
- the role of baptism
- the importance of devotion to Mary.[8]

Participants in the agreement also agreed to an end of "proselytizing" members from each other's folds while affirming the need of all people to be converted to "Christianity."

The obvious problems of committing a denomination to a document that contained some actual divergences from Baptist theology were apparently ignored. The document produced its inevitable response. Criticism came from many directions. Incredulous Southern Baptists who disagree with the current direction of the SBC could not imagine such an agreement with Catholics while admitting the radical differences on many points. These Baptists remembered the leadership's condemnation of churches' gifts through the Cooperative Baptist Fellowship to the SBC for its educational and missionary causes.

James Chancellor of Southern Seminary commented that such an agreement would have been unthinkable in the 1950s and 1960s. He said,

What happened pretty clearly to me is that evangelical Christianity as a whole drew a line in the sand between the broader culture and

---

[7]Associated Baptist Press, 31 March 1994.
[8]Ibid.

themselves over this issue of abortion. When they looked down the line, they saw Catholics on the same side of that line.[9]

Chancellor added that evangelical Protestants had also adopted an

> essentially Catholic stance with regard to life and conception. I have not been able to find any evangelical theologians or prominent preachers who held the position that life began at conception prior to 1970. There has been a rather remarkable shift in theology.[10]

The Foreign Mission Board officially expressed its concern that the joint statement of the group of evangelical and Roman Catholic leaders "is subject to interpretations harmful to the work of foreign missions."[11]

Larry Lewis of the Home Mission Board began to feel the heat almost immediately. He wrote a ten-page letter to his directors saying in part: "You must allow your president to exercise prophetic leadership."[12] He noted that Charles Colson and Pat Robertson signed the document. (Here was a new ecumenism!) He admitted that he did not catch the reference in the document that referred to the Catholic doctrine of salvation through the sacrament of baptism. If he had done so, he said he would have insisted on a rewrite.

Lewis further insisted the document was not about theology. Some of his trustees and many Baptists had a problem with that. One Lewis critic was interested in the passage that referred to Catholics and evangelicals as "brothers and sisters in Christ" and affirms that both traditions represent "authentic forms of discipleship." The critic thought this reference was heresy and departed from traditional evangelical understanding.

When the Southern Baptist Convention met in June 1994, the leadership had sorted out the controversy enough to affirm the document. The body agreed that Catholics and evangelicals should work together on moral and social issues and maintained the right of Baptists to evangelize anywhere anytime. A new ecumenism had emerged that centered on social issues such as abortion, pornography, and homosexuality; religious

---

[9]Ibid.
[10]Ibid.
[11]*Foreign Mission News*, 28 April 1994.
[12]Baptist Press, 3 June 1994.

"acceptance, understanding, and cooperation"; family concerns; a market economy; and a proper understanding of America's role in world affairs.

The executive director of the Christian Life Commission commented concerning a document on environmental concerns:

> The Christian Life Commission has been instructed by our trustee board to do nothing which would be construed as arguing for population limitation and birth control as a means of limiting overpopulation of the Earth.[13]

Recently *Light*, the Commission periodical, featured arguments for and against birth control.

One begins to wonder if this is the harbinger of a future campaign among Baptists against birth control. Thus, Baptists have adopted the Catholic position on a number of issues that they have resisted in the past. Particularly disturbing to traditional Baptist thinking is the idea of joining in the effort on the national scene to secure tax funds for parochial schools. Catholic pressure has continued for generations on this matter and now, joined by the second largest Christian body, Congress may have a difficult time resisting the pressure. With the present attitude of some of the justices of the Supreme Court, the church-state conflict will doubtless intensify.

Marv Knox, editor of the *Western Recorder*, commented:

> The document presents Southern Baptists with a hopeful irony. Isn't it ironic that this agreement between divergent strains of faith has been formed even as brothers and sisters within the same Southern Baptist denomination continue to bludgeon each other? Can we find hope in the recognition that, while they still hold serious doctrinal differences, fervent Christian believers can accentuate common beliefs and rally around common concerns so they can work together for the common good?
>
> Maybe the polar tugs of social causes are stronger than denominational beliefs and identity. Maybe the lines drawn by conservative, moderate, and liberal ideology are sharper than common doctrine and church practice. Maybe the blood of politics is thicker than the water of baptism. But is not the cause of Christ more important than them all? If conservative Baptists can embrace Catholics over the cause of school

---

[13]Ibid.

choice, can they "widen the denominational tent" for the sake of evangelism? And if moderate Baptists can applaud this newfound ecumenism for the sake of interfaith dialogue, can they shake off political division for the sake of missions? God only knows.[14]

The fundamentalist rationale in the beginning for the SBC controversy was that the denomination was turning liberal. The idea was to purify the body with stringent biblical doctrine. Now, the fundamentalists seem to have changed their position by approving a document and movement that admittedly varies from traditional Southern Baptist views on a number of theological dogmas. Although the fundamentalists cannot fellowship with people who give to Southern Baptist mission causes through their own method rather than the established system, cooperation with the Catholic church is allowed.

Having said all that, many moderates welcome the cooperative efforts on social issues. In many ways it is long overdue and holds hope for more collaboration and comradeship in the future. The issue of public money (parental choice of schools) for parochial schools is a different matter altogether, however. Persons who are pursuing this goal should remember that public policy always follows public money and should. This effort to secure public funds for private schools means the intrusion of the government into the operation of the schools themselves. If the schools do not teach religion, they will miss a large part of their mission; and if they do, they will be subject to governmental policy.

*****

Now we are treated to the scene of a "conservative resurgence" that clearly condones the departure from what have been argued as biblical mandates. Further, it has abandoned traditional positions on church-state relations and matters of fellowship with other Christians. We are confronted with a new form of ecumenism, some of which is doubtless good and some of which is basically questionable. Again we consider the problem of whether the "conservative resurgence" was a matter of power and control or the matter of liberal theology.

---

[14]5 April 1994.

Chapter 5

The Catholicizing of the Southern Baptist Convention

During my administration at the Sunday School Board, I was sometimes accused of being the chief censor of the SBC. The point was that, through my associates, the board and I controlled what was published. Some persons who wanted their writings published thought that we should do it without regard to the content. A Southern Seminary professor was unhappy with me because we did not publish a controversial work he had written. In a meeting with the faculty, I commented that we were not passing judgment on his material as to whether he was right or wrong. We were simply following our own policies as set through guidance by the denomination, and his work did not fit our criteria.

This incident raised the inevitable question of freedom of the press and free speech. Actually, the constituents had the right to determine its standards. According to Baptist polity, the institutions, such as the Sunday School Board, were controlled by the constituency—in our case the messengers from the churches. We were influenced as much by the constant stream of comment received from our people as by the actions of the convention. This too was baptistic.

Our concerns were not so much who wrote or composed as what was written and composed. Certainly no effort was made to exclude any person or group of persons, assuming the material met Baptist doctrinal requirements. Before 1969, these requirements were based on Holy Scripture and commonly-held Baptist traditions. The distinction must not be missed. The denomination has the right to determine what it publishes but not what is written, composed, or preached. It is bound by the accumulated will of its people, not the whim of some bureaucrat.

During forty years of service in the denomination, I very rarely if ever saw any effort on the part of the leadership to dictate to the

churches or persons. There was no effort from the national level to pre-
scribe thought, conduct, writing, or preaching. The persons and churches
affiliated with the national body were completely free from any outside
interference. Ecclesiastical authority and "imprimatur" of approval of various books or other writings did not exist.

For generations, the churches did exactly what they thought they
should do regarding the raising and expenditure of funds. The state and
national bodies had no authority to attempt to determine how or if the
churches carried on mission activities. By definition, Baptists had considerable involvement in a wide variety of mission causes whether they were
sponsored by the denomination or not.

Although some congregations supported to a greater or lesser degree
non-denominational causes more than they did the official activity of the
denomination, no effort was made to exclude them from the official causes. The only influence on them was the rather constant promotion of the
denominational causes. If they did not respond, the local brethren might
notice; but if a comment was made about it, the reply was inevitable:
"We are independent and autonomous; we will do whatever we want."

Fundamentalism has brought to the denomination a new approach to
polity, mission giving, and free exercise of religious faith. Individuals and
churches now must accede to the mandated method of participation or be
excluded from the fellowship. The excommunication is not formalized
but just as effective. The national executive committee seems to be march-
ing steadily toward control by intimidation, isolation, and financial
punishment.

Reactions to the Cooperative Baptist Fellowship

Much of the radical departure from traditional policy is aimed at the
Cooperative Baptist Fellowship, the alternative missions group. It was
organized by concerned Baptists who felt the national body was mis-
managing the affairs of the denomination. There was growing concern
about various activities of the convention, particularly the Christian Life
Commission—which in the opinion of many became a political action
committee. The Southeastern Seminary tragedy caused many individuals
and churches to feel that they no longer wanted to support the new
fundamentalism. The high-handed activities of the national executive

committee offended many people, and they no longer trusted it to handle their concerns.

The CBF was finally constituted by the dissidents as a means of supporting some SBC causes while excluding others. To accomplish this goal, the organization set up a giving mechanism that channeled the funds contributed by individuals and churches to the causes they chose. The concept was not new; it merely translated into an organized method what many churches had been doing from the inception of the denomination.

The Fellowship began having national meetings annually, and some of the states followed suit. Participants were immediately accused of starting a new denomination, which some of them wanted to do, although the majority had no such intention. Interested parties simply wanted to do missions and education according to their convictions, while supporting some of the work of the national denomination.

Fundamentalist leaders quickly saw that this movement would soon deprive them of funds. They cried "foul." Those who had earlier called the historic Cooperative Program a "sacred cow" when they did not want to participate, adopted the former moderate position that it was a "sacred how." This method of financing received the verbal support of fundamentalists who had never led their churches to give even the national average to its mission efforts. A few brave souls called on these leaders to match their rhetoric with their money.

Changes in views toward polity and freedom of expression of beliefs, plus opposition to alternative giving plans by fundamentalists, were all considered by traditional Baptists as moves to establish religous authority. Of course, those persons responsible will hotly deny such a ploy, but the record from denominational agencies, institutions, and organizations indicates otherwise.

Home Mission Board

—The Board appointed Rebecca Waugh of New York City as a missionary. Her husband was not appointed because he is a member of the Cooperative Baptist Fellowship Coordinating Council. (The HMB received $556,000 from CBF in 1992 and $304,000 through September

1993.) Also, HMB policy requires that both missionaries and their spouses be appointed.[1]

—The board's executive committee continued the disturbance in a meeting after the June 1994 meeting of the SBC. It voted to establish a committee to study the agency's relationship with state conventions that carry out instructions from contributing churches to disburse gifts to the CBF in addition to or instead of the denomination's traditional unified budget plan. Before that vote, the committee approved a motion to consider changing ways the board relates to state conventions that serve as "brokerage firms" for the Fellowship. The author of the motion said,

> I think we need to rethink how we do missions in states that refuse to be loyal to Southern Baptists. Should we be in partnership with them in the present way?[2]

North Carolina Baptist executive Roy Smith promptly replied in the *Biblical Recorder*:

> The C in CP stands for cooperation, not control. Any action changing the way the SBC Home Mission Board funds projects in North Carolina because the state convention channels designated funds to the Cooperative Baptist Fellowship will generate an immediate and direct response from Tar Heel Baptists.[3]

It should be noted that North Carolina Baptists last year sent more that $5.3 million to the HMB and received $474,000 in grants from the HMB. Smith commented further that North Carolina Baptists are prepared to reallocate missions gifts to take up any slack caused by a drop in HMB funding. "We will continue home missions in North Carolina, with or without the Home Mission Board."[4]

---

[1]*Baptists Today*, 28 October 1993.
[2]Ibid.
[3]20 July 1994.
[4]*Baptist Standard*, 20 June 1994.

Seminaries

—Trustees at Southwestern Seminary approved a recommendation from their academic affairs committee to study the seminary's relationship with the CBF. The study would include the matter of whether the seminary would participate in meetings of its alumni at the CBF meetings. The trustees also debated whether to proceed with presentations previously approved to C. J. and Ophelia Humphrey and Lee and Delores McKellar for "outstanding contributions to the life of the seminary." It seems that the Humphreys had fallen into grievous sin: They supported the Cooperative Baptist Fellowship. Miles Seaborn said the Humphreys' church is an "open supporter," and Wayne Allen said he understood Ophelia Humphrey had spoken on behalf of Texas Baptists Committed. A motion to rescind the presentations was finally withdrawn the next day.[5]
—In February 1994, the trustees of Southern Seminary approved a new policy directing that the Seminary not set up exhibits or sponsor alumni gatherings at meetings of groups it believes compete with the SBC. The move came out of a motion at the SBC meeting by an Oklahoma layman

> that the alumni associations of our seminaries which have exhibited at Cooperative Baptist Fellowship gatherings be discouraged from doing so, and that if they continue to exhibit, the Cooperative Program allocations for those seminaries be withheld and divided among our other seminaries.[6]

The seminaries responded immediately. Southern's president affirmed that he was willing to meet with any group so long as it was not affiliated with the CBF. Therefore, the seminary-sponsored state and national meetings of alumni affiliated with American Baptist Churches will continue.

Concerning the matter, North Carolina editor R. G. Puckett wrote in the *Biblical Recorder*:

> This decision smacks of desperation. Loyalty to the SBC is the stated reason but a close examination of the situation suggests that Southern

---

[5]*Biblical Recorder*, 30 October 1993.
[6]Associated Baptist Press, 4 February 1994.

is losing rapidly, like some other things in Baptist life, and this is a frantic effort to stem the tide. It is a most unwise decision which will further alienate a substantial number of Baptists who will find other places and ways to meet their needs.[7]

Other seminary administrators apparently are following the example of Southern in refusing to meet with groups related to the CBF. Likewise, the Sunday School Board refuses to display materials and services at national and state meetings of the CBF. The CBF is not allowed to have displays at the meetings of the SBC.

State Conventions

—**Florida.** Trustees of the *Baptist Witness* had disagreed over the policies of the paper and opinions of editor Jack Brymer for years. Several commissioners complained about the printing of stories about the SBC controversy and the Cooperative Baptist Fellowship, as well as articles originated by Associated Baptist Press, an independent news service. Their complaints did not seem to match a survey that revealed that 72 percent of the laity and 66 percent of the pastors considered the reporting by the paper to be fair; 71 percent of both categories assess the publication as accurate; and 65 percent of the two categories consider the *Witness* balanced.[8]

Brymer, who had been the editor about ten years, called attention to the fact that in recent years commission members have repeatedly chided him for bias, inflammatory content, and failure to promote changes in denominational life. Yet, each year they have affirmed his performance as being in accordance with the commission's policies and guidelines. Thus, the constituents were receiving mixed signals.

The ambivalence of previous meetings left the editor confused and frustrated. He said he came to realize that he had allowed concern for commissioners' agenda to compromise the paper's commitment to truthful reporting. Suggesting that the paper was bordering on being edited by a committee, he made a strong and forthright statement of his concerns.

---

[7]19 February 1994.
[8]Associated Baptist Press, 30 September 1993.

I can no longer surrender my mind and my pen to the aspirations of factions within our great convention, or even to this commission. I must release my spirit to the greater cause of my calling—to report truth no matter to whom or to where it leads me.[9]

Concerning the problem, one pastor commissioner said that he did not want his church members to read the paper because of his strong disagreement with the editorial policy. Another said that if he gave the paper to new Christians in his church, they would be greatly confused. In a matter of months, Brymer resigned his post. He said that he could no longer endure the harassment from those who, among other things, wanted to shut off reporting by the Associated Baptist Press.

—**Kentucky.** The state executive director and editor of the *Western Recorder* were members of churches that contributed some support to the causes supported by the Cooperative Baptist Fellowship. The issue was focused by a series of letters to the editor questioning the church membership of the two men and their families. Some critics felt that the state leaders should move their church membership or resign their jobs. They saw the CBF as a competitor to the Cooperative Program.

Suddenly, every church was expected to abide by traditional methods, or else be labeled disloyal. Similarly, every denominational employee should be a member of a "loyal" church. The critics were trying to bring a new kind of authority to Baptist life that had never known such strictures. The same questions were raised in other states about seminary professors and other denominational workers.

Marv Know, editor of the *Western Recorder*, confronted the arguments squarely. He made several important points in the article "The 'Southern Baptist Convention *or* the Fellowship?' Question Does not Have an All-or-Nothing Answer":

- The churches in question had channeled their money in both directions as well as to the Kentucky Baptist Convention.
- Other churches had supported such entities as Mid-Continent Baptist Bible College (an independent fundamentalist school), the Kentucky Right-to-Life, and the Gideons.

---

[9]Ibid., 4 February 1994.

- This division of funds between various kinds of causes had previously been a historic and an unquestioned right of the congregation.
- Faithfulness tied to exclusive loyalty to the SBC is a contradiction of history and polity.
- The Kentucky Convention was organized eight years before the SBC and had never been subordinate to the SBC.
- Baptist polity recognizes the total independence of the individual, the church, the local association, the state convention, and other bodies; none owns or controls the others.
- Such arguments as were being raised about loyalty would ultimately destroy both the state and national bodies.
- Churches and their members can rightfully exercise their autonomy.
- Allowing individual churches (such as his own) to choose to support the Fellowship and/or Convention causes is the Baptist method of decision-making, for it emphasizes "corporate responsibility" and defends "individual conscience."

Knox closed the lengthy editorial with this paragraph:

The question posed by the letter writers this week draws a line in the sand for denominational workers like me and families like ours. I feel called of God to minister through this job. But long before that, I felt called of God to be a Baptist Christian. If Kentucky Baptists denigrate my church and deny my personal priesthood by saying I cannot worship with this family of faith, they will have ceased to be the kind of Baptist I am. I will stand with my church.[10]

—**Oklahoma.** At the annual meeting in November 1993, messengers

publicly chastised their retired state convention executive director for his endorsement of the Cooperative Baptist Fellowship. Messengers to the Baptist General Convention of Oklahoma roundly approved a motion asking Joe Ingram to "cease and desist" from his support of the CBF. . . . Messengers approved by an estimated ninety-five percent a motion by Dennis Wright appointing five convention representatives to "call on Ingram to express our disappointment in the action he has taken to lend

---

[10]7 September 1993.

support to any alternatives to the Cooperative Program and to request him to cease and desist from such actions in the future."[11]

In response, Ingram said he did not intend to meet with anyone nor heed the call to cease his involvement with the CBF. He had been a strong advocate and supporter of the Cooperative Program during his ministry and said that he still supported it but chose to make some gifts through the CBF. I personally knew of his dedication to the Convention financing plan. When I was president of Oklahoma Baptist University, Ingram was instrumental in designing a plan of greatly enlarged support of the university through the Cooperative Program. The university still prospers greatly even now due to his foresight and planning.

In December 1993, Gary Cook, pastor of First Baptist Church in Lawton, was replaced on the state convention's strategic planning committee. For a generation, his church has been a leader in the state and a heavy contributor to mission and educational causes. Cook has an outstanding record of denominational service as well. He was a former vice president and trustee of the Sunday School Board and a trustee of Oklahoma Baptist University. He was removed from the committee by its chairman, David Willits, because of his alleged disloyalty: He had served in November as a moderator of a CBF discussion group and had introduced Cecil Sherman, the national CBF coordinator, at a luncheon meeting.

Cook commented that the Lawton church was still a leader in Cooperative Program giving and had raised its Christmas mission offering for foreign missions by 25 percent that year. He said,

> It is grievous to me that I can grow up and be nurtured in my own state by everything that Oklahoma Baptists stand for—if there was ever anybody who is a product of Oklahoma Baptists, I am—and now find myself unacceptable to serve Oklahoma Baptists.[12]

---

[11]Associated Baptist Press, November 1993.
[12]*Baptist Messenger*, 16 October 1993.

The SBC and Executive Committee

—The new direction of the SBC was clearly indicated at its June 1994 meeting. The executive committee had been virtually excluded from sharing funds from the churches channeled through the Cooperative Baptist Fellowship. The total receipts by the executive committee had been less than twenty dollars in three years. The mission boards and seminaries had received more than $9,000,000. The executive committee in its pre-convention meeting voted to refuse any further funds from the CBF and strongly "encouraged" agencies to do the same.[13]

Messengers to the convention passed a motion from the floor directing the agencies to decline gifts that were channeled through the CBF. This action was taken to "maintain fidelity to the convention and avoid compromising the integrity of the Cooperative Program." The discussion centered around the "mutually exclusive visions" of the two organizations. One speaker talked of differences on abortion, nature of scripture, homosexuality, and the virgin birth. His charges were unsubstantiated and completely false, according to CBF leaders. SBC leadership quickly stated that the motion did not come from its executive committee. That it came out of the blue without encouragement from leadership was immediately questioned by long-time observers of the convention.[14]

The motion portrayed the face of protection of the Cooperative Program, whereas discussion of the matter centered around disapproval of the CBF. From a polity point of view, this was clearly the assumption of a radical new kind of power by the national body. The motion was in effect a limitation of the manner in which individuals and churches could contribute to SBC causes.

The Texas *Baptist Standard* immediately called attention to the SBC Constitution, Article IV, "Authority," which states:

> While independent and sovereign in its own sphere, the Convention does not claim and will never attempt to exercise any authority over any other Baptist body, whether church, auxiliary organizations, associations, or convention.

---

[13]*Baptists Today*, 14 July 1994.
[14]Ibid.

The *Standard* reminded readers that the action was a motion, not a resolution. The motion was binding on the agencies.

The editorial said in part:

> Baptists ignore their past and play loose with their future when any Baptist body at any level attempts to exercise authority by directing another Baptist body. Whether Baptists like it or not, those elected by churches to conventions are messengers, not delegates because they take no authority from their church to a convention and in turn the convention has no authority to vest in them to take back to the local church, Baptist headquarters. While the motion called to "avoid compromising the integrity of the Cooperative Program," Southern Baptists must always be careful to avoid compromising the integrity of the SBC Constitution, which preceded the Cooperative Program by eighty years.[15]

Jack Harwell, editor of *Baptists Today,* wrote:

> Many feel this motion was initiated by fundamentalist strategists to force churches to make a choice between the SBC and the CBF, in spite of repeated denials by CBF leadership that CBF plans to become another convention.[16]

—Another assumption of authority came from the SBC executive committee in the same pre-convention meeting. The Historical Commission had published a pamphlet entitled "Who Are Southern Baptists?" The executive committee asked the commission to "cease to distribute" the pamphlet "until such time it deletes any reference" to the CBF in the pamphlet. One sentence in the pamphlet was objectionable.

Guy Henderson of the Mississippi *Baptist Record* editorialized:

> What was this offensive sentence that merited such swift curtailment and was so quickly scissored out of the pamphlet? The villainous sentence was: "Some churches also give money for missions, education, and other causes through such channels as the Cooperative Baptist Fellowship."
>
> Is this statement true? Is it a part of Southern Baptist history?

---

[15]29 June 1994.
[16]14 July 1994.

The answer is yes.

Then why did the executive committee deem it necessary to exercise the heavy hand of censorship? Will Lynn May now have to have the executive committee's approval for other writings? Is the executive committee of the SBC desirous of having all commissions, all pamphlets, all writings pass its scrutiny prior to being published?[17]

Henderson reported that the chairman of the commission and the executive-director asked the administrative committee to act on behalf of the trustees and informed the other trustees by phone. The offensive sentence was immediately deleted. Henderson reported that the change cost about $1,800, or about $100 a word—all this for reporting a historical fact by the Historical Commission! This action was reminiscent of the firing of the executives of the Baptist Press earlier. Sometimes they did not follow the party line. They were never given a reason for their dismissal and had no adequate due process to defend themselves. The problem of power and authority related to the press continued to intrude on the Baptist scene in a variety of ways.

Baptist Censorship

Censorship is relatively new to the SBC, although it has long been practiced by the Catholic Church. In considering this new Baptist type, I am reminded of a passage written by Thomas Merton in which he described his feeling when he discovered in a new book, "Nihil Obstat . . . Imprimatur."

> The feeling of disgust and deception struck me like a knife in the pit of the stomach. I felt as if I had been cheated! They should have warned me that it was a Catholic book . . . the mere fact that they should pass judgment on the character of a book, and permit people to read it: that in itself is fraught with terror. It immediately conjures up all the real and imaginary excesses of the Inquisition. . . . But the imprimatur told me that what I read would be in full conformity with that fearsome and

---

[17]7 October 1993.

mysterious thing, Catholic Dogma, and the fact struck me with an impact against which everything in me reacted with repugnance and fear.[18]

Fundamentalist leaders will argue that no such practice exists in Baptist life, but remember that, along with the matters mentioned in this chapter, the Sunday School Board trustees ordered the destruction of their centennial history because it was labeled "biased." Of course, these kinds of arguments have occurred before in Southern Baptist life, but they were defeated or corrected quickly by a freedom-oriented people. They never became a direction for the denomination that continued for years.

While these many examples of the abuse of power or authority would not be earth-shaking, they do represent a direction toward catholicizing the SBC. The exercise of power in the national body and the attempts for control in the state bodies have never been so blatant or frequent. These incidents and a long list of others similar in nature, many of which are not known to the public, raise again the whole matter of authority in religion. They also pose questions related to free exercise of religion. The problems of relationships between various Baptist bodies are focused in new and alarming ways. Clearly, Southern Baptists are moving in directions that have been rejected by previous leaders and generations.

E. Y. Mullins quoted Cardinal Cushing as saying,

A man enjoys religious liberty when he possesses the free right of worshiping God according to the dictates of a right conscience and of practicing a form of religion most in accordance with his duties to God.[19]

Cushing included in this innocuous-sounding definition several qualifications that sharply limit the freedom involved.

He qualified the freedom by "right conscience." Whose right conscience? What is a right conscience? A "form of religion" raises the questions of what form, from whom, for what purpose, by whose determination, what configuration, and so on. "Most in accordance with his duties to God" elicits another set of potential problems. What does "most

---

[18]*A Thomas Merton Reader*, Mentors (New York: Doubleday, 1974) 236-37.

[19]*The Axioms of Religion* (Philadelphia: American Baptist Publication Society, 1908) 267.

in accord" mean? Who defines duties? Who judges quality of accord or the form of the religion in question? Mullins quoted John Pollard as saying that in this definition is snugly wrapped every religious persecution that ever raged in the world.

Compare these ideas with the system being built by the fundamentalism of the Southern Baptist leadership:

- The definition of a good Southern Baptist is now given to us.
- This definition is often determined by popular vote of a convention body that many people feel is regularly manipulated.
- The agencies sometimes follow suit freely or feel a "mandate" from the convention or the "conservative resurgence."
- National decisions and/or their influence determine membership on boards and committees.
- Leadership positions are not open to persons who do not subscribe to a growing list of requirements for being a "loyal Southern Baptist."
- The requirements for participation are now long and detailed. They include the proper attitude toward women in ministry, homosexuality, abortion, Masonry, the Cooperative Program, the Cooperative Baptist Fellowship, proper forms of cooperation between the states and the SBC, inerrancy, school prayer, and so on. Apparently, now seminary presidents will be required to employ politically-active professors who support the "conservative resurgence."

We are treated now to the use of denominational power—direct or implied—to repress dissent, control the press, criticize state conventions and by implication threaten them, control relationships of seminaries to their alumni, exile dissenters, and submit to political acts by leadership or be labeled disloyal. The list of requirements for fellowship are foreign to the history and traditions of Baptists. To be truly valid, any religious decision must be free, uncoerced, unfettered, and unlimited by human interference and authority.

What Is Authority for a Baptist?

A Dictionary of Doctrinal Terms defines "Authority—The right to judge, control, influence, or be believed." In *The Pattern of Authority*, Bernard

Ramm poses the question: How does God express His authority? Through the Roman Catholic Church, or the ecumenical councils of the Eastern Church, or through religious intuition, or man's best thoughts about God? We would add: Through the executive committee, or the convention meeting, or the Home Mission Board?

Ramm answers that revelation is the key to religious authority and that in Christianity authority is God in self-revelation. He concludes that such a principle represents personal authority. It is free from subjectivism and avoids the resident evils of authoritarianism, the problem of an exclusively written authority and the finite's sitting in the place of the Infinite.[20]

E. Y. Mullins set the matter of authority and freedom of individuals in proper perspective in his statement of the axioms of religion. According to Mullins, an axiom is a self-evident truth that when seen needs no proof of its reality. These self-evident truths are worth restating in the context of Southern Baptists' present problems.

- The theological axiom—The holy and loving God has a right to be sovereign.
- The religious axiom: All souls have an equal right to direct access to God.
- The ecclesiastical axiom: All believers have a right to equal privileges in the church.
- The moral axiom: To be responsible, a person must be free.
- The religio-civic axiom: A free church in a free state.
- The Social axiom: Love your neighbor as yourself.[21]

All of these principles, Mullins insisted, grow out of the mother principle for which Baptists have stood through the ages: the competency of the soul in religion under God.

For even better authority, listen to the Word.

Like living stones, let yourselves be built into a spiritual house, to be a holy priesthood, to offer spiritual sacrifices acceptable to God through Jesus Christ. . . . You are the chosen race, a royal priesthood, a holy

---

[20](Grand Rapids: Eerdmans, 1957).
[21]Mullins, 73ff.

nation, God's own people, in order that you may proclaim the mighty acts of him who called you out of darkness into his marvelous light. (1 Pet 2:5, 9)

All believers are equal before God, and each person has the right to directly approach the Father and not go through some other person.[22] These principles of polity and priesthood are affirmed by a wide variety of Baptists writing from diverse backgrounds.

Scott Walker in *Amidst Babel, Speak the Truth* declares:

> For me, to be a Baptist is to claim the privilege and the freedom of being your own theologian and your own interpreter of scripture, as you are prayerfully led by God's Holy Spirit. You are your own priest.

. . . .

> This diversity allows me to believe what I must believe and to do what I must do as I interpret the leadership of God's spirit for my life. It means that I must respect the right of others within my community of faith to do the same. This is the Baptist way![23]

According to Walter Shurden in *The Baptist Identity*

> Soul freedom is the historic Baptist affirmation of the inalienable right and responsibility of every person to deal with God without the imposition of creed, the interference of clergy, or the intervention of civil government.[24]

In a book about Southern Baptists and written for Roman Catholics, C. Brownlow Hastings said,

> It is easy for us to yield our integrity and responsibility to some accepted authority: beloved pastor, honored teacher, influential book—even an edition of the Bible—respected parents or dynamic church. These all have their proper role of influence, but the final choice of belief and practice must be made in the secret of the soul's naked presence before

---

[22]Ibid., 98.
[23]67, 68.
[24](Macon GA: Smyth & Helwys, 1993) 23.

God alone. I may pray in corporate prayer or use a devotional prayer book, but unless their words are truly my words, I have not engaged God for myself. I have only "said my prayers." I may study the Bible under great teachers and share with devoted Christian friends, but I must finally judge what is truth, not because I find it agreeable to me, but because the inner witness of the Spirit convinces me. I may profit by the testimony of another's experience in the Lord, but I do not need or cannot repeat his experience. I need my own.[25]

The genesis of Southern Baptist problems in this arena are traced to the idea of pastoral authority that subsumes the priesthood of the individual believer. If the pastor believes in his right to authority, he naturally assumes at the state and national level that he and his peers have the right to make decisions for others. The use of threat, penalty, or force—explicit or implied—undoes the whole concept of priesthood. These problems are multiplying.

Some national and state leaders assume that they know what is a good Southern Baptist and what is best for one. They believe they have a right to dictate religious practices and can withhold position, prestige, or recognition. These ideas are contrary to Baptist polity and doctrine. If such leaders are permitted to define loyalty and assert a right to dictate how churches do missions in order to remain "loyal Southern Baptists," we have surrendered our priesthood—we have already lost our denomination.

The Boldest Stroke of All: An Afterword

While the galley proofs of this book were being corrected, the news exploded across the country: "Committee proposes massive overhaul of SBC agencies." Associated Baptist Press releases of 21-23 February gave details of the plan. Some changes have been needed for years, but this proposal is revolutionary. The committee was composed of two pastors, one associate pastor, a lawyer, a restaurateur, a "financial strategist," and the controversial president of Southern Baptist Theological Seminary. The major recommendations are startling:

---

[25]*Introducing Southern Baptists: Their Faith and Their Life* (New York: Paulist Press, 1981) 24.

- Reduce the number of SBC agencies from nineteen to twelve.
- Eliminate the Education Commission, Stewardship Commission, Historical Commission, Baptist Foundation, and Commission on the American Baptist Theological Seminary.
- Consolidate the Brotherhood Commission and Radio and Television Commission with the Home Mission Board to become the North American Mission Board.
- Remove from Woman's Missionary Union the SBC assignments to develop women's ministries and raise money for the two mission boards. Assign the money-raising responsibilities to the mission boards.
- Delegate to the state conventions the primary responsibility for developing and funding the mission strategies within their state boundaries.
- Commission the Sunday School Board to supervise ministries for men and women, stewardship education, and capital fund raising; and assist churches with Christian schools and home-schooling ministries.
- Limit the services of the Annuity Board to serving church employees qualified by state conventions, employees of qualified Baptist associations, employees of state convention and their subsidiaries, and employees of the entities of the SBC and their subsidiaries.

Although the planning had been in progress since September 1993, as Associated Baptist Press reported,

> The executive committee members and officials with the SBC's nineteen current agencies got their first glimpse of the committee's report at the same time Monday night. The study committee succeeded in keeping its work a secret until the formal report was made.

One agency head said that he was given his agency's part of the report on Friday, 17 February. One state executive director said that he was told ahead of time (no time given) but had no opportunity to give input. Insofar as could be determined immediately after the report, it appeared that no state board or board of trustees of any SBC agency had any input to the process.

According to Baptist Press on 21 February,

> The committee indicated that the process of gathering input included an initial letter sent to all SBC agency heads asking various questions about their agencies' duties and vision for the future; committee

interviews with each agency head; follow-up correspondence, along with conversations and questions as needed; several site visits; and input from state convention executive directors and individual Southern Baptists.

Obviously, no organization had an opportunity to study the report and its implications. The secrecy of the committee and the lack of lengthy consideration by other than the seven members seemed to provide another example of the closed-door modus operandi of the fundamentalist leadership. Previous reorganizational efforts had involved lengthy studies with a wide variety of involved persons. Wide publicity was given the efforts with input from impacted entities and interested parties. Reports were issued in time for consideration by affected agencies.

The study committee report for this new plan, however, was given to the executive committee on Monday evening, 20 February, with the vote scheduled for the following day. The executive committee passed the controversial report by a vote of 64–3. The opposition was largely due to the short period of time allowed to consider the matter. The secrecy to the last minute was reminiscent of the report of the Peace Committee report given to the SBC meeting the same evening the vote was scheduled.

In addition to the limited time for study of the report and the secrecy surrounding it, the methodology had several problems.

- The committee had no person on it who had extensive experience in denominational affairs that related to the issues under consideration.
- Trustees who had authority for the agencies apparently were not consulted about their agency and its needs and problems.
- No affected agency apparently had adequate opportunity to study and evaluate the effects of the changes.
- Numbers were conspicuously absent: about the cost of the consolidation; the number of employees affected; the removal costs for two major entities; the real property involved; the legal fees necessary for the hundreds of adjustments necessary in documents, titles, trusts, bequests, constitutions, by-laws, charters, contracts; and on and on.

The report provides for the elimination of several major problems for the fundamentalist leadership. If the reorganization plan is implemented,

- The Annuity Board's reluctance to take orders from the executive committee about whom it will serve will be removed by the action of the
  convention. The board will serve only those who are chosen by the
  fundamentalists. The last tie to the troublesome Cooperative Baptist
  Fellowship will be cut. They can shift for themselves in annuity and retirement matters even though many, if not most of them, are long-time
  participants in the Annuity Board programs.
- The nettlesome problems of the women and WMU will be controlled
  by the elimination of WMU from any meaningful relationship to the
  convention and its programs. The feeble offering that the missions
  boards can cooperate with whomever they choose gives little substance
  to the position of one of the most beneficial organizations that Southern
  Baptists have ever had.
- The need to control the Baptist Foundation's functions and set the rules
  for its financial transactions will be passed into the hands of the group
  that was gathering the power. Many legal and regulatory questions are
  left unanswered.
- The Historical Commission will be a thing of the past, and history can
  be readjusted to suit the fundamentalist scheme of things. Archives of
  the more desirable materials can be maintained by the seminaries.
  Some sealed materials such as the deliberations of the Peace Committee await unknown fates.
- Trustees of the combined agencies will apparently be the second-term
  trustees of each of them. This means that the people who did the questionable acts of "decimation" will be gone. In four years there will be
  a complete turnover of trustees on the affected boards. The "moving
  on" phase can be implemented.
- The power in the denomination will be further concentrated in the
  executive committee, a move that is contrary to the intent of the founders of the organization.
- All of the program assignments carefully worked out by mutual agreement over many years will be null and void. "Ministry" assignments
  will be extremely difficult to determine since many of the agencies
  carry out a variety of ministries that will overlap. Turf concerns will
  escalate.

Conversations with a half-dozen knowledgeable observers reveal one unanimous opinion: "This is a concentration of power." Further comments are equally revealing. A sample follows.

- "This is a dismantling of the SBC."
- "This raises so many more questions than it answers."
- "This report removes WMU from the work and limits the relationships with the state conventions."
- "Now the states will tend to keep Cooperative Program funds to fund their programs."
- "The 'cooperative' part of the Cooperative Program has to go."
- "They are now firing commissions instead of persons."
- "In answer to questions about what various segments of the report meant, most often the reply was 'We don't know.' "
- "We are changing everything without knowing the cost or what the implications of the decisions are."
- "The relationships of the Home Mission Board and the states must change completely. At what cost? What happens to the many programs and missionaries? Will Annie Armstrong offering funds be divided between the states and the North American Mission Board?"

If these recommendations pass the convention, one thing is certain: the power will be concentrated in a few "safe havens" under the complete control of the fundamentalist leadership. Once again, the decisions have been handed down from above. The argument will be made that the convention must approve the recommendations in two successive meetings, which will give the authority for doing these things. That will prove to be of little concern "if the leaders get behind this," as the president of the convention remarked prior to the presentation of the recommendation.

The catholicizing of the SBC continues.

Chapter 6

Church-State and the Culture War

In many ways, the current "culture war" with its concurrent tussle between the church and the state is as old as the country. In the earliest days, there came to this continent a group of Englishmen, who were fed up with the strictures of the Anglican Church and searching for their brand of religious freedom. The Act of Uniformity (1559) did not provide what they wanted from the church. They advocated simpler forms of creed and ritual in the established church and longed for freedom of conscience and worship. They were avid in their condemnation of all laxity of morals. Their understanding of the Christian life was so rigid that by 1564 they were nicknamed Puritans. Webster came to define a Puritan as:

> One who is scrupulously strict or censorious and exacting in his religious life. . . . One who practices or preaches a more rigorous or professedly purer moral code than that which prevails.

As they poured into the Massachusetts Bay Colony and other places during the seventeenth century, the Puritans brought with them a number of ideas that would sway the nation for generations. They were rigidly Calvinistic, strongly oriented toward the printed Word, had no problem with the use of civil power to enforce religous conformity, and felt responsible for transforming the culture. As George Marsden stated, "Calvinism in America . . . demanded intellectual assent to precisely formulated statements of religious truth."[1]

Despite their own longing for freedom of conscience and the free exercise of their religion, primarily the Puritans wanted to reserve this right for themselves. E. Y. Mullins recorded:

---

[1]*Fundamentalism and American Culture*, 225.

As Josh Billings or someone else remarked, "The Puritans came over to worship God according to the dictates of their own consciences and to keep other people from worshiping him according to the'r'n."[2]

Some anonymous satirist summarized a Puritan town meeting by saying:

They voted that "the earth is the Lord's, and the fullness thereof"; they voted that the earth is given to the saints; they voted that we are the saints. When the stern Puritans ruled Britain and America in the 1600s, it was against the law to celebrate Christmas. Laws banned church services and civil celebrations on Christmas day. It was illegal to light Christmas candles or sing carols. Stores were required to remain open, and the British Parliament met on Christmas day. The reasons for such austere measures were several. The most important was the holiday heritage stemming from Old Roman days. Believing Christmas meant observing pagan worship rituals, Puritans made Christmas against the law. . . . But people took Christmas celebrations underground. Churches met secretly to light candles and sing carols . . . but they celebrated in privacy.[3]

The Puritans influenced, if not controlled, the religious scene in America for a century and a half. In 1638 Roger Williams was forced from Massachusetts because he refused to yield his religious convictions to the Congregationalist state church. Princeton historian Thomas Jefferson Wertenbaker referred to the colony as "Massachusetts Bible State." According to Herbert N. Siegel, it was

an oligarchy composed of men who held identical religious beliefs. And history records in vivid detail what happened to citizens who did not follow the rules.

Today at the entrance of the state Capitol in Boston stands a sculpture of two women in Quaker habits, Anne Hutchinson and Mary Dyer, both of whom were banished from the colony and exiled to the

---

[2]*The Axioms of Religion* (Philadelphia: American Baptist Publication Society, 1908) 268.

[3]Tom Stokes, *Western Recorder*, 21 December 1993.

wilderness of Rhode Island. Dyer ignored the banishment and returned to the colony. She was hanged on Boston Common in 1660. The two women had defied church doctrine that prayer to God must be given only in the presence of an intermediary, specifically a church elder. Defying a church teaching was deemed to be heresy, punishable by death.[4]

In Maine, a Baptist preacher named William Screven was arrested and given the option of imprisonment or exclusion from the colony. This virulent plague of religious persecution spread down the coast, infecting other states such as Georgia, North Carolina, and Virginia. The state, controlled by Puritanical ideas residing in the Congregational Church and the Church of England, persecuted religious dissenters of any stripe. Baptists, who from the beginning were dissenters, were particular objects of disdain and persecution. Imprisonment was common for such sins as refusing to baptize infants or preaching without permission.

Modern-day fundamentalists who maintain that the United States was formerly a Christian nation should look again at the religious bigotry that helped birth it. This is not to say that there were not serious Christian influences springing from the milieu that ultimately formed the nation. Many people think that the Puritan influence was a major factor in the problems of slavery and the ultimate solution. Other major contributions were doubtless made from the sometimes biblical principles that sprang from various religious influences.

Marsden spoke at length about such involvements.

> From the time of the Puritans until about the middle of the nineteenth century, American evangelicalism was dominated by a Calvinistic vision of the Christian culture. Old Testament Israel, a nation committed to God's law, was the model for political institutions. Hence, the Christian ideal was to introduce God's kingdom—a new Israel—not only in the lives of the regenerate elect, but also by means of civil laws that would both restrain evil and comprehensively transform culture according to God's will. Jonathan Blanchard (1860) similarly spoke of "a perfect state of society" meaning that "the law of God is the Law of the Land."[5]

---

[4]*Miami Herald*, November 1994.
[5]*Fundamentalism and American Culture*, 86.

Marsden also commented that without the extreme Calvinism of the Puritans, the ideals of Puritanism have been brought into modern times.[6] Close examination of the modern ideas of reconstructionism and those advocating the abolition of the Lemon test in the Supreme Court will reveal a close kinship to the Puritan's ideas of a religious state.

Baptists were hauled along in the early national maelstrom kicking and screaming. Roger Williams, a sometime Baptist, brought substance to the idea of a free conscience by expulsion from Massachusetts in 1638. From that time, Baptists were scrambling for the opportunity to exercise their religious consciences without interference from a controlling church or a dictatorial government. They walked in the shadow of many persons who had since Constantine struggled with the conflict between conscience and church and conscience and government.

Libraries have been written about the problems of maintaining free exercise of religion. Some writers insist that the idea of separation of church and state is the Baptist contribution to Western civilization. Certainly, the Baptist stance on the issue has been clear for the life of this nation—until now.

At this stage in the history of the country, we are treated to the sight and sound of those calling themselves Southern Baptists advocating all sorts of ideas that compromise our blood-bought freedom. Included in these ideas are at least the following:

• laws allowing the schools to foster prayer
• the use of tax money for private parochial schools
• the control of school boards for religious reasons
• the control of school curricula for religious reasons.

A sketchy survey of events from 1993–1994 will give a startling view of the amount of conflict visited on the country by those who feel that God has been cast out of schools by the Supreme Court. The conflict has tormented Congress, the Court, school boards, and Christians, Jews, and Muslims alike.

—Republican Congressman Dick Armey of Texas sponsored a bill that would require one-fourth of federal funds to be given to local

---

[6]Ibid., 99, 135.

communities for educational choice programs, which means parochial schools.

—In a Supreme Court case, a deaf student in Arizona asked that the state pay for a sign language interpreter in a Catholic high school.

—Representatives of main-line religious bodies called for efforts "to prevent our public schools from becoming a battleground over religion and to promote true religious liberty."[7]

—Church-state expert and attorney Oliver Thomas posed this question about the issue of prayer in public schools:

> How can prayer to one's God not be a religious act of worship? And what person of faith would want it to be? Those touting the return of state-sponsored school prayer are confusing the issue by calling for "non-sectarian, non-proselytizing" prayers.[8]

Thomas suggested that constitutionally permissible prayer would be:

- individual student prayer
- groups of students praying on their own in a non-disruptive manner
- Bible clubs praying before and after school if there are other non-curriculum clubs at the school
- church-sponsored, rather than school-sponsored, baccalaureate services.

—Congress approved legislation that would deny federal funds to school districts that prevent constitutionally protected prayer in public schools.

—In Jackson, Mississippi, high school principal Bishop Knox was put on indefinite leave after he allowed a student to lead a prayer over the school's intercom.[9]

—In Texas, more than half of the counties have approved school prayer resolutions. Weston Ware, an official of the Texas Christian Life Commission, said this action demonstrates that some politicians are willing to trade religious liberty for social and religious control.[10]

---

[7]Associated Baptist Press, 7 April 1994.
[8]Ibid.
[9]*Baptist Record*, 18 November 1993.
[10]Baptist Press, 3 February 1994.

—In Kentucky, concerned educators call for the involvement of Christians in the public schools. Such involvement enriches both the schools and the Christian children who study there. Also, Christians have a mandate to participate in important aspects of society such as public schools.
—The Baptist Joint Committee on Public Affairs affirmed that Christians have these rights in public schools:

• Schools can teach about religion.
• Religious holidays can be explained and secular celebrations observed.
• Release time programs may allow students to attend classes in religious instruction in an off-campus facility.
• Public schools are required to accommodate the religious exercise of students under the free-exercise clause of the Constitution when that can be done without disrupting the learning process or interfering with the rights of others.[11]

While this recitation could continue for volumes, I will choose limited comments on the school situation. About 450 Southern Baptist churches operate Christian schools and many others are considering opening schools. Nationwide, 11.2 percent of America's school-age children are educated outside the public schools.[12]

Pollster George Gallup says that Americans repeatedly have spoken in favor of the idea of choice in the matter of schools, but also repeatedly have spoken against plans to fund private schools with public money.[13]

People for the American Way recently reported on efforts to ban, burn, and otherwise destroy books, films, and other materials. In some schools, these efforts have removed works ranging from *Huckleberry Finn* to *Schindler's List*. On the other side of the coin are the efforts by the "left-wing" to develop campus speech codes, dismiss faculty and staff, establish "political correctness," and control campus publications.[14]

The issues are clouded and confused for Southern Baptists and the establishment in Washington. The traditional voice of Baptists on such issues, the Baptist Joint Committee, is often in conflict with the new

---

[11]Associated Baptist Press, 10 February 1994.
[12]Ibid., 8 October 1994.
[13]*Western Recorder*, 30 November 1993.
[14]*Miami Herald*, 7 September 1993.

voice on such matters, the SBC Christian Life Commission. These organizations express basically two distinct points of view on the school issues and many others.

The Baptist Joint Committee on Public Affairs supports the traditional Southern Baptist view of free exercise of religion with no interference by the state and no use of tax monies for the support of religion. The Christian Life Commission holds to the old stance on the free exercise of religion, but is willing to compromise the separation of church and state when it comes to government aid for religion. This view has its roots in its Puritan forebears.

More than eighty religious leaders of many denominations, including at least thirty Baptists, worked for three years on the document, "A Shared Vision: Religious Liberty in the Twenty-First Century." Concerning the school and other problems, the statement said in part:

> We oppose direct or indirect government funding of parochial schools at primary and secondary levels and of persuasively sectarian colleges and universities. On the other hand, government aid to certain social service programs sponsored by religious organizations—such as homes for children and the elderly and hospitals—enjoys a long history. Aid to religious institutions that provide manifestly secular services (e. g., hospitals) does not pose a threat to religious liberty if services are provided on a nondiscriminatory basis. However, if an institution indoctrinates its clients with religion or discriminates based on religion in its admission policies, it should be deemed ineligible for government aid.
>
> In sum, public schools should not advance religion, but should accommodate the free exercise of religion. They may not confer a benefit on religion, but may lift governmentally-imposed burdens on the free exercise of religion. They may not promote a religious perspective, but may protect the religious exercise of students.[15]

The conflicts in society over such matters as prayer in schools, legal abortion, school management and curricula, rights for homosexuals and the place of women in society have been greatly aggravated by the rebirth of virulent fundamentalism. How to resolve the wide differences that exist in the most pluralistic society in history is a constant source of conflict and even violence.

---

[15]*Baptists Today*, 8 September 1994.

Add to this instability the fact that many of the minority groups that once longed for integration into the society now insist on preserving their distinctive cultures, including the language differences, morés, and religious traditions. Traditional denominations seem to be losing their claims to loyalty of the clergy and laity. Divisions between major segments of religious bodies are causing even more conflicts that confuse the issues confronting society as a whole. Many aspects of these growing differences end up in court or the legislative bodies.

Fundamentalism seems quite willing to allow or even insist that cultural and societal differences be settled by legal and governmental action. The insistence on closer relationships between church and state raises a plethora of problems about violation of the rights or consciences of others.

Who will make such decisions? On what basis? What criteria should be used to determine issues of conscience? How do these issues relate to the First Amendment rights of all citizens? Will the largest number of persons with a vote decide the conscience and religious issues of the minorities? Will they be treated in the fashion Baptists and other dissenters were in the early days of our nation?

Attempts have been made throughout our history to resolve these issues equitably. In 1971, the Supreme Court formulated what came to be called the Lemon Test. It requires that governmental actions shall:

• have a secular purpose
• neither advance nor restrict religion in its primary affect
• avoid excessive entanglement with religion

For persons who want government to remain neutral toward religion, these criteria have worked reasonably well. They have prevented government meddling in religious practice except where there has been a "compelling state interest."

With the organized emergence of fundamentalism in the Southern Baptist Convention (and many other places), the demands for a change in these rules have accelerated. The Christian Life Commission has agitated rather vocally for the adoption by the Supreme Court of a less binding or directing set of regulations. It "recommends a test based on a legal article by University of Chicago Law School professor Michael McConnell." The suggested test includes the following guidelines:

- Does the state action allow or accommodate independent religious choice?
- Does the state action interfere with the religious liberty of non-adherents by inducing or coercing them to alter their religious practices?
- Does the state action go beyond accommodation and show favoritism toward one religious choice that would not be shown to other religious or non-religious choices?
- Does the state action use the taxing and spending power of government to provide some financial incentive, benefit, or penalty to a particular religious activity that is not given to other religious or non-religious alternatives?[16]

While these guidelines appear to protect private opinion, they open the door to all kinds of governmental participation in religious activities and religious pressures in governmental affairs. Whenever this has been obtained in history, the governmental power has always bent religion to its own purposes. With the present state of American politics, inevitably the groups with the most political power will prevail in any disagreements that arise.

According to the CLC guidelines, it appears to be quite acceptable for the government to support, encourage, and finance religious causes if they are equally available to all. This is a deadly trap that would ultimately produce entanglements that could change the character of religious activity. Again, when government and religion mix, religion loses.

The words of the legendary George Truett, spoken on the Capitol steps in 1920, seem particularly apropos in these troubled times.

That utterance of Jesus, "Render therefore unto Caesar the things which are Caesar's, and unto God the things that are God's," is one of the most revolutionary and history-making utterances that ever fell from those lips divine. That utterance, once for all, marked the divorcement of church and state. It marked a new era for the creeds and deeds of men. It was the sunrise gun of a new day, the echoes of which are to go on and on until in every land, whether great or small, the doctrine shall have absolute supremacy everywhere of a free church in a free state. . . . Christ's religion needs no prop of any kind from any worldly

---

[16]*Western Recorder*, 8 February 1994.

source, and to the degree that it is thus supported is a millstone hanged about its neck.[17]

Recently, a broad coalition of religious groups such as the Baptist Joint Committee, the Christian Life Commission, the Catholic church, and the various Jewish groups united around the passing of the Religious Freedom Restoration Act. In 1990, the Supreme Court ruled that government no longer has to demonstrate a "compelling interest" before restricting religious freedom. After the ruling, it must have only a "reasonable interest." Led by Justice Scalia, the Court declared by a 5–4 vote that the "compelling" standard is "a legal luxury we can no longer afford." The coalition that led in the passage of the law that effectively reversed the Court's action said that within a very short time, about sixty issues had arisen because of it.

These and a hundred other such matters have intensified the conflicts in the society. Because of the stand of fundamentalists and other Christians, many people feel that this is the time of "Christian bashing." Some insist that the only group in the society that isn't protected by "political correctness" is the Christians. Lumping fundamentalism and conservative Christianity together has created an unwholesome atmosphere in which to solve some of these problems.

The fundamentalist movement has some legitimate gripes in various areas. In discussing Stephen Carter's *The Culture of Disbelief*, Kenneth L. Woodward said:

> Religion of every stripe is now threatened by state-enforced "public secularism." In the court of public opinion, he charges, the nation's liberal elites have "come to belittle religious devotion, to humiliate believers and, even if indirectly, to discourage religion as a serious activity"—although he believes that law, politics, the media, and the universities pressure devout believers to treat religion as merely a private matter and "God as a hobby."
>
> The metaphorical wall of separation "originated in an effort to protect religion from the state, not the state from religion." Today, he believes, the "regulatory ubiquity of the modern welfare state" threatens

---

[17]Quoted by Stan Hastey, *Baptists Today*, 26 May 1994.

the autonomy of religion far more than religious fanaticism endangers the body politic.[18]

To simply list the religious issues and cases before the Supreme Court would tax both time and space. Rather than reaching an accommodation that can be accepted by most if not all religious groups in the country, the issues continue to multiply and intensify. The attempts of the religious right to capture school boards across the country is producing untold conflict and will accelerate in the near future.

Baptists traditionally have stood for citizen participation in civil and governmental affairs. Much emphasis has been given in the last generation particularly to the responsibility of Christians to live out their convictions in the culture. Both interest groups and ministers have encouraged such participation.

Christian citizenship should not be confused, however, with politicizing the church and the denomination. Partisan politics in the church even for positive ends has dire consequences. It can easily evolve into a contest for who has the most votes on any issue, however mundane.

One other matter of gravest importance is the oft-repeated admonition of the Christian Life Commission that righteousness or morality can be legislated. This is true only in the most limited sense. Legislating for the protection of society such matters as murder, theft, and rape is necessary and sometimes effective. Strangely, law seems to restrain only the lawful.

If the ends of spiritual religion can be achieved by using legal channels, it means one of two things: Either the religion is not Christian, or Christ died in vain. The ruminations of the Spirit led intellectual giant, Paul of Tarsus, to deal with this issue at length in Romans 7. The idea of the purification of society by legal means has been around a long time. This not to say that we do not need law and laws, but rather that the Christian doctrine of the need for salvation has abundant application to the issues.

The methodology for changing society used in the biblical teaching is sometimes radically different from the modern practices. One modern illustration of the difference in methods is seen in the conflict over abortion. The Christian Life Commission and many other organizations have joined the shouting and screaming picket lines in spirit if not in person.

---

[18]*Newsweek* (20 September 1993) 56, 57.

After years of encouraging protest, it has issued a lengthy paper acknowledging that one should not murder an abortionist.

Religious freedom is definitely under assault. It can be described in many ways and is often discussed in metaphorical terms whose meaning sometimes eludes us. James Dunn, the much maligned but very effective leader of the Baptist Joint Committee on Public Affairs, put the matter quite clearly and succinctly. Speaking to the William H. Whitsitt Baptist Heritage Society, he listed what he considers to be six of the most important threats to religious freedom.

(1) *A politicization of religion.* Don't be fooled by those who conflate political agendas with "God talk." One of the most serious threats to the moral authority of the religous community is the shortsightedness of those who sacrifice the permanent on the altar of the temporary. . . . One of the most serious threats to civility in society is the medieval use and abuse of religion as a weapon in polemical politics.

(2) *The religious right.* Fueled by fear and flirting dangerously with hate, . . . it employs a bottom-up rather than a top-down strategy and targets do-able objectives such as school boards and trains its troops for political action. Stealth candidates backing an agenda including ultimate abolition of public education are advised to conceal their true colors until elected and if exposed, to disown "anti-Christian bigotry."

(3) *Revisionism.* Rewriting history is a growth industry. Critics in high places contend separation of church and state was not the intent of America's founders but a latter-day innovation. Despite such arguments, church-state separation is the law of the land.

(4) *Roman Catholicism.* No informed observer of the political scene can honestly ignore the millions of dollars being spent right now to get public monies for parochial schools. (Some "Baptists" are involved in this pursuit now!)

(5) *Reconstructionism.* The Coalition for Revival, rooted in R. J. Rushdoony's writings, hails seventeenth-century colonial America as a period when civil law was based explicitly on biblical principles. Though it has received wide public attention, the group may not be statistically significant. Reconstructionists aim to establish a theocracy in America and each one of them would like to be "theo."

(6) *Commodification.* The rise of churches built on consumer-oriented marketing principles threatens religious freedom by weakening traditional Baptist emphases on experiential religion and religious liberty.

The bland leading the bland have no time for history and little interest in denominational distinctives.[19]

American church-state conflict dates back to the days of the early colonists. Although the Puritans came to America for religious freedom, in reality they were intolerant of persons whose religious views differed from their own. Through the years, Christians have felt their culture has allowed them few rights. In opposition, the modern fundamentalists seek to impose restrictions on the government and involve it in matters that will benefit the conservative religious cause. Backed by the new Christian Life Commission, they pressure for prayer in school, government funding of religious schools, and control of school personnel and curriculum. Their efforts represent a major challenge to the Lemon Test in which the government remains neutral in religious issues. This principle of the separation of church and state was the intention of our constitutional forebears but is now greatly challenged.

[19]Associated Baptist Press, 12 May 1994.

Chapter 7

The Anatomy of Fundamentalism Southwestern Baptist Theological Seminary

The anatomy of Fundamentalism was exposed and naked when the trustees of Southwestern Seminary fired President Russell Dilday on Wednesday, 9 March 1994. The event occurred at a regular meeting of the trustees amid rumors of pending drastic action. It was not a new story since rumors had circulated for years that the termination of the president was imminent.

On the prior evening, the committee met with Dilday. He was evaluated on nine criteria and received positive marks on all nine. On some of the criteria he received high trustee marks including the use of language such as "great, wonderful, glorious."

This evaluation, while appreciated by the president, perplexed him. He asked about the rampant rumors that he was to be fired. He received the blunt reply: "There is nothing to those rumors." The *Baptist Standard* reported on 16 March:

> Despite the denials, it became obvious that the dismissal was to be a fact and had been planned weeks ahead. One trustee who voted against the dismissal motion told the (*Baptist*) *Standard* that another trustee told him he had known about it for at least two weeks before the meeting and told him what the vote count would be an hour before it was taken.

On Wednesday morning, trustee chairman and Dallas lawyer Ralph Pulley requested a meeting with the president and a small group of trustees. In this meeting, Dilday was offered a retirement package if he agreed to resign. He replied that he had no intention of retiring at that time: "God led me here, and I had no leadership from the Lord that this was the time to retire." Dilday said that he "asked under what charges, what rationale, would they dismiss me."

The chairman replied, "We don't need a reason. We have the votes to do it, and we will. And it will be with no provision for anything if you don't accept the early retirement plan."

The president told the trustees, "You have to do your business as a board. My business is to determine my calling in life, and I am not planning retirement. So let's go. You do what you have to do."

The trustees entered a closed-door session. A group of students gathered outside the room, praying and singing. After seventy-five minutes, Dilday emerged to tell them that the Seminary no longer had a president. When asked why the president had been fired, Pulley replied that the institution "needed new direction to move into the twenty-first century."

To add insult to injury, the trustees in the company of armed guards (not campus security) changed the locks on the door of the president's office, as Dilday said, "before I got out of the building." They changed the access codes in the computers since, as one trustee said, "He is a computer whiz." One trustee said that the action was taken according to "business-world protocol." Obviously, they did not trust the president to retrieve his personal effects from the office or computer.

In a subsequent press conference, Pulley said that the adverse reaction was expected and that it would subside. He would not give a reason for the firing, however, commenting that reasons were "not pertinent." Yet, two days after the termination, the trustees issued a press release saying that they and Dilday had "irreconcilable differences." They gave little detail; they simply criticized Dilday for continuing to speak out on political issues, a violation of an agreement set by the trustees. Dilday told reporters in a post-firing statement: "The only word that ever cropped up that I heard (in the closed-door meeting) was insubordination, which I don't think is worthy."

Immediately trustees distributed letters to students and faculty. Two versions had been prepared, one indicating that Dilday had retired and the other that he had been fired. (Some faculty members actually received the wrong letter.) John Earl Seelig, a long-term vice president who was said to have been fired by Dilday in 1990, was asked before the event to be in charge of public relations. It was reported on campus that he had pre-pared the material for release to the students and faculty.[1]

An interesting sidelight to the entire affair was the fact that chairman Pulley was widely reported to have long been a foe of Dilday. When the presidential search committee recommended Dilday as president in 1978, Pulley presented as an alternative candidate his brother-in-law, Huber Drumwright, dean of the theology school. Trustees defeated Pulley's motion and elected Dilday. Later, Pulley lobbied Dilday to name Drum-wright vice president for academic affairs, but Dilday chose John New-port. The *Western Recorder* reported, "Longtime observers close to the seminary said that rejection solidified Pulley's opposition to Dilday."[2]

Responses to the Firing

The response to the firing was immediate, loud, and very vigorous from students and faculty, individual and corporate financial contributors, insti-tutions and agencies, editors of state Baptist papers, state and SBC leaders, seminary trustees, and others. Outraged persons from all over the nation began to register their opinions of the firing by phone, church newsletter columns, telegrams, phone calls, and visits with Dilday and members of the trustees.

Students and Faculty

—In a five-column headline that read "Students Bitter at Southwestern Baptist Seminary President's Firing," the *Fresno (California) Bee*, report-ed that students jeered the chairman of the trustees in a chapel meeting and shouted "Why? Why?" Several hundred students and faculty met with Dilday on the lawn of the president's home on the morning after the firing. Also, students scheduled a meeting for 21 March to decide what response to give to the firing.[3]

---

[1]The previous Information and citations come from personal conversations with Dil-day and media representatives, Associated Baptist Press, Baptist Press, and state papers.

[2]15 March 1994.

[3]11 March 1994.

—On the day after the firing, the faculty unanimously approved a letter to each trustee that said: "We do not concur with either the action taken by the (board) with regard to our president, nor the manner in which the action was carried out."[4]

—The theology faculty issued this statement: "President Dilday was an excellent administrator who led the seminary with a spirit of Christlikeness and kept the school doctrinally sound."[5] Similar declarations followed.

—On 13 April, Jack Coldiron, distinguished professor of voice, sent his notice of retirement to individual members of the trustees. He told Miles Seaborn, to whom the letter was addressed, that despite a lifetime of nurture from the SBC, his "belief and confidence" in the convention "have gradually eroded" as fundamental-conservatives now controlling the convention have effected their reforms. With the firing of Dilday, "the last vestige of trust was ripped apart, and I have decided it is impossible for me to work with you any longer."[6]

Financial Contributors

—Kenneth Cooper, an international expert on preventive medicine and a longtime supporter of Southwestern, resigned his life membership on the advisory council of the seminary in protest of the "unwarranted, disrespectful, and embarrassing" firing of Dilday. (Other council members were reported to tender their resignations as well.) He also resigned as chairman of the council's current fund-raising campaign and canceled his $30,000 pledge to the seminary. In a telegram to the trustees announcing his resignation, Cooper commented, "I will no longer offer my services in any capacity in support of Southwestern Baptist Theological Seminary."[7]

—On 15 March, Marilyn McNeely Dunn asked seminary administrators to remove the portraits of her parents from the school of church music that her parents helped establish. She reasoned that the seminary had

---

[4]Baptist Press, 24 March 1994.
[5]*Baptist Standard*, 4 May 1994.
[6]Associated Baptist Press, as quoted in *Baptist Standard*, 4 May 1994.
[7]Associated Baptist Press, 15 April 1994.

come under the control of the type of people that the McNeelys found "repugnant." As she said,

> All who knew my feisty father will join me in the strong suspicion that though he went home to be with the Lord ten years ago and now hangs framed in Cowden Hall, he will climb off that wall and take his leave since the seminary is no longer the one he knew and loved.[8]

—Spokespersons for three West Texas foundations that have channeled hundreds of thousands of dollars to Southwestern said that the funds will be halted, placed under review, or given only for specific purposes.[9]
—Kelley Brown, president of the Tom and Evelyn Linebery Foundation and vice president of the Scarborough Foundation of Midland, told the *Baptist Standard* that no more funds will be given by the foundations to the seminary because of the dismissal of Dilday. In the last few years, the foundation had given more than $700,000 to the seminary and more than that in years past. Until the firing, a gift of $6,000,000–$9,000,000 was under consideration. Brown said that before any money is given again, "We will take the position that we want to know who are serving on the boards of trustees and how they stand on the controversy."[10]
—The Panhandle Baptist Foundation, established by C. J. and Ophelia Humphrey of Amarillo, who were to have been honored with the B. H. Carroll Award on Founder's Day, notified the seminary that it was putting further contributions on hold.[11]
—Frank Pollard, a noted pastor from Jackson, Mississippi, and the chairman of a committee to request support from Southwestern alumni for a $36,000,000 effort, told the *Baptist Standard* he had notified the seminary that he could not

> "in good conscience" be involved in raising money for the school at present. . . . I am personally hurting because a friend I loved has been wronged, the seminary abused, and the denomination once again embarrassed.[12]

---

[8]Associated Baptist Press, 17 March 1994.
[9]Baptist Press, 18 March 1994.
[10]Ibid.
[11]Ibid.
[12]Ibid.

—Additional financial results were immediately evident. The firing cost the seminary in gifts and pledges "at least $15,000,000" according to a memorandum sent to members of the Southwestern Council by its current and past chairman.[13]

—A potential donor was on campus the day of the firing. His contemplated gift was in the financial vicinity of $6,000,000. He left the campus after the firing, uncommitted.[14]

—Other potential gifts already had been canceled. One donor had planned for the seminary to share with another school a $14,000,000 gift. Another person was contemplating leaving the seminary half of a total estate valued in the millions.[15]

Institutions and Agencies

—In a written statement, Baylor University president Herbert Reynolds called the action a

> sad day in Baptist life. I was not at all surprised by those actions on the part of fundamentalists who have ravaged so many of our Southern Baptist institutions and agencies over the past fifteen years.[16]

—Students and faculty at Brite Divinity School at Texas Christian University sent consoling messages to Southwestern.

—The seminary's disarray was the subject of concern by the Association of Theological Schools (ATS), one of the school's accrediting agencies. In a rare letter of censure, the Association said,

> We view with utmost seriousness the dismissal of Russell Dilday. Such precipitous action on the part of any board of trustees is a clear violation of accepted governance practices and places in jeopardy the vitality and basic integrity of the institution.[17]

---

[13]Associated Baptist Press, 29 March 1994.
[14]Anonymous source.
[15]Anonymous source.
[16]*Fresno Bee*, 11 March 1994.
[17]Associated Baptist Press, 22 March 1994.

It called on trustees to reconsider the firing but did not threaten to place the school on probation. In July ATS announced that it would make a follow-up visit to Southwestern in the fall. The acting president, William Tolar, said he would ask the accrediting agency to delay the visit until the new president had settled in, however.[18] In February 1995, the seminary was placed on probation for two years.[19]

Editors of State Baptist Papers

—**Oklahoma.** Glenn Brown commented in the *Baptist Messenger*:

> Deep, gut-wrenching anger is what many Southern Baptists are registering at the firing of Russell Dilday as president of Southwestern Seminary. Even some of the conservative pastors and leaders who have supported the conservative resurgence have expressed dismay at what took place and the manner in which Dilday was treated. . . . There was no battle for the Bible at Southwestern. It is biblically solid. . . . Even the trustees acknowledge Dilday is a very capable administrator and the school prospers by nearly every measure. Thus, the move to fire the president, in spite of rumors that it was imminent, appears to many to be an unwarranted action, lacking in substantive cause.[20]

—**North Carolina.** *Biblical Recorder* editor R. G. Puckett wrote:

> In the days of yesteryear, the western frontier of America was often characterized by a "law and order" maintained through the six-gun and lynching rope. Cattle rustlers and horse thieves, when captured by quickly-formed posses or vigilante groups, were judged, convicted, sentenced, and executed on the spot. Russell Dilday is neither a cattle rustler nor a horse thief. He is a moral man with an exemplary family. He is known as conservative in his theology, gracious in his spirit, and kind in dealing with others. Why then was he fired by the trustees in a manner reminiscent of an old-fashioned lynching party?[21]

---

[18]Baptist Press, 15 July 1994.
[19]Associated Baptist Press, 2 February 1995.
[20]24 March 1994.
[21]2 April 1994.

Puckett concluded that the answers given by trustees and SBC leaders were inadequate.

—**Alabama.** The *Alabama Baptist* reported that Dilday's dismissal "gives critics of Southern Baptists more ammunition to use against us."[22]

—**New Mexico.** John Loudat of the *Baptist New Mexican* said:

> Satan can use this event to cast a dark cloud on all the work of Southern Baptists around the world. You better believe he would love to use this to blow us out of the water.[23]

—**Tennessee.** *Baptist and Reflector* editor Fletcher Allen wrote that while the board's authority to fire Dilday is unquestioned,

> Christian actions are on trial. . . . There must be a better way to settle differences. Baptists deserve answers, more facts. Until they get them, they have little reason to hope for the best.[24]

—**Texas.** Presnall Wood of the *Baptist Standard* was particularly concerned. He commented: "The issue in Dilday's firing was not Dilday's belief in the Bible, but it was power. It was control. It was denominational politics." The action has

> ushered the institution into a day of instability that could hurt the largest evangelical seminary in the world. If the firing and the way it was done is an example of the direction the Southwestern trustees are going, the seminary is in for even greater trouble.[25]

—**Louisiana.** Lynn Clayton of the *Baptist Messenger* predicted the firing

> will prove to be a cataclysmic event of recent Southern Baptist Convention life. Whatever is going to happen in convention life, Russell Dilday's firing will hasten by ten years.[26]

---

[22]Ibid.
[23]Ibid.
[24]Ibid.
[25]Ibid.
[26]Ibid., 26 March 1994.

—**Kentucky.** Marv Knox of the *Western Recorder* headed his editorial, "They lied to Dilday; have they been lying to you?" He was concerned that one day before the firing, trustees told Dilday that there was no substance to the firing rumors. Knox concluded the editorial with these words:

> The conservative political party has claimed the SBC needed to be taken over, saved from liberals. Thousands of good, earnest, God-fearing, Bible-loving Southern Baptists contributed to the cause by voting the party ticket. Now, that party is in such control of the SBC that its leaders "don't need a reason" for firing a respected and faithful seminary president. They still don't have any heretics to show for all their hunting, and numerous indicators of denominational health have declined. Is it because party bosses have been lying to Southern Baptists, just like they lied to Russell Dilday?[27]

State Conventions

—**Kentucky.** Executive director William Marshall commented on the firing in his regular column in the *Western Recorder*:

> Since no public charges have been made as to why Dilday was fired, and the trustees have refused to be specific, the trustees have left themselves open to a Southern Baptist "public" outrage which cannot but negatively impact their role and the role of trustees elected as "stewards" of other Southern Baptist institutions. . . . The furor already rising in Texas over this event will further sweep many other Southern Baptists into an even more painful awareness that Southern Baptists are in deep trouble. . . . This incident will have awesome repercussions, yet to be imagined.[28]

—**Missouri.** The executive board voted 31–6 to send a letter to the trustees of SWBTS to protest their manner of firing Dilday. Some board members argued that the action should be protested, while others did not

---

[27]15 March 1994.
[28]Ibid.

want to bring the debate into Missouri or act in an unchristian manner. Others argued that it was not unchristian to protest unchristian behavior.[29] —**North Carolina.** In a meeting 24–25 May, the general board passed a statement called "Cooperation Through Autonomy" reaffirming "The North Carolina Baptist Way." It discussed the problems the fundamentalist movement had caused and acknowledged that every agency of the SBC had suffered some degree of discord and disruption. It cited the Dilday firing and the problems of the Annuity Board with the SBC executive committee and others. The action expressed

> our keen disapproval of and disappointment in those events which have taken place in the SBC. . . . At the same time we do hereby reaffirm and recommit ourselves to the principle of autonomy, from which emerges all other guiding principles of our state convention, The North Carolina Baptist Way.[30]

The statement reaffirmed local church autonomy, the right to distribute funding, North Carolina cooperation, the rejection of any creedal litmus test, and dedication to the task committed to the church.

Roy Smith, executive director of the state convention, sent a strong letter to the chairman of the Southwestern trustees protesting their action in firing Dilday. He made it clear that the firing had made his job of raising money for missions significantly more difficult.[31] —**Northwest Baptist Convention.** Executive director Cecil Sims announced in a 23 May letter to Edwin Young, president of the SBC, that he would make a motion at the SBC meeting requesting the resignation of Southwestern trustee chairman Ralph Pulley, vice chairman Lee Weaver, and secretary T. Bob Davis. He stated,

> My motive is two-fold. First, I honestly believe the actions and judgment of the trustee leaders is such that they have betrayed the trust given them by the convention and the seminary. Secondly, the voice of dissent must be respected and given an opportunity to express itself.[32]

[29]Associated Baptist Press, 21 April 1994.
[30]*Biblical Recorder*, 4 June 1994.
[31]Ibid.
[32]Baptist Press, 26 May 1994.

(Although Sims had researched the SBC constitution and bylaws and the charter documents of the seminary and found nothing that would suggest the motion was out of order, parliamentary maneuvering defeated his attempt.)

—**Texas.** Executive director William Pinson, who is usually very cautious, said:

> A host of Texas Baptists are deeply disturbed about the action of some of the trustees to dismiss R. H. Dilday as president of Southwestern Seminary and are equally concerned about the effect it might have on the Lord's work in Texas and beyond.[33]

Jerold McBride, president of the state convention, expressed his sentiments:

> It is a sad day for the SBC because those within the convention who kept hoping that reconciliation would in time come, now have every reason to question their hope. All but seven of the trustees of SWBTS acted in a manner that has inflicted irreparable damage both to the seminary and the SBC. . . . The decision to fire Russell Dilday is consistent with the nature of political fundamentalists to purge those who do not submit to their authoritarianism. The trail of their victims is long and tragic.[34]

On 26 March, moderate Baptists met with leaders of the state convention to discuss ways to respond to the crisis. After some extended discussion, the participants decided to work through established denominational channels and not pursue radical measures.[35]

In its 7 June meeting, the executive board denounced the firing of Dilday and voted to consider establishing an alternative school for training ministers.[36]

The executive board passed a resolution formally recording its disapproval of the firing of Dilday and reminding the seminary trustees of "their moral obligation" to provide an equitable and generous severance

---

[33]*Baptist Record*, 17 March 1994.
[34]*Biblical Recorder*, 26 March 1994.
[35]Associated Baptist Press, 29 March 1994.
[36]Ibid.

package and not to infringe on Dilday's freedom to speak or restrict his right to serve Christ under the dictates of his own conscience.[37]

SBC Leaders

—Ed Young, president of the SBC commented on the action of the trustees:

> I'm sure they were thinking about the direction the seminary would take in the next decade and felt this was the proper time, evidently, to look for a new president. . . . They're trustees; we've entrusted them with the responsibility for these institutions fulfilling the purpose for which they are established.[38]

Young also sent a telegram to Dilday assuring him of prayer.

—Morris Chapman, president of the executive committee, indicated that the decision to fire Dilday was a trustee responsibility.[39]

—Henry Blackaby, director of the Office of Prayer and Spiritual Awakening for the Home Mission Board and consultant to the Foreign Mission Board and Sunday School Board, commented that many people were responding to the firing of Dilday in the same way the world would respond. "We're not consulting our brothers; we're just reacting. The knee-jerk reaction can be worse than the action." He acknowledged that the trustee action was "precipitous" but warned that "men will have to give account on the day of judgment for every careless word they have spoken."[40]

—On 21 April, top leaders of the SBC met privately in Atlanta apparently to consider damage control in the Southwestern debacle. Associated Baptist Press reported:

> At least fifteen leaders of the conservative movement were seen leaving the meeting . . . including former presidents Adrian Rogers of Memphis

---

[37]Ibid.
[38]Baptist Press, 17 March 1994.
[39]*Baptist Record*, 17 March 1994.
[40]Baptist Press, 25 March 1994.

who presided at the six-hour meeting, Charles Stanley and Bailey Smith of Atlanta, and Jerry Vines of Jacksonville.[41]

The participants agreed not to talk to the press about the meeting but acknowledged that they had talked about several matters of mutual interest. —Texas trustee Ollin Collins wrote these words to eight key figures in the conservative movement, including six former SBC presidents, complaining about their strange silence since the firing:

> I say strange silence because it just seems strange that when we finally did what you men had been leading us to do, and saying needed to be done for some ten years now, . . . it was as though we had leprosy and nobody wanted to touch us or be associated with us. We really feel like we have been hung out and left by our self, and nobody that we have respected has stepped forward to support the action.[42]

—Chairman Pulley, on the other hand, said that he had received strong support from SBC leaders. Within days, Collins received a phone call from James Draper, president of the Sunday School Board, and Jerry Vines wrote of his support in his church newsletter that he mailed to 8,000 pastors. He said he was authorized by former presidents Rogers, Smith, and Stanley to speak for them. Collins also received supportive letters from Rogers, Vines, and Lindsay, pastor in Jacksonville.[43]
—Mark Coppenger, executive committee vice president for public relations, saw the firing as a part of "the transition process." He recited a long list of the changes of agency heads and cited what he called progress in most areas of the work.[44]
—In an article in *SBC Life*, Coppenger took the Baptist media to task for the Dilday reporting. He criticized Associated Baptist Press, the Cooperative Baptist Fellowship, Baptist Press, Religious News Service, *Christianity Today*, Southwestern's faculty, and the secular press. Coppenger's principal point was that Southwestern's trustees had good reason to fire Dilday, but the press had neglected to report on those good reasons.[45]

---

[41]Associated Baptist Press, 26 April 1994.
[42]Ibid., 24 Mary 1994.
[43]Ibid.
[44]*Biblical Recorder*, 26 March 1994.
[45]Associated Baptist Press, 7 June 1994.

Trustees

—Larry Brown of New Jersey told board members that he had served on the boards of major secular corporations and had never seen such a "mean spirit" as that demonstrated by the seminary trustees. John Babb of Nevada told trustees he had seen sheepherders get better treatment than Dilday.[46]

—Wayne Allen, pastor of First Baptist Church, Carrollton, Texas, voted against firing the president. In several forums, he defended Dilday. Allen said that the biggest dispute between Dilday and trustees was over the Cooperative Baptist Fellowship. Allen said Dilday was trying to keep some moderate churches and Fellowship supporters from abandoning the school and that

> the trustees finally came to the place where they didn't want anything to do with anyone identified with the Cooperative Baptist Fellowship. It had become a major issue in the last two years.[47]

—On 23 March, conservative leader Jack Graham, pastor of prestigious Prestonwood Baptist Church in North Dallas, was quoted in the *Dallas Morning News* as saying that the president was fired with "little if any, compassion." The way he was dismissed only fuels the belief that conservatives are "unloving and mean-spirited." Wayne Allen concurred, saying that Graham's statement shows that not all fundamentalists agree with the trustee board's behavior. "I think it's helping them see that there have been actions taken that aren't Christian." Allen also said that he would ask the SBC executive committee to investigate the board's actions. Shortly after conversations with other trustees, however, he abandoned that intention.[48]

—Floridian Jim Leftwich told the Florida *Baptist Witness*,

> In short, he (Dilday) didn't demonstrate a willingness to be under the leadership that God had placed over him at the seminary or at the

---

[46]*Baptist Standard*, 16 March 1994.
[47]Associated Baptist Press, 22 March 1994.
[48]Baptist Press, 24 March 1994.

convention. . . . The trustees had stated "in no uncertain terms" they didn't want the seminary used as a platform for the Baptist moderates' Cooperative Baptist Fellowship. . . . I would not call Dr. Dilday a classic liberal, but his views in that book would be called veiled new-orthodoxy. A wavering view of Bible inspiration leads to a multitude of divisions in Bible interpretation.[49]

—Alabama trustee Paul Balducci defended the firing. He indicated that a very serious matter in the firing was the invitation to Keith Parks to speak at the seminary. Concerning the book discussed by Leftwich, Balducci said: "That reason doesn't reflect my view. In fact, I went back and reread his book, and I had a hard time finding problems with that."[50]

Trustee Action

On 21 March, trustees issued another press release in an attempt to calm the ground-swell of protest. The trustees said that they dismissed Dilday

because of mismanagement of the institution, and doctrinal and policy differences that caused gridlock between him and trustees and Southern Baptist Convention leadership.

The release also accused the president of insubordination and cited a decline in enrollment of 1,000 students in less than ten years.[51]

Also on 21 March, some trustees addressed a pastors' group. In giving examples of Dilday's failures, they cited his opposition to forming an anti-abortion group on campus, his defense of a professor's speech on the role of women—which trustees said was influenced by feminist thinking —and his alleged indifference to charges that conservative students were being belittled by some faculty and students.

In other action, the trustee officers announced that they would send letters to 40,000 pastors and directors of missions on 31 March. This effort moved from "we don't need a reason," "irreconcilable differences,"

---

[49]Ibid., 26 April 1994.
[50]Ibid.
[51]Ibid.

and "mismanagement and insubordination" to a new litany of presidential problems.

The "irreconcilable philosophical differences" were illustrated by Dilday's invitation to CBF leader Keith Parks to speak at commencement, disagreement over the type of training offered in the seminary's school of church music, and an administrative reorganization plan offered by Dilday that trustees found "unacceptable."

The letter faulted Dilday for an "unwillingness to cooperate" with the board, demonstrated by repeated criticism of SBC leaders and board members, failure to adhere to "directives" that he avoid political involvement in SBC life, and a relationship with trustees marked by "constant confrontation, both individually and collectively."[52]

For the first time, trustees accused Dilday of liberalism. They charged that in his book, *The Doctrine of Biblical Authority*, he used "his high office in a denominational institution" and took sides in the debate over the nature of scripture by shifting

> the emphasis from the nature to the purpose of scripture. . . . From a decidedly biased position, Dr. Dilday is dedicated to berate, misrepresent, and assail those who hold the Bible to be God's inerrant, infallible and authoritative Word.[53]

Dilday's Response

Dilday responded that the criticism concerning his book was

> an absolute misreading of my book. . . . My total commitment has been, is, and will be that the Bible is the inerrant, infallible and authoritative word of God. It is that philosophy I have used in accepting faculty for recommendation and to which the curriculum of our school is committed. . . . I am appalled and stunned by the inaccuracy and misrepresentations and untruths in this letter from some of the leaders of the board of trustees.[54]

---

[52]Associated Baptist Press, 31 March 1994.
[53]Baptist Press, 21 March 1994.
[54]Associated Baptist Press, 31 March 1994.

Concerning the "generous offer" of a retirement plan if he retired, Dilday commented that the idea was "absolutely false."

> It was offered in a confrontational spirit, which I looked at long enough to realize while generous in total it was really a buyout, almost an effort to bribe me to leave, and no matter how generous I could not in good faith accept it.[55]

According to Dilday, it was "troublesome because it can be arbitrarily terminated by trustees." At issue were three conditions:

> (a) To keep as his primary and ultimate purpose the well-being and good of SWBTS (the seminary) as an institution for training men and women for ministry and will let this be the basis for conferences, interviews, speeches, lectures, etc., in which he may be involved while drawing benefits from SWBTS
> (b) To refrain from any action or activity that may be deemed not in the best interests of SWBTS, specifically including (but without limitation) working with or promoting any entity not in harmony and cooperation with the Southern Baptist Convention, while drawing benefits from SWBTS
> (c) Should the executive committee of the board of trustees of SWBTS deem that Dr. Dilday has not acted in good faith with regard to this agreement, the committee may in its sole discretion terminate any benefits which have not been paid.[56]

Dilday denied any concept of gridlock, that the trustees were on record as saying they did not want to change the direction of the music school but only add another emphasis, that he had made a bold effort to reduce administrative expenses, and that he had not engaged in denominational politics at all since the agreement with the trustees in 1989.

In reply to the accusations about his dealings with the CBF, he said,

> As to my supposed sympathy with the Cooperative Fellowship, I am on public record as not endorsing the Fellowship as the way forward in the convention. I have taken no action that would imply anything other than

---

[55]Ibid.
[56]Ibid.

that my total commitment has always been to support the Cooperative Program and the Southern Baptist Convention. That reference in the trustee letter is simply a false statement.[57]

By 17 May, the fired president told the press that he would vacate the seminary house by the deadline set by the trustees (June 7), but that the severance package was still not finalized. He said,

> My effort in negotiation is to avoid being muzzled or limited in my activity and to give the severance some sort of permanence so we can make further plans.[58]

The Dildays moved out of the seminary presidential home on the scheduled date. The closing on their new home had been delayed twice, Dilday said, because the trustees wanted to put a first lien on the property, which caused the mortgage company to balk. The impasse was resolved by separating the housing fund (previously provided) from Dilday's severance package that was still in dispute with trustees.[59]

Despite the unhappy situation of the previous months, Dilday responded to the continuous support of friends, both known and unknown. On the evening of 6 June, about 1,100 friends gathered in Dallas to honor Betty and Russell Dilday. The master of ceremonies and president the the Annuity Board, Paul Powell, commented that probably never before had so many people come so far to "honor two jobless and homeless people." Some fifty persons and companies contributed to support the banquet. Dilday said that since the firing, though there had been a lot of doubts and downsides, he and his wife had been able to retain their sense of humor, a gift from God. He said the word "friends" had come to have new meaning and that it was "great to be in a fellowship where love is unfeigned."[60]

Russell Dilday also responded positively to the opporutnity for service at Baylor University as distinguished professor of homiletics at the new George W. Truett Theological Seminary and as special assistant to

---

[57]Baptist Press, 31 March 1994.
[58]Associated Baptist Press, 17 May 1994.
[59]Ibid., 7 June 1994.
[60]Ibid., 9 June 1994.

the university's president. Dilday said he sought employment for at least three or four years because

> Unreasonable and arbitrary conditions enforced by the (trustee) chairman made it impossible to depend on the severance as our income from month to month.

He said attempts to resolve the problem yielded only answers that were "curt, arbitrary, and inflexible, giving no indication of good-faith negotiations."[61]

The Anatomy of Fundamentalism

The true nature and form of fundamentalism was starkly revealed and displayed in the Southwestern debacle. To use an analogy Texans would understand, "The carcass lay visible for all to see in the chilling howl of a Blue Norther." (When the storm thunders in from the north, Texans are fond of saying that there is nothing between them and the North Pole except a barbed wire fence—and it is frequently down.) As the details of the controversy were gradually uncovered, by early summer the bones lay bleaching in the Texas sun.

Whichever characteristics of fundamentalism are used (see Chapter 1), the Dilday firing was an unmistakable portrait of the aberration. The trustees seemed to act without regard for Dilday or his family. They thought the reasons were "irrelevant." They didn't "need a reason; we have the votes." They used questionable criteria in locking Dilday out of his office and changing the access code in the computers. Such reasons as were finally devised after the fact evidenced inflexibility. To the trustees, the end justified the means. Clearly, they expected conformity from all segments of the seminary community. Persistent militancy was the keynote of the "negotiations." Arrogance seemed to dominate the trustee positions.

The Southern Baptist Convention suffered a severe blow with the termination of Dilday. The fallout went far beyond the individual and his plight. While the seminary was seriously damaged, the real problems

---

[61]Ibid., 29 July 1994.

were much larger. The reputation of the denomination, carefully built over more than a century, was seriously impaired. The Christian witness of Southern Baptists had already been hurt severely by previous actions of the fundamentalist leadership.

Now, conservative Christianity is once again lumped with fundamentalism. The growing opposition to "the religious right" on every side is reinforced in its belief that all conservatives fall in the category of fundamentalism. The conservative trustees who abhorred what happened to Dilday will bear an unworthy label for perhaps the rest of their lives. The 1920 definition of fundamentalists as "people . . . preoccupied with the message of God's salvation of sinners . . ." that fit millions of Baptists cannot describe the trustees of Southwestern Seminary; they were preoccupied with something else.

On 6 July, Baptist Press announced that Kenneth S. Hemphill, church growth specialist and former Virginia pastor, was the choice of the presidential search committee to succeed Dilday. On 12 July, committee chairman Miles Seaborn confirmed the announcement. Shortly after, Hemphill was elected and labeled "a mainstream" selection.

Chapter 8

The Great Silence

"When the Lamb opened the seventh seal, there was silence in heaven for about half an hour." (Rev 8:1)

The silence from the multitudes in the SBC has lasted for a decade and a half. From the time fundamentalism won the victory for control of the Southern Baptist Convention, a strange silence has engulfed a very large segment of the people. The silence was exceedingly strange, considering the fact that we have been properly labeled "not a silent people" by Walter Shurden.[1]

When I was responsible for some part of the work of the denomination from 1961 to 1984, the silence was frequently broken by someone with an opinion or complaint. Grievances, real or imagined, were regularly aired. This free expression was not persecution or non-cooperation; it was the democratic Baptist way. This conduct had nothing to do with being a loyal Southern Baptist or a cooperating brother. There were few measures of loyalty, and those were often resented. Every Baptist had the right and even the responsibility to dissent if he or she thought the denomination was straying. These rights were often exercised.

Yet, for a decade at least, there was a deafening silence from vast numbers of the constituency concerning the fundamentalist takeover. Of course, dissatisfaction with the "conservative resurgence" was expressed in hall talk, private conversations, and small group discussions. But insofar as organized, vigorous opposition in official circles was concerned, the silence reigned.

In spite of the silence, private conversations and interviews indicated that the majority of the officials of the denomination—from the directors of missions in the local association to the presidents of the national agencies—opposed the movement. Most of the state executive directors, college presidents, and other state leaders were conspicuously missing from the conflict.

---

[1]*Not a Silent People*, rev. ed. (Macon GA: Smyth & Helwys, 1995).

When I was a denominational official, I would comment that if Baptists ever learned how much power the state executive director actually had, they would abolish the office. Inherent in the office was a reservoir of trust in the executive. Most often, this person served honorably and efficiently, rarely abusing the position. State executive directors probably were the only ones who could have harnessed enough following and votes to curb the fundamentalist takeover.

State directors primarily limited their opposition to private communications of various natures and took no sustained organized action against the coup, however. To them, peace in the fellowship of the state organizations was essential to their function. One of their major responsibilities was the raising of money from the churches to fund the state and national educational and missionary causes. Many, if not most, of the leaders hoped in vain that the controversy would remain on a national level and not invade their domain.

Furthermore, these leaders had been born and bred administratively in the democratic principle that the majority rules. When the SBC votes became roughly 55 percent for the fundamentalist agenda and 45 percent for the "moderate" side, the state leadership felt an obligation to abide by the vote of the majority.

At this juncture the convictions of many of the state leaders collided with an agenda they knew did not fit the Baptist heritage. They felt their jobs required one course of action and their understanding of Baptist polity and theology another. Since peace was felt to be essential to the proper functioning of the body politic, many state directors privately complained about the course of the denomination but did not organize to confront it. Of course, some persons felt that their jobs depended on their relative silence.

For fifteen years, the most serious problem in the denomination was the relative ignorance of the vast numbers of the laity about the SBC controversy. The fundamentalists did a much better job of informing laity about their views and enlisting them to attend convention meetings than did the moderates. Laypersons were at a distinct disadvantage in the conflict in that they had little source of information except the pastor. Many pastors did not educate their members about the problems and/or blindly held to the view that the controversy does not affect them.

A minority of lay persons received their only information from state Baptist papers. Many of the editors discussed the controversy in very guarded terms, however, often because their jobs were on the line. Occasionally when the battles broke into the public press, the laity saw a glimpse of the problems. For example, in South Florida, the *Wall Street Journal* sometimes brought the sad news. Despite the lack of involvement by many traditional Southern Baptists, some pastors and informed laity in the various states have actively sought to control the hand of fundamentalism. (These efforts are outlined and explicated in *The Struggle for the Soul of the SBC,* edited by Walter Shurden and published by Mercer University Press.)

The silence of the great middle constituency of the SBC, both ministerial and lay, is difficult to understand. Some clarity came to the discussion with the discovery that multitudes understood the controversy as a battle between "two groups." They did not wish to be identified with either "side." Many of the moderates saw the problem as a takeover by alien forces of the denomination and their attempts were to save the denomination. The differences were to some obscure, but to others very real.

One young pastor discussed this battle of the two sides with me several times and then wrote a letter to me presenting his ideas. He articulated a viewpoint that had not been clear to me at all. I have come to believe that his opinions represent a large number of the ministers, especially the young ones who have not known a denomination at peace during their ministry.

The pastor, who wishes to remain anonymous, is a graduate of a Baptist college and Southwestern Seminary. He is articulate, thoughtful, and an excellent preacher. With his permission, his lengthy discussion is given below. While I will summarize some portions for brevity's sake, the major portion will be printed verbatim. I feel this view opens a new understanding of the reluctance of many persons to join the battle against present-day fundamentalism.

Dear Dr. Cothen:

The decision where to lead my church in terms of denominational affiliation has been most difficult. I have been in a private struggle with this issue from the very onset of my pastorate here. I have prayed as well as sought wisdom from people whom I trust. I have laid awake at night rehashing philosophical viewpoints and theological positions. And throughout this struggle, I keep coming back to a personal position of the inability to wholeheartedly identify with either side. I do not necessarily need to agree on every issue, but I do need to be able to identify.

In this letter, I hope to communicate some of my views on SBC/CBF issues, realizing that in some areas I may either be misinformed or uninformed. It is my prayer that upon reading this, you can help me find a position toward which I can, in good conscience, lead my church. . . . It is not my intent to criticize, but rather my only desire is to find a place to stand.

Presuppositions and Background

I bring to this struggle a background of being raised in a Christian home with two parents who honestly believed in God and wholeheartedly supported the church. My sister and I were loved and nurtured in an almost idyllic home setting. I became a Christian at the age of eight and spent my days thereafter in the church learning and growing in the Christian faith.

(A paragraph follows on the fine Christian home in which he was reared.)

I was taught from a very early age to look at both sides of an issue. Often if I took a strong position on something, my mother would take the opposite view just to show me that there were two sides to every argument. Because of my upbringing, my personality is more of a "both/and" orientation rather than an "either/or."

For example (and this may sound strange), I would tend to say that both Calvinism and Armenianism are each true. To simplify, I honestly believe in the deterministic view that God chooses some and does not choose others, while at the same time I believe that man has free choice. Both are somehow paradoxically and simultaneously true.

Each view seems to me to be a different perspective on truth rather than, in and of itself, exclusively true. I believe this because I see strong biblical evidence for both positions, and I have observed it in the practical realm. I admit that I cannot completely comprehend how both can be true, but that isn't difficult for me because there are many theological concepts which I, through faith, embrace without the luxury of complete understanding. When I bring this "both/and" mindset to the SBC/CBF debate, I cannot seem to tip the scales in either direction and feel comfortable.

(He then gives a warm discussion of his home church, which in its SBC orthodoxy greatly influenced his ministry.)

You can bet that when I committed my life to ministry, I vowed to be a "Cooperative Program pastor"—a minister of the Gospel who would carry on the torch of missions support. I think it is rather ironic that young ministers like myself who were so influenced by the architects of the "SBC machine," are now in such a dilemma to decide between our inbred loyalty to the SBC/Cooperative Program and our sense of what is theologically and philosophically true. My forefathers taught me an undying loyalty to the SBC, and now they have abandoned the very structure which I was taught by them to revere.

I believe that this controversy has had much of the same kind of effect on my generation as Vietnam and Watergate had on the generation of the 60s and 70s. Vietnam and Watergate destroyed trust and made people skeptical of American politics and, worse, has left many with an overall disrespect for our political leadership. Good men like your friend Jimmy Carter were treated by some as a "laughing stock." I generally vote Republican, but it is unbelievable, even to me, how our current president is being treated.

It is with the same skepticism that I and much of my generation now look at denominations. (By the way, statistics tell us that denominations are on the decline.) We are now asking whether or not we can trust any kind of denominational "machine" again. And I also find myself not at all desirous of any kind of denominational leadership on either side. I cringe when I think about what happened to you and the way you and many of your contemporaries were treated. I don't think I could endure that as gracefully as you did.

As I try to discern my position, I cannot ignore the people and churches who have been the greatest influences in my life. First and foremost would be my parents. I have already talked about them, but I am who I am mainly because of who they are. Here are some more of the major influences in my life.

(He then gives a lengthy recital of the excellent church staff members of his home church and the good influence they had on his life.)

Another great influence in my life was my first church position. When I came to the _____ Baptist Church, I considered myself a "strict fundamentalist." My position was due mainly to the strong conservative influence of my college BSU. So, I began my ministry by doing conservative things. I told the young people to burn their albums and they couldn't wear shorts on the mission trip.

The first of three pastors during my time at that church was a moderate/liberal. He and I have remained good friends through the years in spite of the fact that he was only there for three months of my ministry in that church. . . . He was a nice man whose main focus was people and preaching. His degree of scholarship almost made him seem "out of place" in that small, country church. At the time he reinforced my thinking about "liberals," which was that they were satisfied without church growth and evangelism. I have since developed a strong appreciation for his ministry. He is now with the CBF.

I spent most of my time at that church enduring an interim period. The interim pastor was a little comical fundamentalist who would shake his head profusely when he preached. He preached the same sermon every Sunday and even chastised me one Sunday from the pulpit for being late with the choir. He was about seventy-five years-old at the time and decided that he was the one who needed to be the pastor of the church. Through some underhanded tactics, he won some of the older members to his side and thus began division in that church that lasted for years.

The pastor they finally settled on was a "card-carrying fundamentalist." He was not very intelligent, and he had come from a background of drinking and carousing. He preached very strict religion from the pulpit, but at the same time would tell off-colored jokes to all the guys. I admired his enthusiasm, distrusted his judgment, and realized very quickly that he would not serve as a "role model" for my ministry. I also realized that it probably wouldn't be fair to judge all strict fundamentalists by him.

Please see the dilemma here. While on the one hand I did not like the complacency of the first pastor, I did like his scholarship and his treatment of me and others; on the other hand, I didn't care for both the lack of scholarship in the preaching of the second two and their treatment of people, but I did admire their enthusiasm and zeal. Therefore, when I went away to seminary, I was rather unsure as to which way I would choose to go and where I would serve.

When I went to seminary, my first job there was at First Baptist Dallas. I had been given a recommendation to work there by my church staff. The same kind of dilemma reoccurred in my work there. I was proud to be working at such a prestigious church and could see many great ways in which they were affecting Dallas for Christ, but at the same time I had some real problems reconciling some of their philosophy and in the course of time began to see that they were twisting scripture to fit their socio-political viewpoints.

For example: I had a discussion with a college professor. He told me that he did not believe that Jesus drank fermented wine (he said it was grape juice). I personally thought his thinking was rather ridiculous. I have chosen in my life not to drink, but I realize that this stand is based more on wisdom than a "proof text." Everything which came out of the mouths of either the college staff and students or FBC employees was laced with robotic conservatism—almost like it was more out of fear than conviction.

Even so, there were still many employees and staff who were genuine Christians and who practiced their faith with undying loyalty to Christ. I was impressed with that church, despite the weaknesses I saw. They support a great deal of social work and many kinds of ministries and are a beacon in that city. I could never wish in a hundred years that that church would fail. I genuinely believe that Dallas needs for that church to be strong.

It seems to be that the conservative/fundamentalist churches are the ones which are growing. With their growth comes financial stability and with financial stability comes the adding of ministries. I often hear moderates criticize the fundamentalists for the lack of "doing it unto the least of these." But from what I have observed, it is the larger churches, most of which are fundamentalist, which do the most social work. I have not been exposed to a great number of churches, but from what I observed, First Dallas does more social work than any one I have seen. First Fort Lauderdale (Florida) does quite a bit also. I have not observed any particular lack of concern for the poor or underprivileged on the part of the SBC fundamentalists. It is certainly not the "main thing" for them, but it never has been (for the SBC) as far as I have seen.

My real shift from a strictly conservative position came when I joined the _____ Baptist Church in Fort Worth. They were more of a praise and worship church than I preferred, but there were several single girls there and so I opted for the girls. _____ was the pastor and since I dated his daughter, I was able to spend some personal time with him. He was an extremely humble man and exemplified an extremely positive mind set. But as I read between the lines, I also found that he had been mistreated in his last church over politics. He was a conservative but would not bow to the "gods of rhetoric," and he was forced to leave his previous church after a long successful ministry. This made me angry for him, and I slowly began to see that this conservative movement was not all it was cracked up to be. (He) eventually died of cancer, and I attribute much of his illness to the way he was treated.

(At this point, the pastor gives a lengthy tribute to the wholesome influence on his maturation and ministry of Dr. Leon Marsh of Southwestern Seminary.)

I need to say at this point that in spite of my experiences, while at seminary, I remained aligned with the SBC takeover. I believed every bit of what I heard concerning the need for a new direction. I was pleased when the fundamentalists won in Dallas. But, at the same time, I really did not pay that much attention to it. I remember my friends and myself joking about how the Southern Baptists can't get along. These issues had not really affected me to this point, but if you had asked me, I would have told you that I sided with the fundamentalists.

My first full-time position after seminary was ironically the ____. It was a moderate/liberal church fully equipped with women deacons, a governing church council, no Sunday night services, and an AIDS support group. We were more allied with the ecumenical community than with the other Southern Baptist Churches. Our services (as you experienced) were formal and repetitive. I had never been in such a church, nor did I ever imagine that any SBC church was like this. I went to that church mainly because I was attracted to _____ and the big city. I had always imagined that I would end up in a city church. I came recommended by _____, and I trusted their judgment. I do not regret going to that church, although I would not choose another one like it.

The pastor, _____, and I got along very well. We were at opposite extremes theologically, but we agreed philosophically on many issues. I remember asking (him) when I was there in view of a call if he supported biblical inerrancy. He answered "yes," but later I would find out that his brand of inerrancy was far different than mine. I learned not to ask that question again.

After I had been in that church for only three months, the pastor announced that he was going through a divorce. It was a real shock, and I began thinking about the implications of serving in a church with a divorced pastor. Would I be marked for life? At the announcement of his divorce, he resigned and gave the church the option of reinstating him. The vote was 246 to 2 in favor of him staying. This is the first time I had ever had to come to grips with my convictions concerning qualifications of church leaders. I found myself emotionally wanting him to stay, but at the same time wondering whether or not it was right for him to remain as pastor.

In addition to the divorce, there were occasions when homosexual couples would visit the church. I have always had the philosophy that anyone should be able to come to the church, but I always wondered what would happen if they wanted to join or asked the pastor to marry them. There were also church members there whom I would call "universalists," who would teach things like that hell was fiction in their Sunday School lessons.

Having said that, I am deeply grateful for what I learned from the pastor. He taught me to pastor. He did everything he could to help me press toward my goal of becoming a pastor. He was a man who was very secure in himself, and there was never any jealousy on his part. He showed nothing but a deep respect for my theological positions. Again, I do not regret going to that church. God used that experience to prepare me for the pastorate. I do not know where I would be if I had not gone there.

My experience at _____ did force me to come to grips with who I am as a called minister. If I was tired of conservatism in Texas and "rebelled" by going to that church, then the lesson I learned was that I am not a liberal. In the practical side, I saw how liberalism can be a real hindrance to personal growth and church growth. I also learned that unbridled acceptance without any foundation of truth is not healthy to church life. People want to believe in something, and they want boundaries. I believe this is biblical as well as practical.

(Then he addresses several paragraphs to me.)

There are good men on both sides of this issue to whom I owe great debts of gratitude. These men have invested their time and energy into my life in ways that I could never repay. For that I am grateful and yet fearful of any disappointment which I might create.

I do not regret any stop I have made along the path of my life. Each one has prepared me in character and experience to do God's work wherever I may go. At each stop I have accumulated friends with whom I still keep in touch. At each place I have observed the advantages and disadvantages of a particular theological or philosophical approach to ministry. I believe I have come away "balanced," but at the same time I am unable to, in good conscience, give my full support to either side of the controversy. Here are some of the specific issues with which I struggle:

(1) Truth vs. Freedom

One of the basic underlying issues which I have observed in this controversy is "truth vs. freedom." The fundamentalists espouse "truth" as their highest ideal, whereas with the moderates it is "freedom." Both sides revere both ideals; it's just that each respective side holds one higher than the other. That is where the communication breaks down between moderates and fundamentalists (aside from egos). It is almost like they are speaking a different language.

On the issue of biblical inerrancy, I hear the fundamentalists holding up the truth of scripture above any other presupposition. On the positive side of the argument, I believe that scripture should be the sole foundation of faith. I believe the Bible is the inerrant, infallible word of God. I concur with what the Baptist Faith and Message says about the scripture.

I also believe that some adjustments needed to be made to what was taught in the seminaries (if indeed there were really professors who taught contrary to a high view of scripture and/or Baptist orthodoxy). I do think we need to be very careful about what is taught as truth in our schools. If for no other reason, we need to be careful because I see how utterly vulnerable I was to the opinions of my teachers. So throughout my journey I have concluded that truth is very important; I seek it every day. On the negative side of this truth issue is the fact that the "truth" is often violated in the name of truth. Truth can become an idol.

[A visitor] told an extremely mean joke about President Clinton. I personally do not think that President Clinton is particularly credible nor is he, in my opinion, a good president. But at the same time, my inerrant, infallible Bible tells me that I ought to respect my leaders. There should be no question about this scripture since it was written at a time when Christians had every right to verbalize their disgust at the "powers that be."

That is what I mean by violating the truth in the name of truth. Many good men and women who have been faithful to God have suffered from this kind of action. Truth does stand alone, as God exists whether I think He does or not, but this kind of "siding with the truth" is not in and of itself "siding with God." Therefore on the one hand, I agree with the fundamentalists on their views of truth, but on the other hand disagree with their enforcement of it.

Freedom, on the other hand, seems to be the highest ideal of the moderates. The moderates I have been around seem to echo the cry, "Give me liberty or give me death." On the positive side, I think that freedom is a basic fundamental right of mankind. Every man is ultimately free no matter what his circumstances, since you cannot take away the freedom to think for one's self. I see freedom as important to individuals as well as churches. I would never want be in a denomination which was controlled from the top down. My denomination does not understand my people like I do and does not experience my situation day in and day out like I do. So I need the freedom to "do church" in the way I see fit. I need the freedom to make mistakes and to say what I think, even if it does not completely agree with "denominational policy." Freedom is an important value to me, and I need it in order to be of maximum effectiveness.

On the other hand, the negative side of this issue as I have seen in the moderate camp is that freedom, like truth, can become an idol. Sometimes I feel like the moderate view of freedom is as closely tied to the Democratic party as truth is to Republicans. I believe that as the political climate in our country has been swayed toward an exaggerated view of freedom, so has much of the religious community followed. I know moderates who will vote down the line Democratic and then equate truth with whatever the mainline Democrats are saying. If the Democrats are pro-abortion, then these moderate Christians will support a woman's right to choose in the name of freedom.

It is ironic to me that the Republicans are often considered the most patriotic because they are most apt to exercise military action—all done in the sacred name of freedom—whereas the Democrats also hold this ideal, but in a completely different context. Maybe that is why we need both. In the same light, their religious counterparts view freedom in two different contexts. The fundamentalists view freedom as the lack of opposition—that is why they search out and destroy anything which gets in their way—whereas the moderates view freedom as the lack of restriction. That's why they did not stay and fight; they moved on and began a new organization.

Another negative is that I must ask the question: How far does this freedom extend? Surely there are lines to be drawn even in the moderate camp. I have never heard from any of the moderate leadership as to how far they will go in their freedom. I have heard some attempts, but have never had this question answered to my satisfaction.

In the name of local church autonomy and freedom, will we allow a homosexual to pastor a convention church? What if a church abandons any theological resemblance of being Baptist? How will a convention whose highest ideal is freedom maintain theological integrity in its missions organizations and seminaries? How is the CBF different from the United Methodists or the Presbyterian USA who love freedom but are declining denominations? What or who will see that the CBF maintains a climate of theological orthodoxy?

I cannot concur with either truth or freedom (exclusively) as being the highest ideal of a denomination. Both CBF and the SBC are adamant about each. They interpret them differently, and they each hold one as being more supreme, but I believe in both/and. Truth must be tempered by grace and freedom and freedom by truth. I feel that since we have split, this crucial balance is now missing from both. The Bible says that Jesus was "full of grace and truth," and I cannot seem to find this balance in either.

(2) Baptist History

Our Baptist heritage has been used by both sides to support their respective arguments. The fundamentalists use history to support their claim that Baptists have always been a "people of the book" and (of course) a people committed to truth at all costs. When I was a seminary student, I read Russ Bush's book on our Baptist heritage. It was written solely to prove that from our inception Baptists have been committed to biblical inerrancy. The moderates use our Baptist heritage to prove that we have always been a people committed to freedom.

One of the problems with both views is that they are used out of context. I think that there was a time when these views did not conflict. Both truth and freedom existed simultaneously in Baptist life, and people did not even think about which one of the two was most important. There have been times in our history when the two, existing simultaneously, have been an historical embarrassment. For example, when the SBC split from the Triennial Convention, it was certainly in the name of freedom but this freedom was the right to slavery. At the same time, they had a misconception of truth, which allowed them to own the slaves in the first place.

As I have looked at Baptist history, most all the denominational problems I have seen come back to this issue: an unbalanced or even dishonest view of freedom and/or truth. Sometimes I think the current debate is no exception to this. It seems that as the gulf has widened between "conservative/fundamentalist" and "moderate/liberal," freedom/truth have followed. As I said before, there was a time when freedom and truth were not so much in conflict, and there was also a time when the distance between mainline denominations and their various factions was not as wide as it is today. There seems to be a new framework in operation today, politically and religiously, and it is forcing people to one side or the other.

One of the reasons I have so much trouble choosing sides is that I agree with both and disagree that they should exist apart. I think the Baptists were the last major denomination to idealize both truth and freedom as a whole. It was the key to our success. But we have chosen to follow the world and its political climate and become "either/or" rather than "both/and." At the same time it also seems that when Baptists have been able to balance the two, great things have happened. Some of our past evangelistic victories are an example. Our organizational structure is another.

Again, I see the current opinions of Baptist history as both/and. Neither is exclusively accurate. We have always been a "people of the book" and a people committed to truth as well as a "people committed to freedom." I deeply value our Baptist heritage, but I also keep in mind as I listen that history is usually told with an agenda.

(3) The Agenda(s)

I have read and studied both the SBC as well as the CBF propaganda newsletters. I attended the CBF meeting and the Southern Baptist Convention (1993). When I hear SBC speakers and read their writings, almost everything is laced with "the agenda." I hear and read "Stay the course," "infallible word of God," "return to truth," and on and on the rhetoric goes. When you listen to an SBC leader speak or read his writing, you can almost predict what he will say. It's almost like he has to say the "code words" before his discourse will be legitimate. It is very difficult for me to take these men seriously because behind all these words is a political agenda which, in actuality, has very little to do with the words themselves. I don't like hidden agendas in politics or religion. It is dishonest.

Having said that about the SBC, I also hear the agendas of the CBF. Their "catch phrases" reflect the other side of the "truth/freedom" debate—phrases like "free Baptists," "freedom of conscience," "freedom to worship and practice faith as one chooses," "autonomy of the local church," and "priesthood of the believer." Like the conservative rhetoric, all of these ideas in and of themselves are biblical and true. But, I feel, the agenda is political. And like the fundamentalists, these ideals end up being used to rally people around a cause and not necessarily for the purpose to which they were intended. The real rallying point for all Christians should be Christ and missions. I feel like both sides agree on Christ (maybe).

The agendas involved remind me of partisan politics. The Republicans and the Democrats will do almost anything to cut the throat of the other, even if it means compromising important legislation. It seems these days that the SBC and the CBF are nearly the same. They have severed their ties at the expense of myself and many of my friends and my church. The current battle is "cut throat." The fundamentalists are cutting off any ties with the CBF at great expense to them and the cause of missions. The CBF cuts the throat of the SBC by its very existence.

I feel that agendas and not convictions are the cause. And in both the CBF and the SBC, the main agenda does not seem to reflect that of missions and evangelism.

(4) Issues

I feel that as I have watched the SBC/CBF debate, the issues have been the weapons of choice. I disagree with using issues this way because it too is dishonest. That is what the issues have become in the CBF/SBC debate. All of a sudden, the fundamentalists start having this "deep concern" for the Bible as God's infallible word. Years before it was their "deep concern" for something else. I cannot believe that these men care so deeply about infallibility. Do you think that when they get together to play golf they talk about how wonderful it is that God's word in infallible? I seriously doubt it. They talk about their conquests—who showed who and who told who.

The resolution on homosexuality at the 1993 convention was a smoke screen for excluding more churches. Homosexuality does need to be addressed in the SBC but not as a weapon. This business about praying for President Clinton is a smoke screen for "vote Republican." They never prayed for Bush (like they do for Clinton), and Bush faced difficult challenges in his presidency (like the Gulf war). I thoroughly disagree with using prayer for anything other than for what it was intended to be used.

The CBF also has its smoke screens. I hear "freedom" used as a weapon to accuse the fundamentalists of tyranny. I think hurt feelings are the root of moderates' problem with the fundamentalists—not issues. I also believe that the moderates have gone too far in embracing feminism. I think they have done this as a way to gain ground quickly with churches who embrace women in ministry. I fully support a woman's right to do as she feels God has called her, but to make this issue a rallying point is, in my opinion, not a wise move for the CBF. This issue is characteristic of my lack of decisiveness. The fundamentalists almost persecute women, and moderates elevate them to a higher place than I believe they should be. I do not feel comfortable with either extreme.

The moderates criticize the fundamentalists for their political involvement and influence, but the CBF seems to embrace "political correctness" with the issues. Both the CBF and the SBC have had either a former president or a vice president at their conventions. I think both are political and exert political influence whether directly or indirectly.

(5) The Future

I have thirty years to retirement, and I must look at where the CBF and the SBC will be in the years to come. It seems that any kind of reconciliation is beyond question, at least while the leaders of the two sides are in power. I don't think either side is at all interested. The only exception to this is the intervention of God. I do believe that God could make this happen.

Both sides are currently in a reactionary mode. Some of the unity which both sides now experience may not be around when the ties are completely severed. I think that the fundamentalists will begin devouring one another very soon (if they haven't already). I also feel that it is inevitable that the SBC will be faced with the decision of moderating or losing still more churches, more political clout, and more missions dollars. Whether or not they opt for suicide is yet to be seen.

The election of Jim Henry was a sign to me that most Southern Baptists are getting tired of the rhetoric and desire to get on with the business at hand. Jim Henry is far from moderate, but I think his election was indicative of the fact that Southern Baptists are tired of politics. I think future leaders of the SBC may very well be more moderate and less oriented toward politics. At the same time, I do not see this happening any time soon because the architects have systematically replaced nearly all leadership with their own people.

On the other hand, I worry about the future of the CBF. As I have previously stated, I do not see what will keep this group from becoming so liberal and diverse that they lose sight of their common goal of missions. This freedom, acceptance, and inclusiveness can be a real help to the cause of missions because it can allow for a diverse mission and diverse resources. But at the same time, if not kept in check, it can be a hindrance just from trying to promote a unified purpose with limited resources among such a diverse group. If a universalist-type church, a church with a homosexual pastor, and a conservative church all come together to try to agree on a philosophy of missions, where will that leave evangelism, and who will determine the qualifications of the appointees—the men and women who will represent the CBF denomination and the cause of Christ?

This is where I really have trouble with the CBF. I cannot see how the future will bring anything but more liberal leadership. There is nothing in the philosophical make-up of the CBF which I have seen which could preclude these kinds of problems. Before the split, the perception of the SBC was diverse yet primarily conservative. There were always screaming fundamentalists to keep the convention "in line." I don't see any checks and balances in the CBF. The very nature of the organization forbids any of this kind of activity.

I wonder what will happen if a CBF pastor stands up in a meeting and calls for a more conservative approach to denominational activity. Will it remind these people of the past and cause them to summarily dismiss any kind of constructive reform? One of the main reasons I am fearful of joining the CBF is the future. When the CBF was formed, it took with most of the moderates and liberals in the SBC. I am fearful that this lack of balance and view of freedom will create an environment which I cannot, in good conscience, support.

At the same time, it is difficult to support SBC causes because of the lack of respect and love they have shown. No one can tell me what either the CBF or the SBC will become in the future. They are both on a different course from the former SBC. As long as they are separate, they will not be able to recreate the kind of environment to which I have looked forward since my calling to the ministry.

Dr. Cothen, there is much more that I could write. I am not angry at anyone so much as I am angry that we split. As you can see, I have some deep disagreements with both sides. Whenever I begin to lean to one side, my doubts and convictions pull me back. When Russell Dilday was fired, I was angry enough to leave the SBC; but I did not want to react to this based on emotion.

At this point I cannot stand up in front of my church and recommend any kind of action because I don't fully agree with either side. It would be dishonest of me to try to influence my church in either direction, since I do not know which way to go myself. I also have fears about our church's reaction to the possibility of aligning with the CBF.

I want desperately to get this thing settled so that I can feel good about my support. It would be really nice to be able to support Lottie Moon or the CBF Christmas offering with the same kind of enthusiasm I once knew, but I can't. I even dread having to face it again.

In this letter, I am opening myself up to you in a way that I have not to anyone else about this issue. . . . In this letter, I am not trying to sound like an intellectual, nor does my thinking reflect any book I have read or man or woman I have talked to. This is completely freehand with no input from anyone else. I apologize for taking so long.

Your friend,

I cannot accept all of my friend's arguments or understandings. I think he misses some crucial points. For example, most of the CBF people have not split off from anything. Most are still members of Southern Baptist churches, and some of their regular contributions go to SBC causes—in many cases a much larger percentage than the present SBC leaders give to SBC causes through their churches. In the moderate gifts through CBF, they are doing what SBC leaders have been doing for years and in some cases for their entire ministry. It seems to me that he does not believe that the same limitations of scripture and the leadership of God apply to CBF that have applied to the SBC.

There are other points of difference, but the points of view mentioned are worthy of being heard. I fear that they are representative of those held by a host of ministers, especially the younger ones who have never known the SBC at peace. At the end of this chapter, I will include a parable written by the young pastor that is both interesting and disturbing but worth pondering.

Jenne Harmon, a layperson from Terrell, Texas, cast some light on the same subject in an article she wrote following the Southwestern Seminary debacle. She said in part:

> In response to the reader who asked in a recent issue, "Where were Texas Baptists when this happened to our institutions?" I can only speak for myself. But I apologize to you and repent before God for having stood idly by as events of the past fifteen years took place. The depth of anguish of many Texas Baptists is accentuated by the realization that Southwestern Seminary was the last institution to fall under control, and we have awakened to the truth too late. Our lack of an earlier response was due to several factors:
>
> (1) the desire to have Christian love and unity in our churches and conventions
> (2) the failure of our leaders to inform the membership of the controversy (which was often related to the first reason, but sometimes to fear of fundamentalist power)
> (3) the use by radical fundamentalists of the authority of the Bible as their rallying point, making those who oppose their cause seem to be

opposing the Bible and its message—a position not lightly chosen by those for whom Jesus is Lord.[2]

It seems that the writer of that letter has hit on another matter that, in honesty, demands some recognition. To what degree did fear play a role in the long silence?

Carlyle Marney, with whom I more often disagreed than agreed, had the notion that fear on the part of the ministry was a major factor in the life of most of them. I was shocked to read recently his evaluation in the words of his biographer.

> Marney developed a set of metaphors to describe these tragic men: (typical professional holy men) even on our best days (note he included himself) we know ourselves to be *shaken reeds*, vacillating with each blowing wind; we are *smoking lamps*, sputtering and even smothered by the rages of our culture; we are *earthen vessels*, "absorbing and passing along in our gospels the extracts of our own prejudiced, provincial places"; and we are *untempered mortar*, unable to hold anything or to bind anything among the new structures in the world of thought. Sometime around age fifty ministers become *spent arrows*, exhausted from the futility of struggling against culture, disillusioned with their achievements, but still hoping for some affirmation of how they have invested their time. As a group they command little respect; history seems to have passed them by.
>
> As a professional group, they are neither better nor worse than other comparable groups. . . . Ministers become tragic men when they are beholden to denominational or congregational structures for their means of existence. Young prophets are usually co-opted into systems and structures which control them; they buy in so deeply that they can no longer speak or act as men of conscience. Men and women who at one time aspired to a prophetic role become house priests because of economic necessities. The professional ministry as we know it is beholden to a culture that follows after other gods than Yahweh. It is in this sense that the "tragic men" live in "tragic houses"[3]

---

[2]*Baptists Today*, 14 July 1994.

[3]John J. Carey, *Carlyle Marney, A Pilgrim's Progress* (Macon GA: Mercer University Press, 1980) 117-18.

Marney's evaluation doubtless came out of his understanding of his own problems together with his knowledge of other ministers.

The concept of fear of fundamentalist leaders and punishment has been a factor in the lives of many modern ministers, although the subject has received little attention. It is a very delicate matter to look into the mirror of self and see the stark terror that kept one awake last night. One is forced then to ask: Where were the John Lelands, Richard Furmans, Roger Williams, Issac Backuses, John Smyths, and martyrs who bolstered the cause of the free exercise of religion with their lives and blood?

We are not talking about the control of an organization by people who in the main did little to build it. We are talking about the multitude who stood by and allowed precious principles of freedom and the heritage of Baptists to be ignored at best or savaged at worst. This is not a discussion of leaving or staying with a denomination. It is a discussion of right or wrong. "To him that knows to do good and does it not, to him it is sin."

Consider this parable, used by permission, written by the young pastor who wrote the letter:

Anatomy of a Division

Once upon a time there was a body. It was not a perfect body, but it was big and strong and useful and it accomplished much. This body was composed of many parts. Each part had a different function which served the good of the body.

The body grew stronger and stronger, until one day a rift developed. The antibodies which always served an important role in the body's function decided that they were not given the credit they deserved. So all of the antibodies got together and held a secret meeting. The question was asked, "How can we antibodies assert ourselves and gain the recognition and control that we really deserve?"

And then the answer was spoken, "Why not tell the parts that there are too many germs in this body? No part of the body likes germs. Then, the body will finally come to recognize that without us, that disease would surely reap havoc and compromise our function. The head will surely be proud and stand behind us for this is an honorable pursuit." It was agreed that this would be the strategy.

And so the antibodies carried their message to all the parts of the body. "There are too many germs in this body, and if you will give us your allegiance, we will rid this fine organism of all impurities." Many of the parts of the body agreed with the message and willingly pledged allegiance to the antibodies. Still others were not convinced that the body carried as much disease as the antibodies claimed, so they held back their allegiance. The heart found itself in an especially difficult situation. It was torn between the two sides, trying exhaustively to pump nourishment into all the body, while at the same time attempting to adapt to the refusal by some parts to perform their function. Meanwhile, the head ached.

Then the antibodies convened again in secret. They said, "There remain some organs and body parts which refuse to pledge allegiance. They hold the body back from our control. We cannot conquer the heart if these parts remain." So, in a slow and calculated manner, the antibodies began to disconnect the organs and parts which stood in their way. At first it was subtle, and only a few smaller parts were disconnected. But then they began to disconnect some of the major organs and replace them with mechanical, robotic parts—parts which would obey the antibodies. Many of the body parts cried out in protest, but the antibodies assured them that this amputation was completely necessary because the part or the organ was infected with germs. This went on for a while until the antibodies had replaced nearly every dissenting part with another. And at last, after a great struggle, the antibodies gained control of the heart. The dissenting parts and organs were devastated. They had served the body with great sacrifice for many years.

So they said to themselves, "Well if this body doesn't want us, then we will just form our own body." And so they set out to form another body. Many of the parts and organs decided to go along. As it turned out, at least at first, the two bodies weren't completely separate. They were sort of like Siamese twins, sharing some parts and organs but with two different hearts and two distinct bodies.

The first meeting of the dissenting organs was held, and there was great unity among them. They decided to call themselves the "Fellowship of Loving Organs and Parts (F.L.O.P.)." They decided first and foremost that freedom would be paramount in their body. Each part of the body is free to function in the way it was created to function. There would be no use for antibodies since each part was supposed to take care of itself. There would be no restrictions as to who could be a part so long as that part contributed nourishment to the body.

Meanwhile back at the ranch (in the first body), the antibodies held another secret meeting. At the top of the agenda was the notion that the second body had become a parasite. It was stealing precious body parts from the original entity. Although it was contributing a significant amount of nourishment to the original body, it was felt among the antibodies that there must be a clean break so that their plan might fully come to fruition. It didn't matter that the original body would be compromised in this process. What did matter was that the original body would be under the complete control of the wise antibodies. Meanwhile, the Head continued to ache.

At the same time, the Fellowship of Loving Organs and Parts decided that they could no longer support the main body and that a separation was imminent. This separation would not be easy. To separate Siamese twins would mean great pain and the risk that one or both might not survive. Finally, the day of the surgery came. Both bodies stood their ground, and no compromise was even mentioned. Both said, "Better to die than to compromise." The antibodies cried out, "Better to die than to allow germs in our body." The Fellowship said, "Better to die than give up our freedom."

And so the surgery was performed. It was bloody. It was a mess. The minor parts of the body cried out in anguish and pain. They screamed and begged for mercy that this would not continue and that this problem could be solved. But the leaders of both bodies stood solemnly, unflinching to the pain of separation.

The operation was finished. It was a clean break. And to everyone's dismay, both survived. Both bodies lived on, enjoyed great unity, and recovered from the surgery . . . until . . . As the years went by, they both discovered that they had a problem. At first, both ignored their troubles and focused on the good days after the surgery. But the pain and dysfunction soon became unavoidable, so they went to the doctor. Both bodies were found to be terminally ill.

You see, the antibodies certainly did rid their body of infection and disease. The whole body was under their control in a disease-free environment. But the problem was that the antibodies were made to fight. And as soon as the body was free of disease, they began to divide and fight among themselves. They continued to attack themselves and the remaining organs until soon the body found itself dying and useless.

On the other hand, the Fellowship of Loving Organs and Parts got an infection. At first it was small and localized, but soon it spread. And soon, this body found itself eaten up with germs. Everyone knew that the germs needed to be expelled from the body, but there were no antibodies to do so. Even if there had been antibodies, it was specifically stated that no antibody activity could be allowed in this body. And so, because of the infection, the fellowship body also found itself on its death bed.

As they both lay dying, they still stood their ground. They refused to even entertain the notion that they might have been created to function together and that separation meant death. But there they lay, stubborn, uncompromising, refusing to even make eye contact until they died. And the head really ached.

The young pastor's parable is haunting. While it is a parable and cannot be made to stand on all counts, it is disturbingly instructive. In any case, it represents a point of view that has not been adequately represented in the SBC controversy. It expresses potential issues among Baptists, just as the pastor's letter calls attention to very real issues. Both writings seem to imply the results of years of silence and lack of involvement over areas of contention in Baptist life.

Chapter 9

The New
Southern Baptist
Convention

The controversy was said by fundamentalists to be about theology. The entire denomination was convulsed over what was supposed to be a theology that was leading the people into liberalism. Several professors and writers were accused at length for what was labeled error in their theology. Schools were thus contaminated by association, and some faculties were decimated or seriously disturbed. The entire package of fundamentalist objectives was sold to the unsuspecting or somnolent constituents based on the accusations of liberalism. A careful survey of the present scene reveals some rather startling evidences of a new theology.

A New Theology

The shift of emphasis and the adoption of new approaches to worship and "doing church" are bringing to the SBC some striking changes. For instance, there is a subtle trend toward what one writer calls "user-friendly" theology. This rather strange phenomenon manifests itself in many different ways such as radical new forms of worship, selling the church to unbelievers, and challenging basic Christian concepts of humankind's relationship to God and God's work.

Worship

Consider the matter of the worship services today. Raymond Bailey's comments are apropos.

> When Moses heard God, he was filled with awe. Fear and trembling are common responses in biblical accounts of divine-human encounter. A

sense of awe is often lacking in contemporary worship. Modern worship too often has the character of a country hoedown or a pep rally. There is no sense of the majesty, holiness, and power of God. We want to reduce the creator-redeemer to a fun-loving indulgent buddy. God is worthy of adoration. He is the mighty one who evokes a sense of smallness before his grandeur.[1]

This reaction is fairly typical of those from thoughtful people awash in frivolous trivia in an irreverent world.

Ron Owens of the Home Mission Board addressed the problem at a Glorieta meeting.

What many churches call "worship" is often evangelical entertainment and not a response to a holy God. . . . Worship has become a cover word for services. We sing about God, we talk about what God is doing, but we do not spend time in awe of who He is. . . . Because (true) worship focuses on God's holiness, many people experience deep conviction. Worship demands a moral change in response to Holy God. Conviction, however, makes unbelievers and carnal Christians uneasy, and churches have adapted their services so outsiders can be comfortable. We want dead people to enjoy themselves. Worship can never be seeker-friendly. Worship is for God alone, not a bait to catch an unsuspecting sinner.[2]

Many churches schedule "special emphases" or guest performers to attract the attention of the public. Mini-spectaculars are held in some churches at worship time, followed by brief sermonettes. (R. G. Lee used to say that "sermonettes by preacherettes make christianettes.") The criterion of success seems to be the number in attendance and the reactions of the attendees. Many persons believe that enthusiasm for a performance is becoming a substitute for the moving of the spirit of God.

The idea of the entertainment element of church services has been legitimized by the pastors conference prior to the annual SBC. The convention meetings themselves have sometimes appeared to be extravaganzas with all the appurtenances of a political rally. The practices have

---

[1]*Amidst Babel, Speak the Truth*, 117.

[2]*Baptist Standard*, Sarah Zimmerman, Home Mission Board News Service, 17 August 1994.

spread as the smaller church pastors "do church" in the fashion they have learned from the leaders of the large churches.

Marketing

The topics mentioned are in the same vein as the often-heard idea of "marketing the church." Broadman and Holman recently published a book by Jerry Wilkins that emphasized marketing concepts such as product development and evaluation, packaging the product, determining the target audience, and communicating the benefits of the product to aid Sunday school growth. Wilkins commented,

> Actually, marketing is a concept that is easily baptized. Advertising is just telling the benefits so that customers will use the product. When you apply it to the gospel, that's evangelism![3]

A firm in Birmingham, Alabama, specializes in marketing and design for churches. It "goes on pushing the edges of the traditional church limits on marketing." Recently, it released to a local newspaper an ad for a church disguised as a movie ad in the movie section. The firm emphasizes "target" audiences but thinks the gospel is for all—but any one church is not for all.

One church, apparently stung by the ridicule of the community, rented a billboard to reply. It posed a question, followed by a message:

Which of the following best describes the church at the intersection of
_____ and _____ Street?
   A. Six Flags Over Jesus
   B. The Church at the Immaculate Intersection
   C. _____ Country Club: the Home of the Old, Cold, and Gold.
   D. Fort God
To see if you have the best answer, come visit us Sunday.

Persons who responded to the message heard the pastor preach on the four themes. When that same pastor began his service at the church, he was introduced to the city on the same billboard. Superimposed on a

---

[3]*Baptist Press*, 7 July 1994.

picture of Elvis Presley's head was the pastor's body. The message read, "Come meet our new pastor."[4]

Many people believe that marketing the church presents as many problems as it attempts to solve. Leonard Sweet told a conference of communicators:

> Ministry today is the ability to evoke experiences of the transcendent. It is not giving people something to believe in. . . . The methodology employed in targeting boomers based on tailoring churches to their likes and dislikes has special problems for a "gospel that's based not on pierced ears but pierced hands. . . . Go too far to accommodate preferences in the way the gospel is presented, and the content is in jeopardy.[5]

As Sweet suggested, the secularity of the methods and content of the efforts at "marketing" is accompanied by another problem. The influence of the culture on the church will not be in its best interest.

Theologian Millard Erickson told a seminary audience, "The tentacles of secularism have crept into the church, encouraging an easy believe-ism." He suggested that we are facing a danger because, in trying to reach people, we will try to make it easier for them to come to Christ. Erickson continued,

> The gospel meets the deepest human need, but in our desire to reach across the bridge to the other side where the unbelievers are, we must make certain that they come across to Christ.

He labeled the present problems as "serious business," a battle, a race.[6]

Church historian George Marsden was reported to be interested in this set of issues. He said that evangelicals' fascination with marketing techniques has made them more likely to imitate culture than engage in serious theological reflection.

> As evangelicals succeed, they become better at analyzing church growth and finding marketing techniques that will work best. They have

---

[4]Ibid., 8 March 1994.
[5]Associated Baptist Press, 12 April 1994.
[6]Baptist Press, 15 April 1994.

become increasingly responsive to what will work—to what people want to hear.

The most effective marketing methods, however, often have little intellectual emphasis and make few theological demands. Evangelicals have been influenced by the shift in American culture away from the intellectual and theoretical to the psychological and the relational. Churches, therefore, have tended to amplify self-development within a relational community.

The trend has left little place for serious intellectual reflection on the faith or its place in the culture. . . . My impression . . . is that the intellectual mission of evangelicalism plays a minimal role in most evangelical circles today.[7]

Preaching

The idea of easy believe-ism seems particularly appropriate in the light of the methodology of much modern preaching. The listing of sermon topics in various places is an interesting study. Many churches are getting band-aids for terminal illness if one is to believe the announced subjects. Increasingly, the Sunday subjects are focused on money management, treating stress, dealing with anxiety, family discord, courtesy, depression, prosperity theology (God wants you to have the best house, car, education, boat, bank account, and send your money to me), and similar matters. This is spiritually equivalent to ignoring the cancer and treating the skin eruption. One pastor's topics for the fall read as follows:

• Surviving My Schedule
• Taming My Temper
• Avoiding Fatal Attractions
• Dealing with Disappointment
• Cultivating My Friends
• Making up My Mind

While these subjects are not wrong to discuss and may have interest for the hearers, one wonders how they relate to the central eternal verities

---

[7]Ibid., 11 October 1994.

of God and scripture. One must assume that they will have some biblical underpinning and thus of themselves are not evil. Perhaps these topics occupy the minds of the audiences, but do the answers reverse the divine order of things?

The divine order of things revolves around the fact that God is, man is flawed, God has the answer to the flaws, and God has a purpose for a person and a church. Finding God's purpose and living it equips the individual to find solutions to problems or strength to bear them. God is not a servant to be summoned at will and dismissed if inconvenient. God is God, and we are men and women, and God is sovereign. Divine help is indeed available, but the matter of God's purpose in our lives is paramount, and our momentary wants or needs are subordinate to God's will.

If the modern presentation of God as the mender of our hurts and satisfier of our wants leaves out the crucial nature of the gospel revelation, this is a heresy more subtle and dangerous than outright falsehood. While this easy "believe-ism" is evident, another more subtle kind of amalgamation is taking place in the churches. It suits some moderates and is practiced by a substantial number of super-church fundamentalists.

The president of the Southern Baptist Convention, Ed Young, proudly announced in 1993 that many non-Baptists attend his church and he does not try to make Baptists out of them. It was not clear whether he was referring to visitors or new members. Inevitably, many of these persons become "non-Baptist" members. Add to this the following story.

A former president of the convention tells of the statement by Young concerning his attitude toward the governmental requirement of making public buildings accessible to persons in a wheel chair. Young is reported to have said that he had no intention of doing so since persons in wheelchairs make people in church uncomfortable. Young subsequently told seminarians in New Orleans that a key to successful ministry is to never make people in church uncomfortable.[8]

If reported correctly, clearly this attitude contradicts the teaching and ministry of Christ. A large portion of the gospel story is the ministry of Jesus to the sick and handicapped. Secondly, it introduces a new theology to the Baptist scene. It basically denies the need for a sense and conviction of sin and a necessary experience of repentance. It refutes the idea of taking up a cross, a clearly uncomfortable experience. Then the

---

[8]Baptist Press.

question arises: Are the persons who have come into the church what we would traditionally call Baptists?

The message of conviction for sin is an uncomfortable one and makes the human spirit writhe in misery since the modern culture does not admit that sin exists, but it corrupts the human spirit all the same. If, as the president of the SBC said to the seminary audience, nothing is to be done to make people uncomfortable at church, the doctrines of God's condemnation of sin and the death of Christ in our behalf are to be left off the agenda. If this is done, the gospel is compromised, and liberalism has come to fundamentalism.

Further, the idea that one must have a high sense of self-esteem, about which we hear so much these days, is precarious when placed beside the scriptural teaching about the real human nature. One is treated regularly to the sight on television news of someone trying to help criminals or juvenile offenders have a sense of self-esteem. Somehow this seems strange, in the light of the need for them to recognize wrong-doing and straighten up their lives. Here one walks a tight rope, teetering between secular humanism the fundamentalists claim to hate and compassion and the edicts of the revelation of God.

Consider that repentance means, among other things, that the lifestyle must be changed. Orders must be taken from God and not our peers. If there is nothing wrong with us, then repentance is unnecessary. If there is nothing wrong with persons in a secular culture, then the gospel is to them nonsense. Herein is one of the reasons the church is taken so lightly by society. We have too often tried to lure persons into a costless relationship with Christ that simply says, "Believe and everything will be all right." Perhaps this course will help our statistics compare favorably with other big wheels.

In this era of a lack of biblical emphasis, consider the matter of the cost of New Testament Christianity. According to the scripture, being a Christian involves carrying a cross on a daily basis. Christianity most certainly involves one in a constant struggle against the forces of the culture, influence of peers, snares of Satan, and endless temptations to give in to popular society. To maintain Christian morality and conduct generally in today's world requires constant reliance on the power of God and the cultivation of the graces of the gospel. The Christian life is not easy, and to present it as a smooth way to problem-solving is to misrepresent Christ.

Role of the Pastor

Modern fundamentalism emphasizes the idea that the pastor is the ruler or deciding power in a congregation. This idea has had great currency in the history of the church, but it is not a Baptist or biblical idea. The passages used to assert this doctrine by fundamentalism are often misinterpreted or misunderstood. They are often interpreted in isolation without proper reference to the context and general teachings of scripture.

A "ruling" pastor cancels the priesthood of the believers when he makes decisions for the church or individuals. He diminishes the possibility of responsible development by individuals, removes from the congregation the ability to determine the will of God for the body of Christ, flies in the face of the history of Baptists, and compromises the integrity of the body. Further, a "ruling" pastor frequently involves the congregation in bitter controversy over the direction of the church. Perhaps as many churches have split over this issue as any other.

Many of the terminations of pastors in the SBC in the last few years have had their roots in the authoritarian rule of a pastor. This theology has spread rapidly in the churches as the pastors have heard their role models trumpet their successes as rulers of the churches. A considerable number of men with superior gifts have won the confidence of the people, who surrendered power to the pastors because they trusted them. Any successful pastor has considerable power, but it must be earned, carefully handled, and lightly used.

Church Membership

Consider also the modern movements that reduce and compromise the meaning of biblical church membership. One church bulletin said,

> Although baptism is not a requirement for membership at _____, yet we seek to follow Jesus' command; and baptism by immersion is offered to any who would choose it.

A number of "mega-churches" seem to follow the advertisement of the church that would accept "any baptism that you are satisfied with." Also, some churches no longer maintain membership roles.

Numerous churches now do not have the name "Baptist" in their names. The label seemingly implies an offensive connotation in the community, and congregations do not want to discourage prospective members. One wonders if persons who attend such churches are taught what Baptists have historically believed about scripture, the need for redemption, and our other beliefs.

The relaxation of church membership requirements is not a trivial matter. These unbaptized persons, maybe unbelievers, not indoctrinated as Baptists, will move from church to church where they will become just church members like all the rest of us. Since, as someone has commented, "Anyone can join a Baptist church if he can get down the aisle," we are approaching the hazard of approving the idea of an unregenerate church membership without even knowing it. Much of this departure from traditional positions has been "legitimized" by "super-church" pastors who are said to practice some part of this "user-friendly theology."

Baptist Calvinism

The attitude of today's theology seems to involve the assumption that "We are right and you are wrong if you don't accept what we say. That means you are not what you ought to be and can't associate with us. The power is in our hands, and we will use it to do what we want to do. No dialogue is required since that will be compromise. You may join with us if you do it our way—if not, leave." This may be fundamentalism, but it is not Christianity. This attitude of exclusion and rigidity is seemingly akin to Calvinism and threatens to produce new trauma.

In 1982 some young pastors, who were Baptist Calvinists, formed a group called the Founders Conference. They were concerned that Baptists had lost their theological moorings. From a small group of seven, their meetings now draw about 250. Others have taken up the refrain. The discussion about Calvinism versus Armenianism has continued in the denomination for more than a century but only rarely has produced serious controversy. Honest convictions shared by some persons and not others have been a common occurrence among Southern Baptists.

Now, concerns about the differences between Calvinists and Armenians have broken out anew. With the coming of Albert Mohler to the presidency of Southern Baptist Theological Seminary, new interpretations of the school's Abstract of Principles have been widely publicized. Additionally, Mohler has declared himself to be a "five-point Calvinist."

The five points of Calvin's theology are:

(1) All persons are *totally depraved,* usually meaning that every person is a sinner and cannot save himself/herself. This tenet of Calvinism is usually interpreted to mean that all persons are not as corrupt as they might be, but that every part of their character is affected.
(2) *Unconditional election* decrees that those who are saved are saved because God has chosen them to be saved, and they gain salvation through no merit of their own.
(3) *Perseverance of the saints* is the idea that salvation cannot be lost. Baptists usually call this idea "once saved always saved."
(4) *Limited atonement* implies that the death of Christ effectively bought salvation for only a limited number of people, the elect, rather than having the potential to save all.
(5) *Irresistible grace* holds that God's grace in Christ is so complete that the elect are compelled to profess faith in Christ.

Southern Baptists have usually accepted the first three doctrines but rejected the last two ideas. The "whosoever will may come and take of the water of life freely" (Rev 22:17 KJV) folks believe that salvation was intended for anyone who would believe. Some passages signal the free will of persons; others seem to indicate God's initiative (John 6:44).

Since Mohler assumed the mantle as a spokesman of the fundamentalist cause, he has drawn much interest and fire, particularly from his announcement of his five-point Calvinism. Immediately, much of his faculty disagreed with him. One report said that his pronouncement even drew fury from some of his trustees.

Theologians continued the discussion as the press exhibited limited interest. Some persons affirmed the assertion, claiming that these ideas were bedrock fundamentals of the Baptist faith. Others, including some evangelists and pastors, decried this rebirth of an old heresy. Most of these would agree with the historical position of the denomination in the acceptance of the three dicta.

The history of the SBC reveals a continuing interest in evangelism and missions, efforts that many people believe are incompatible with at least two of the Calvinistic principles. These are the same arguments that swept England in the late eighteenth century when cobbler William Carey said he was called of God to proclaim the gospel in a distant land. Jesse Fletcher summed up the Baptist-Calvinist confrontation in these words in *The Southern Baptist Convention, A Sesquicentennial History*: "The oldest Baptist fault line runs along the theological question of God's sovereignty and human free will."[9] Fault lines sometimes bring earthquakes and major upheaval.

The Example of Jesus

While many of these changes seem to be much ado about very little, they represent a radical departure from tradition. Tradition may not be so important in this kind of culture, but the departure represents a "drift toward theological liberalism" that makes anything done by the old leadership of the SBC seem trivial by comparison. And I thought of Jesus.

Although Jesus electrified his generation with the unusual and condemned much of its tradition, careful analysis will reveal that his departure from religious tradition always arrived at the mind and purpose of God. He deliberately turned aside from the temptation to worship Satan who promised him the world if he would do so.

Jesus taught his disciples:

* Repentance for sin is the way to forgiveness.
* The gate is narrow, and a lot of folks miss it.
* Similarity to the world often defines the absence of God.
* If you follow me, take up a cross, not an easy chair.
* Those blessed of God are poor in spirit, not necessarily with high self-esteem.
* "Neither do I condemn you; go and sin no more."
* Those who are merciful to others will find mercy.
* The pure in heart are the ones who will see God.
* Love those who hate you.
* Forgive the offenders seven times seventy times.

---

[9]For a fuller treatment of this problem, see articles by Mark Wingfield in the *Western Recorder*, 8 November 1994.

Jesus did not organize Jewry to take on the Roman government, which crucified its foes. He did not try to vote the Pharisees out or destroy the Sadducees because they did not believe in the resurrection. He went to the heart of the matter: humankind's need for God and God's love for the sinful creature. He talked about the relationship of one person to another: "Love thy neighbor as thyself." Nowhere did he even suggest force, except when he personally drove out the moneychangers.

A Changing Polity

The Southern Baptist Convention for more than a hundred years was a strange organization insofar as its decision-making and governance were concerned. When the national body acted on some issue by passing a resolution or even a motion, states, associations, and churches may or may not have noticed. None of these independent bodies felt the obligation to follow suit. On occasion, some state body would vote the opposite view, and the work proceeded according to the will of the independent body. National committees held little control over the business of state conventions, associations, agencies, and institutions. A sense of openness was maintained, but as the fundamentalist agenda increasingly occupied the attention of the SBC, serious governance changes began to take place.

Directives from the SBC

Previously, the convention avoided issuing instructions to the institutions and agencies since they had trustees elected by the convention. Care usually was exercised to fix responsibility with the trustees who noted the convention actions and acted responsibly.

Early in the transition, resolutions passed by the convention became bases of action by trustees of the agencies and institutions. The Home Mission Board considered any resolution as binding on it in employment actions and determining policy. As the convention took action regarding women in ministry or other matters relating to possible personnel decisions, the HMB set policy on these matters following the resolutions of the national body.

The problems increased as the understanding grew that all levels of denominational life were expected to follow the lead of the national body. Problems introduced into the states because of such actions were either ignored or pursued by some persons who felt they were commissioned to correct error.

As the abortion hysteria grew in the country, and as the Christian Life Commission made the issue its central concern, agencies began to follow what they perceived to be the will of the convention. Seminary faculties and students were urged to make the issue a cause celebré. Many state bodies followed suit, and literature was filled with the issue.

Shortly, the issues related to homosexuality were introduced into the business of the convention. Although most Baptists agreed that the practice of homosexuality was not right according to scripture, many felt that more passages dealt with adultery and fornication than homosexuality.

The political agenda of the political and religious right was again dragged into the affairs of the denomination. Two churches in North Carolina took actions that seemed to favor or at least accept the homosexual lifestyle. Following action at two annual convention meetings, the constitution of the SBC was changed to declare that churches that act to "affirm, approve, or endorse homosexual behavior" are "not in cooperation" with the SBC and therefore not eligible to send messengers.

For the first time, a constitutional change was made to condemn a particular course of conduct. In fact, the constitution did not even define a Baptist church or set forth any parameters within which a church must fall. The convention had for more than a hundred years avoided passing judgment on individual congregations for any cause. Whatever the merits of that particular case, the door of Pandora's box was thrown wide open for similar actions against any congregation that might offend the powers in charge. The precedent had been set to exclude real or imagined offenders of whatever nature or disposition, particularly if the offense is publicly unpopular. The results of such drastic departure from traditional Baptist practices were not long in coming.

Earlier I made reference to the motion at the 1993 SBC meeting to unseat messengers from President Clinton's home church. Fortunately, saner heads prevailed, but only after a bitter and painful appearance by representatives of the church before the credentials committee. The convention was embarrassed nationally because someone who did not understand Baptist polity tried to punish a church according to his own prejudice. He seemed to have been led by the conduct of convention leadership to believe that it was possible to discipline a church for some real or supposed infraction.

Although this attempt at virtual excommunication of a church failed, the basic problem remains. If churches can be excluded for one cause, another issue of equal heat or popularity may surface, and the painful unbaptistic procedure can be repeated. The national body in its pronouncements on one issue or another had created a climate in which individuals or groups could, with the blessings of the majority, violate Baptist polity to achieve personal or group objectives.

Concerning the incident related to the church in Little Rock, the editor of the *California Southern Baptist* wrote:

> That such an issue should arise at the very convention meeting where messengers affirmed local church autonomy and the priesthood of the believer is an irony which escaped few who witnessed the unfortunate episode. The issue raises anew the ugly specter of vendetta which, recent history notwithstanding, has no place in Southern Baptist life.[10]

The convention took another drastic step in its 1994 meeting by instructing its institutions and agencies not to accept any funds channeled to them by the Cooperative Baptist Fellowship. This action violated policies that had existed from the beginning of the convention. Never had the SBC tried to tell the churches how they were to conduct their affairs or allocate their funds. One by one the institutions and agencies in their next trustee meetings followed the convention's instructions.

SBC Executive Committee

Adding to directives from the SBC, the national body has an executive committee that is the Convention ad interim, meaning that this committee acts in place of the convention between annual meetings. It reviews audits of agencies, gathers reports, and performs other routine housekeeping chores. Its principal functions are the channeling of funds and preparation of the allocation budget for convention action. Carefully prescribed procedures are to be followed in this task.

---

[10]24 June 1994.

According to tradition, every cause had an opportunity to present its needs. The budget committee then tried to recommend the allocations according to need and priorities. The task was never easy. Even in the growing years, there was never enough money to satisfy the burgeoning causes. Yet, during nearly forty years of observing this process, money was seldom, if ever, used as a threat or lever to achieve a hidden agenda.

During the nearly thirty years of Porter Routh's leadership of the executive committee, the committee took care not to invade the autonomy of the various institutions and agencies, although Routh would sometimes plead their cases behind the scenes and occasionally in public. He was often reminded that he had no power to dictate what any entity should do in a given circumstance. He frequently reminded new members, who came often from operations of a state board of directors, that on the national scene, the committee did not direct the affairs of the agencies and institutions.

In the new day of the convention itself, however, a new spirit in its executive committee surfaced. The committee felt that it was a legislative body charged with the responsibility for directing the affairs of the convention. For example, the committee sensed the need to correct the Historical Commission's inclusion of one sentence about the CBF in a pamphlet. (This story is told is some detail earlier in this volume.) In one of the most disturbing actions of the new regime, the executive committee initiated a series of actions aimed at the Annuity Board, which manages the investment portfolios of retirement plans in the amount of four billion dollars for a multitude of interests in Baptist life.

The executive committee's subcommittee on program and budget questioned president Paul Powell of the Annuity Board about the investment policies of the board. Members were exorcised over the perceived investments in corporations that related to abortion activities. Powell outlined the investment policies that prohibit investment in companies directly related to abortion activities. He said the Annuity Board could not monitor charitable contributions of corporations to such organizations as Planned Parenthood. This explanation was inadequate according to some members of the subcommittee, however. The subcommittee suggested that the million dollar annual contribution to the Annuity Board for distribution to underfunded pensioners be cut. Again money became a weapon.

According to committee rules, no quotes or attributions are allowed, so the members had complete anonymity in making their threats. Associated Baptist Press reported that

> A variety of punitive actions against the Annuity Board were discussed, ranging from completely defunding the board to asking a different agency to administer relief funds. . . . During the debate, a committee member suggested the only way to get the Annuity Board's attention would be to gain control of its trustee board the same way conservatives gained control of the executive committee and other SBC trustee boards in recent years. This member said the Annuity Board had been left alone because it was not a center of power.[11]

To give clarity to the situation, Powell issued this statement to acquaint the committee and the public with the board's policy on abortion:

> The Annuity Board of the Southern Baptist Convention has long held a position of opposition to the wanton destruction of life inherent in the practice of abortions. Several years ago the trustees approved a staff recommendation to deny medical plan benefits for abortion. In our investment decisions we will avoid, or divest in orderly fashion, equities in any company that is found to have a service or product that is publicly perceived as uniquely aiding, supporting, or promoting abortion. This commitment grows out of a deep personal, biblical-based conviction that is shared by the president, the trustees, and the officers of the Annuity Board.[12]

At the next meeting of the executive committee in September 1994, the subcommittee insisted that the Annuity Board conform to the views of the members of the committee. This was the fourth time in a year the committee had dealt with the investment policies of the board.

Editor Michael J. Clingenpeel of the *Religious Herald* responded to the executive committee's actions in an editorial entitled: "Don't Mess with the Annuity Board." His first paragraph opened with these words: "Message to Southern Baptist ministers—the Southern Baptist Convention executive committee is tinkering with your retirement." He recounted the

---

[11]5 March 1994.
[12]Baptist Press, 23 February 1994.

incidents recorded above. He called the effort seriously flawed for several reasons: the board's opposition to abortion; the problem of good returns on investments; and in a global economy the difficulty of segregating funds since firms such as RJR Nabisco sells Oreo cookies, Planters peanuts, Sanka coffee, Kool-aid, Post cereals, Maxwell House coffee, and Velveeta cheese. Clingenpeel further stated that the real issue was control, not competence or ethics.

> The SBC Executive Committee and its officials possess an uncontrollable need to micromanage the plans, policies, and practices of SBC agencies and any entities related to them. They are control freaks who give verbal assent to local church autonomy, but practice a polity that gives power to a denominational hierarchy in Nashville. Their preferred direction of decision-making flows downward to the churches rather than upward from the churches to Nashville.[13]

Editor R. G. Puckett of the *Biblical Recorder* also expressed deep disturbance at the executive committee's actions:

> The executive committee has not only experienced an attitudinal revolution but also a cultural one. The mood, the tone, the methods and attitudes in doing the Lord's work are totally different from the pre-1979 days. For years, the executive committee has been moving toward a centralized power-base which many of us warned about, but it is firmly entrenched now. Despite carefully chosen words such as "request" instead of "instruct," the bottom line is that the executive committee is trying to run the entire convention, including every agency and institution. The Annuity Board is a case in point. Such is not the Baptist polity that made the denomination what it once was.[14]

In closing Puckett rejoiced that he was a part of the "North Carolina Way," a reference to the declarations of independence that had come out of the state.

---

[13]Quoted in *Baptist Record*, 31 March 1994.
[14]15 October 1994.

Closed Meetings

Also in the realm of control, SBC leaders are using a device previously avoided whenever possible: closed meetings. Formerly, executive sessions were used only as a last resort and usually limited to the discussion of matters related to personnel or legal problems. Fundamentalists quickly discovered that the subcommittee use of "background rules" with no quotes or attributions was a good way to avoid personal responsibility for comments or actions.

Before long, some leaders wanted to close important meetings altogether. Selected examples follow:

—The Executive Committee held a closed session with armed guards outside when it fired the Baptist Press leadership.[15] In time, committee meetings were closed to the press when the subject was controversial.

—Editor Jack Brymer of Florida complained when he was not permitted to attend the meeting of the program and budget subcommittee of the executive committee while it discussed how the ten million-plus dollars from Florida would be spent.[16] He was soon without a job.

—The trustees of Southern Seminary held closed meetings frequently as they wrestled with their problems. They used a closed meeting off campus to elect the new president.[17]

—Southwestern Seminary used a closed meeting to fire its president and elect a new one.

—The Foreign Mission Board used a closed meeting to elect its new president. To add insult to injury, it added an executive session to its regular meeting schedule. Baptist Press reported that "The executive session will allow for confidential interchange between trustees and the board's senior executive team."[18] No one seemed to note that there had been open dialogues between trustees and the executives for more than a hundred years.

The list of closed meetings could continue. In some cases this procedure was simply formalizing what had gone on for years in the form of caucuses called with sympathetic trustees. Privately-made decisions were

---

[15]Baptist Press, 18 July 1990.
[16]*Western Recorder*, 22 March 1994.
[17]Associated Baptist Press, February 1993.
[18]28 April 1994.

formalized later in plenary meetings. Now the atmosphere of secret meetings allows any loose canon to fire at will at any target. They present other problems also:

- They allow discussion of convention business without public knowledge, a knowledge essential to cooperation.
- Secrecy prevents identification of the true nature of the problems and the persons advocating courses of action.
- Secrecy allows decisions to be made without adequate public input.
- Secrecy avoids proper pressure of public opinion on both the boards and staffs involved.
- Secrecy means that discussions and votes will be held without public accountability and simply announced by public vote. The rationale of a decision, objections of some participants, and true issues are not publicized.
- Secrecy protects the private use of power for personal reasons.

Censorship of State Papers

With the machinations of the convention—its executive committee and the trustees of the institutions and agencies—the polity of the SBC has changed radically in the last decade. Increasingly, state papers have been limited in their access to information as well. SBC president Ed Young told the executive committee that the editors did not need to be in the business of investigative reporting but should print the good things about the denomination. (One wonders what actions would be visited on the unsuspecting if his advice were followed.)

Editor Jack Brymer of the Florida *Baptist Witness* resigned rather than accept restrictions on what type of articles he would publish. At a ceremony honoring him with a presentation of the Associated Baptist Press Religious Freedom Award, Brymer commented on his fellow editors. He remarked that too many of his colleagues opt for silence on controversial issues. He said that the greatest threat to political and religious freedom

is not the adversaries . . . be they secular dictators or religious ayatollahs, but good and decent people who choose silence as a defense. We all know it is criminal to remain silent in the face of even the slightest threat to one's freedom; yet, far too many of us in the religious press are guilty of doing just that.

Brymer said the "dilemma" that led to his decision to resign came after his board "suggested that the choice of news copy selected for publication be based not on which is the most truthful, but which is the most politically expedient."[19]

*****

Because of changing Baptist polity, the mechanisms are now in place to excommunicate churches that depart from the party line. The mere existence of a procedure in the constitution to exclude churches for any cause is a threat to other potential offenders. The refusal of the convention to receive funds contributed to its causes through the Cooperative Baptist Fellowship effectively sets the stage for the exclusion of those churches that wish to follow their own consciences.

The exclusion of any congregation or group of congregations by this means is essentially by nature not baptistic. The use of money as a threat by national bodies or leaders as a way to control an agency or institution is a radical departure from Baptist polity. The protests of denial by convention leaders are ineffective when one observes such activity as the harassment of the Annuity Board.

The use of directives, control, secrecy, censorship, exclusion, threat, and power present questions about the future of the SBC. The Convention is already reaping a most disturbing harvest. Ties between the national and state conventions are showing evidence of strain.

New State Relationships

For the century prior to 1979, ties had developed between the Southern Baptist Convention and the state conventions. The relationships were under constant study, and minor adjustments were made as often as necessary. The ties were entirely voluntary since each convention was independent and autonomous. Each level determined its own affairs,

---

[19]Associated Baptist Press, 28 October 1994.

disbursed money according to whatever agreements were in vogue at the time, and generally cooperated with other bodies as it chose.

Over the years, agreements were made as to the particular enterprises each convention would sponsor. The states owned and operated the colleges, children's homes, and hospitals. The national body operated the seminaries and controlled the foreign and home mission enterprises.

After long negotiations, the states and the Home Mission Board agreed on cooperative efforts in various programs. The HMB invested funds back into the states for these joint efforts. The states were largely responsible for raising funds for these projects, though the national body promoted the Cooperative Program and mission offerings. The state conventions determined the division of funds between the state and national causes. Various aspects of these agreements changed from time to time, but the major provisions of the arrangements were of long standing.

As the fundamentalist forces took over the national body, the relationships with the states began to change. The new leadership either did not understand the delicate nature of the partnership arrangements or wished to change them to suit their method of operations: control. As the politics of the convention began to affect the state bodies, various state entities began to flee to safety. Hospital systems such as those in Tennessee and South Carolina sought autonomy to avoid the controversy over such issues as abortion.

Colleges in the states were threatened early on by the politics of the convention. Several of the top institutions in the SBC states sought independence. Baylor in Texas, Furman in South Carolina, Mississippi College, and Samford in Alabama all changed their charters to make the boards of trustees self-perpetuating. Later, Mississippi College negotiated a compromise with the Mississippi convention to allow the state body to approve the trustee nominations. In the case of a difference of opinion about who would serve, however, the trustees would have the final say.

Such changes indicate the restless and fearful reaction in the states about the direction of the SBC. Because of the new directions, some states have chosen or are considering alternate avenues of mission giving.

Texas

In Texas, the strongest of the state conventions financially and numerically, dissatisfaction with the national trends had been growing. The

Baylor move toward independence had created a storm. When the South-western Seminary trustees fired Russell Dilday, the winds of dissent gained hurricane strength.

In its fall meeting in 1993, the convention commissioned a committee to study ways to enhance mission giving in Texas. The need arose in part because of the actions of the national body and in part because of the dissatisfaction of the churches with the direction of the national convention. The SBC leadership was greatly concerned with the growth of the Cooperative Baptist Fellowship and its new mission ventures. Since moderate Baptists were excluded from any meaningful participation in the national body, they were seeking new ways of doing missions and education.

Following months of study and consultation with a variety of interests, the Texas Cooperative Missions Giving Study Committee brought to the state board a remarkable report. It said in part:

> That the BGCT will recognize and distribute as Texas Cooperative Program contributions from the churches given in any or all of the following ways:
>
> (1) Gifts to the adopted budget of the BGCT and the adopted budget of the SBC according to the annually adopted percentage allocation between the two
>
> (2) Gifts to the adopted budget of the BGCT (Texas missions and ministries)
>
> (3) Gifts to the adopted budget of the BGCT and to other worldwide Baptist missions and ministries. These may include such entities as the Southern Baptist Convention, any agency of the Southern Baptist Convention, Woman's Missionary Union, the Cooperative Baptist Fellowship, the Baptist World Alliance, and other missions and ministries within the Baptist family.
>
> Note: The BGCT will continue to recognize the decision of a church to delete up to a total of five line items in the BGCT budget and/or the SBC budget.[20]

Previously, only undesignated funds were called Cooperative Program gifts. These had been used as informal indicators of a church's cooperation with the denomination.

---

[20]Toby Drim, *Baptist Standard*, 17 August 1994.

The public announcement of the committee action brought another wave of protest and confrontation. A minority report was written attempting to keep a "pure" Cooperative Program. The national convention's action instructing its agencies to refuse gifts given through the Fellowship intensified the conflict in Texas as well as other places.The issue centered around whether the churches could make their contributions to causes they chose and have them called a part of the Cooperative Program. The committee studying the matter said yes; the minority said no. The BGCT met on 31 October 1994 to decide the matter.

When the Texans met in Amarillo, they were in no mood for further submission to the fundamentalist ideals of the SBC. The minority report from the study committee was defeated by an estimated two-to-one majority. A substitute motion to redefine the committee's proposal was defeated by an even larger majority. The committee report was adopted by a large majority. Texas had decided to do missions in its own way.

The newly re-elected president, Jerold McBride, commented that the vote should deliver a message to the Southern Baptist Convention that Texas Baptists favor "state's rights over federal control." Another prominent pastor who spoke against the change in rules for counting mission money said the change would send shock waves across the Southern Baptist Convention. (This was probably the understatement of the week.) Richard Land of the SBC Christian Life Commission told reporters, "This was the beginning of the end of the Baptist General Convention of Texas."[21] (This was probably the overstatement of the century.)

Walter Carpenter, a Houston attorney and Home Mission Board trustee, reacted even more adamantly as he filed a charter for the "Texas Baptist Convention, Inc." should the need arise for a new convention. He indicated that the inclusion of the Cooperative Baptist Fellowship in the BGCT budget could trigger this move. He said that he was not in the loop of leadership decisions—"I merely do what I am asked to do."[22]

---

[21]Associated Baptist Press, 3 November 1994.
[22]Baptist Press, 6 October 1994.

Florida

The problems of relationships multiplied in Florida. The Home Mission Board voted to "investigate state conventions that forward (at the request of their churches) contributions to the Cooperative Baptist Fellowship."This unprecedented action brought immediate responses from many sources including John Sullivan, executive director of the Florida Convention. He said, "They have no right to investigate us, just like we have no right to investigate them."[23]

Immediately, a special study committee was called in Florida to consider the relationship of the state to the Home Mission Board. The committee recommended that the state retain the $1.3 million in funds that formerly would have been channeled to the HMB. Since the state normally received from the HMB for joint mission projects only about $600,000, the state could assume responsibility for all home mission work in the state. The plan called for designating all other SBC funds to the appropriate causes excluding the HMB. This move represented a radical departure from usual practice, although many Floridians felt it was no more radical than the HMB "investigating" the financial practices of a state convention. The study committee approved the plan, and it was unanimously approved by the full budget-allocation committee.

Larry Lewis, president of the Home Mission Board, said that he was

> appalled and aghast that a budget planning committee would recommend that the state convention cooperative allocation exclude the Home Mission Board or any major agency of the SBC. . . . From my perspective, that strikes at the very heart of what the Cooperative Program is all about—the states and the SBC cooperating together in the funding of our mission work around the world and at home. We're living with the reality that state conventions are radically redefining what the Cooperative Program is.[24]

Lewis neglected to comment on the radical investigation of one Baptist body by another or the necessity of studying how a state convention handled designated funds from the churches.

---

[23]Ibid., 22 August 1994.
[24]Ibid.

The Home Mission Board called a meeting to discuss the matter with several state mission leaders. The chairman of the HMB trustees, Bob Curtis, said,

> our purpose is not now and never has been, nor will it ever be, to investigate any state. . . . We have no authority to dictate what states can do regarding their work or funds.[25]

The meeting was apparently conciliatory. John Sullivan of Florida described it as "very open." The HMB committee planned to meet with all state executive directors before making a report to the board.

Also, the chairman of a committee appointed by the SBC Executive Committee to examine the programs and organizational structure of the SBC asked Sullivan of Florida to delay the implementation of this new plan for home missions until further consultations could be held. Sullivan agreed and commented:

> This is neither compromise nor capitulation, but a desire to cooperate with brothers in seeking solutions to sensitive problems and to insure the aggressive ongoing mission of winning this diverse and dynamic state to Christ.[26]

Virginia, North Carolina, Georgia

Other states are involved in funding changes. In Virginia, churches are allowed to support any of three budgets: the traditional Cooperative Program, one that funds the CBF, and one that is a hybrid of the other two. North Carolina churches can choose an alternate Cooperative Program budget that steers money away from some SBC agencies to moderate alternatives. Georgia Baptists have authorized a study of whether churches must cooperate with the SBC to be in good standing with the state convention.

Whether the conflicts between the state and national conventions can be worked out without further decimation of the Southern Baptist

---

[25]Ibid., 1 September 1994.
[26]Ibid., 9 September 1994.

Convention is not clear. To assure its future, the national body must revise its dealings with other Baptist entities. The rule of authority is beginning to chafe severely in the states. While in some places fundamentalism is strong enough to keep the state bodies in line, in other states moderates are strong enough to insist on genuinely baptistic practices. Interestingly, the problems are most severe in the traditionally strong Southern Baptist states.

The psychology of testing loyalty is a non-baptist concept. The exclusion of individuals or churches or state conventions because of a relationship to the Cooperative Baptist Fellowship will bring more and more conflict. It is a no-win situation for all concerned. The only solution that will not bring chaos is for the national convention to recognize that it cannot control the actions of individuals and other Baptist bodies. Whether the present leadership recognizes the severity of the problems or their long-term implications is questionable.

SBC Fundamentalism and Women

The issue of female leadership and ministry in the SBC provides another example of denominational conflict and change. For nearly a hundred years, women were not permitted to serve as messengers to the meetings of the convention. For many more years they were not allowed to serve as trustees of the agencies or officers of the convention. Something of the aura of the "southern belle" attached itself to the women of the SBC. Women initiated their leadership roles in the SBC through WMU and later through service in the local church and association, seminaries, denominational agencies, and state conventions.

With most advances in female leadership, fundamentalists have reacted negatively. They have attempted to manipulate the activity of WMU and limit the hiring of women as teachers in seminaries and ministers in the local church. They have spoken loudly against the ordination of women ministers and deacons and accused the Cooperative Baptist Fellowship of being a front for the "women's issue."[27]

---

[27]*Baptists Today,* 4 February 1994.

Woman's Missionary Union

While various women's groups interested in mission activities flourished in many places, it was not until 1888 in Richmond, Virginia, that women organized Woman's Missionary Union, an auxiliary to the SBC. The ladies could not be a part of the general body, but they would affect its affairs in significant ways for generations.

The purpose of WMU was to support the mission efforts of the convention. Mission education, prayer support, and collection of funds for the various projects became the passion of the organization. It sponsored mission education programs for children as well as women.

The mission boards soon came to recognize the organization as a worthy partner in their tasks and joined with WMU in various activities considered mutually beneficial. In time, the spring home mission offering, named for pioneer mission-minded Annie Armstrong, became the second most important source of funds for the Home Mission Board. The Christmas foreign mission offering, named for pioneer missionary to China Lottie Moon, became the largest single source of support for the Foreign Mission Board.

As the partnership with the mission boards became more and more productive, what had been a WMU activity became a church cause. As late as the 1960s, this was a reason for concern in parts of the convention, particularly in Virginia. On the positive side, the joint effort raised much more money for the mission boards. On the negative end, it removed control of the offerings from the women and gave it to the pastor and church. As the fundamentalists gained controlled of the SBC, the executive committee and other groups, including the mission boards, claimed the offerings as their own. The women were once again pushed into the background and in effect were told to go back to the kitchen.

As the fundamentalist power grew, WMU problems grew. Because of its auxiliary status, it was governed by a board that the SBC could not control. The Home Mission Board president announced that the board would like to "marry" the WMU. Former SBC president Adrian Rogers said that the auxiliary should be "hard wired" to the SBC and have nothing to do with dissident Baptists. The executive committee of the SBC made overtures to the WMU to become an agency of the Convention; thus, control would shift. WMU said no.

As the efforts to control met with little success, the long romance began to wane. More and more harsh comments were made publicly about the lack of cooperation from the women. Threats were made to begin another women's organization. Joint efforts were minimized or canceled.

WMU leaders saw the handwriting on the wall. Overtures were made to them by the newly organized Cooperative Baptist Fellowship. CBF wanted some help in mission education and materials. WMU was so inclined. Other opportunities were available to produce and distribute mission education materials

WMU voted to expand and revise its ministry to include all types of Baptist groups, not just Southern Baptists. Reaction was swift. Moderates were delighted; fundamentalists were furious. The latter accused the women of choosing sides in the controversy. WMU officials replied quietly that they were doing only what the Sunday School Board had been doing for many years: supplying Christian materials to whatever group wanted them.

The Foreign Mission Board, the recipient of the most money for the longest period of time due to the WMU efforts, criticized the WMU for voting to assist any entity not controlled by the SBC. Executive committee leaders requested an urgent meeting with WMU leaders to discuss the matter.

WMU stood firm. Under a barrage of criticism and innuendo, misinformation and accusation, the women maintained their "cool." Their responses were measured and Christian. Various efforts were made to break the impasse, but no solution was found. The women's organization reiterated that it would continue its support of the SBC mission efforts and not change its basic purpose. In the middle of the furor, James Draper, president of the Sunday School Board, urged his fellow executives to be "very careful how we react."

The president of the Home Mission Board urged WMU to redouble its efforts because of projected income shortfall. Shortly, however, he told Florida Baptists that the Annie Armstrong offering belonged to the HMB, and he would strongly contest any use of the name by Florida for multiple purposes.

Seminaries

—Southern Seminary had been a co-sponsor of a conference on women in the church. Southern's new president told the presidents of the consortium sponsors that the seminary could not participate since the meeting was "so controversial." Mohler said that his decision to withdraw sponsorship was based on the selection of keynote speakers as well as a suggested list of workshop topics and leaders.[28]

—In 1984, Southern Seminary trustees elected Molly Marshall as an instructor in theology and granted her tenure in 1988. Her gender and theology were sources of controversy during her service at the seminary. Until the election of Albert Mohler, the administration supported Marshall even while some trustees called for her dismissal. In the 1980s her status was often debated but supposedly settled when the trustees exonerated the president and faculty members accused of heresy after the adoption of the "Glorieta Statement" and the signing of the "Covenant."

In June 1994, the administration informed Marshall that charges seeking her dismissal would be initiated if she did not resign. A memorandum from David Dockery, vice president for academic affairs, indicated that the charges would center around two matters: (1) her alleged "failure to relate constructively to" the Southern Baptist Convention, such as "teachings that might be in conflict with motions or resolutions passed at the SBC or support of/involvement with the Cooperative Baptist Fellowship"; and (2) alleged "violations of the Abstract of Principles," the seminary's governing theological document.[29]

Marshall responded that she was given no opportunity to present her defense and that in effect, there was no due process. She said she was told that her trustee adversaries had both the votes and the will to fire her. One commentator opined that the matter sounded rather like old-fashioned western justice: "We are going to give you a fair trial and then hang you."

While her theology had been discussed from the beginning of her tenure, many observers believe that her gender was primary in the decision, although Mohler denied that to be the case. He said,

---

[28]Associated Baptist Press, in *Baptists Today*, 28 October 1993.
[29]Associated Baptist Press, 23 August 1994.

The issue is not the gender of the professor, but the substance of what the professor teaches. Even though I believe the New Testament excludes women from teaching authority and the pastorate in the church, this does not mean women should not teach on the faculty of the seminary or even in the school of theology.[30]

Response to Marshall's dismissal was widespread. Guy Henderson, editor of the *Baptist Record*, said,

What kind of theological double-speak is this? It sounds like the Pharisees are back in town. "Excludes women from teaching authority" . . . but they can teach theology in the seminary? It seems more like unhappy trustees forcing an issue rather than an erudite seminary president. Let's be consistent. If women are not to pastor a church, neither should they teach theology to preachers. . . . Shades of Dilday! He that is without theological aberrance should cast the first stone.[31]

Marv Knox, expressed similar sentiments in his editorial in the *Western Recorder*: "Was Theology or Gender Molly Marshall's Undoing?" The independent association of faculty members at the seminary adopted a resolution that expressed their "outrage" over the forced resignation of Marshall describing it as "unjustified and untimely."[32]
—At Southwestern Seminary, the opposite kind of action related to women was occurring. The trustees, on the recommendation of new president Ken Hemphill, elected Karen O'Dell Bullock as the first woman on the theology faculty. She and other women had been adjunct teachers, but she was the first woman elected to a faculty appointment. Guy Henderson's "theological double-speak" found another illustration:

Hemphill said some trustees raised concerns about electing a woman to the faculty, but he noted she would teach *church history,* not *theology.* Bullock assured Hemphill that she is under the authority of the seminary president as a faculty member and her husband in her home.[33]

---

[30]Ibid.
[31]1 September 1994.
[32]*Western Recorder*, 30 August 1994.
[33]Associated Baptist Press, 20 October 1994.

Baptist Sunday School Board

—The board canceled a national meeting of Christian women. The meeting had been developed by the board and WMU. The cancellation was unilateral on the part of the board; WMU was not consulted. The board spokesman said the meeting was scrapped because the board did not want to conflict with a local church holding a similar meeting about twenty-five miles away.[34]

—Late in 1993, the board announced the beginning of a new ministry aimed at women, the purpose of which was to involve women in Bible study, prayer, and outreach. Immediately a director was employed and began laying plans. The board announced that the move was not in competition with WMU but to work with it. WMU indicated it was not sure it wanted the help.[35]

State Conventions and Local Associations

—In Oklahoma, Anne Graham Lotz (daughter of Billy Graham and sister -in-law of Denton Lotz, general secretary of the Baptist World Alliance) was removed from an evangelism conference program. A pastor complained that a woman should not preach to men.[36]

—In Kentucky, an association split three ways over the issue of women's ordination.[37]

—In California, the state convention refused to seat the messengers from the Nineteenth Avenue Church because its pastor was a woman. A year later, by a narrow margin, the convention reversed its decision.[38]

—First Baptist Church of West Jefferson, North Carolina, was expelled from the Ashe Baptist Association for ordaining a woman deacon.[39]

—The executive board of Galveston Baptist Association requested the transfer of the director of the Baptist Student Union at the University of

---

[34]*Baptists Today*, 20 January 1994.
[35]Ibid., 16 December 1993.
[36]Ibid., 4 February 1993.
[37]Associated Baptist Press, 21 October 1993.
[38]Baptist Press, 17 November 1993.
[39]Stan Hastey, *Baptists Today*, 17 February 1994.

Texas medical branch because she had produced "irreconcilable differences" growing out of her ordination to the gospel ministry.[40]

*****

These reports concerning negative treatment of women at various denominational levels confirm that fundamentalism is a widespread phenomenon and promises women more problems in the future, along with problems over money.

And Then There Is Money

By the 1990s, the financial momentum generated by many years of teaching about Christian stewardship had begun to slow. The denomination's income had not kept up with inflation for a number of years. The actual number of dollars had declined for several years.

The controversy had begun to affect the state conventions in spite of their hopeful rhetoric. As they began to experience financial shortfalls, it became evident that the inevitable had happened. The churches were feeling the pinch of economic stagnation and the uncertainty caused by denominational infighting. The almost frantic national efforts to increase giving to the Cooperative Program fell on many unhearing ears. Churches and pastors began to wonder if they should not keep the money at home —for after all, missions began at home.

Some churches and leaders were disturbed by what they considered the wanton waste of mission money on extravaganzas, world travel by denominational leaders, joint ventures with non-Baptists, and constantly increasing budgets of those leaders who seemed to be engaged in defeating the Democrats. Some churches were concerned about the treatment of Woman's Missionary Union, or the election of fundamentalist leaders for the institutions, or the vitriolic language used by leadership against those who disagreed. Some persons were just concerned.

The usually prosperous Sunday School Board, which received no mission funds, was beginning to experience economic hardship. Circulation of curriculum materials, Broadman Press, and the bookstores were

---

[40]Associated Baptist Press, 30 August 1994.

crucial to the board's financial health. The key to its ongoing health depended on the circulation of magazines and periodicals. By 1993, Sunday school literature sales alone were down 8 percent, representative of the overall decline of periodicals. President Jimmy Draper told the board that it is "in the process of dying" and will fade away unless drastic steps are taken to revive it. Only four of the publisher's seventeen programs made a profit the previous year.[41]

Extensive plans were designed for reorganization and budget administration. Experts in finance and marketing were hired to stem the tide. Departments and divisions were combined or eliminated. Serious changes decimated the student, music, and church administration departments and eliminated the church recreation and media-library departments.

Serious "downsizing" of staff was announced. By the September meeting of trustees in 1994, by termination or retirement or resignation, the board had lost 599 employees but hired 480. The net reduction was only 121.[42] Many department and division leaders were removed or transferred to other responsibilities. The trustees voted to close four bookstores. They also announced that while revenue was up from the last year, budget shortfall would be about $13 million. The board had authorized loans for operations of about $13.6 million, acknowledging a "cash-flow problem"[43]

By the 1992–1993 budget year, the Cooperative Program receipts by the SBC were 1.23 percent below the previous year. Every agency received less money that year than the previous year. The seminaries and mission boards were taking drastic reductions in budgets due to the shortfall. At the end of the 1993–94 fiscal year, however, the executive committee announced the best year yet in Cooperative Program gifts. Mission funds rebounded after a long drought.[44]

The Cooperative Program increase was reported to be about $6.3 million. Associated Baptist Press reported almost immediately that

almost a fourth . . . are dollars that would not have been counted as Cooperative Program last year. . . . Those numbers include more than

---

[41]Ibid., 8 February 1993.
[42]Ibid., 29 September 1994.
[43]Ibid.
[44]Ibid.

$1.2 million in restricted funds from Baptist state conventions and another $201,000 sent directly to the SBC for the unified budget. Before a change in the executive committee's accounting practices adopted last year, those funds would have been reported as "designated" gifts and not included in Cooperative Program totals.

And while 1993–94 totals exceed the 1989–90 record by $2.1 million, the denomination lost ground in spending power. To buy what $140 million would purchase in 1990, the SBC would have needed to take in more than $159 million in 1994 dollars, based on annual percentage estimates of increased costs of living.[45]

Whether this total dollar increase continues is a doubtful assumption due to events in the states.

Of even greater concern are the results of a survey on the priorities of Southern Baptists. The Inter-Agency Council of the convention commissioned a survey to study the concerns and interests of the people in the churches. Ministry areas of the local church ranked in this order:

(1) outreach/evangelism/witnessing
(2) ministry to families
(3) prayer ministry
(4) training/Bible study
(5) ministry to groups within the church
(6) ministry to groups outside the church
(7) home and foreign missions.[46]

If the survey represents the preoccupations of the local Baptist churches and people, tougher days are ahead for the denomination.

Attitudes

One incident out of hundreds illustrates clearly the attitudes accompanying the fundamentalist power plays. In a meeting with religious leaders, President Clinton commented that his view of abortion was essentially that expressed by the SBC in 1971. The convention reaffirmed the 1971

---

[45]3 November 1994.
[46]Baptist Press, 19 February 1993.

resolution in 1974, and took a similar position on the subject in 1976, 1977, 1978, and 1979. When asked about his position, the President said, "Well, did we learn something about the Bible in the last twenty-three years?"

In response, James A. Smith of the Christian Life Commission said,

> The reason the Southern Baptist Convention resolutions have changed is not because we learned something about the Bible. Instead, we elected new leaders who believe the Bible. The former leadership of the SBC—including the Christian Life Commission and Baptist Joint Committee—rejected the clear evidence of God's revealed word, which holds human life to be sacred and worthy of protection. These leaders have a burden to bear regarding their rejection of God's word and acceptance of worldly wisdom.[47]

Leaders of the years mentioned include presidents Carl Bates, Owen Cooper, Jaroy Weber, James Sullivan, and Jimmy Allen; agency heads Baker James Cauthen, Duke McCall, Olin Binkley, Harold Graves, Milton Fergurson, Robert Naylor, Foy Valentine, and Porter Routh; and dozens of others who could hardly be called either ignorant of God's word or unbelievers.

When President Clinton talked with me about this incident, he said that he was shocked to learn that the present leadership seemed uninformed on previous SBC actions. He assured me that he was not pro-abortion but pro-choice. He sounded rather like the 1971–1979 actions of the convention.

A New Southern Baptist Convention

Whatever else can be said about the SBC, it is no longer the same body in doctrine, polity, procedures, or cooperative effort in education and missions. The careful attempts to put a good face on the problems are now of small consequence. Texas state president Jerold McBride commented that "When the earthquake hit Texas, we finally took it seriously."[48] The

[47]Associated Baptist Press, 4 October 1994.
[48]*Baptist Standard*, 9 November 1994.

resultant shock surely must alert SBC leadership that coercion will not continue to function effectively.

William Brackney, principal of McMaster Divinity College in Ontario, Canada, told the North American Baptist Fellowship that Baptists in North America must address

> the issue of who we are; or there may be little need for us collectively. Unlike the comfortable Christian faith many Baptists in North America enjoy today, the earliest Baptists were individuals and "dissenters" who suffered for their beliefs. . . . Believers baptism and their insistence on religious liberty put Baptists in the "dissenters" group.
>
> [In the colonies] Baptists made nuisances of themselves, antagonizing the authorities over infant baptism, taxes to support ministers and other religious institutions; and early Baptist leaders paid dearly for this.
>
> Fundamentalism more than any other issue gave Baptists a national identity in the early twentieth century. . . . As a result of the wars of fundamentalism, Baptists broadly came to be seen as protectors of primitive Christianity in modern clothing.[49]

Brackney credited Southern Baptists with changing that image nationally and worldwide. Because Southern Baptists agreed on missions, evangelism, and congregationalism, they created "an image of growth, stewardship, and internationalism for post-war America." He commented that it is different today since Baptists are more divided than ever.

> They have strayed from their beginnings. The loudest and most obvious and most-often quoted Baptists in the United States seem to be nowhere near the historic principles of older Baptist bodies.[50]

The new Southern Baptist Convention seems to stand in that distant lowland.

---

[49]Baptist Press, 4 May 1994.
[50]Ibid.

Chapter 10

The Lingering Chill

"Now that the battle for the Bible is over, we can move on" is an often-heard cliché. Several problems come to mind over such a view. One may question whether there was ever a battle over the Bible. "Moving on" implies that all is forgotten or even forgiven or will be ignored. The whole concept denies the Old Testament idea of repentance and restitution concerning past wrongs and the New Testament concepts of love and compassion. Some of the participants may move on, but the chill lingers and spreads. The damage will not be repaired by simplistic assumptions.

The waves caused by dropping the fundamentalist rock into the SBC pond still spread to the far reaches of zion and in places reach tsunami (tidal wave) proportions. Placing blame and denial do not suffice to eradicate the damage done to every segment of the denomination.

"The Controversy Doesn't Affect Us"

One western convention executive director was heard to say, "I am glad we don't have to fool with that controversy here." He was referring to the fact that some other states had more problems with the argument than he had. He was also still in denial that a problem existed that affected his work. For fifteen years, similar statements have been made by various denominational leaders, pastors, and lay people.

In trying to alleviate the trauma, many laypersons and some pastors have said that the controversy has been "a preacher fight." In a sense, of course, the preachers have led in the problems because they have had a better understanding of or more concern about the issues. Theology and denominational issues have too often belonged to the clergy only in a body that acknowledges the priesthood of all believers.

As sick people often deny that they have a problem, Baptists in many places have denied a real problem. For some, the denial phase has lasted for fifteen years. This negation has not slowed nor diverted the problems, however. The disease has eaten away at the vitals, while some good people have denied its existence or felt that the disease had attacked someone else. For pastors or laypersons to hide behind the denial syndrome is to invite more rapid fragmentation of their domain. Despite the denial, all Southern Baptists are or will be seriously affected by the controversy, although many churches will not be directly involved for many years. Yet, the new theology discussed in chapter nine will most seriously affect most, if not all, churches as the years go by.

The transfer of membership from one church to another will alter the makeup of individual churches. With the perfunctory examination of new members, the nature of the congregation will change. As churches export members who have been entertained week by week, not experienced believers baptism, or had little or no training in Baptist doctrines, a new kind of membership will spread in New Testament churches.

The controversy is already seriously affecting churches as they call new pastors. Many search committees are already questioning prospects as to whether they are "conservative or moderate." Considerable numbers of pastors have reported long and difficult sessions with committees over their status in the controversy. Many others testify that they have been examined in detail by committees on doctrines, biblical understanding, affiliations, and sympathies. Many churches are very concerned that they do not hire a moderate, while others are frightened by bringing in a fundamentalist who will introduce the conflict into their church. No longer can numerous churches achieve a unanimous call of a pastor.

Churches, like ministers, are now labeled as conservative, moderate, or liberal. The designations are really not very descriptive of the true nature of many churches, however. Most of them are conservative theologically, even if they are labeled otherwise. To illustrate this sad state of affairs, the example of a new western Kentucky church is instructive.

About seventy members of an existing church started meeting in another location and calling their church by a different name. At a business meeting in the original congregation, three motions were made trying to link the church to the fundamentalist movement in the SBC. Two motions passed, stating that the church would remain "a Southern Baptist church" and that the church no longer would allow members to designate offerings through the church to the Cooperative Baptist Fellowship. This move alone indicates a radical departure from usual Baptist procedures. Various sources commented on problems such as the new pastor's move in a more conservative direction, the method of the pastor's call to the church, the nomination of women as deacons, and the new pastor's authoritarian style of leadership. In one relatively small congregation many of the denominational problems were introduced.

The seminary problems have now invaded many congregations as well. Churches have known good ministers from a given seminary but now realize that the school has changed radically in recent years. No longer can a church rely on the alma mater of a minister to determine where he/she will fall in the denominational scale. Church leaders and laypersons are questioning what has happened to theological training. Now the decimation of Southeastern, the fundamentalizing of Southern, the firing of the popular and conservative president of Southwestern, and the coming retirement of the presidents of New Orleans and Midwestern seminaries—well, these raise a lot of questions.

Add to the milieu the birth of new divinity schools or seminaries at Hardin-Simmons, Baylor, Gardner-Webb, Samford, Wake Forest, Mercer, Richmond, and who knows where else; plus the Baptist "houses" or special offerings at Duke, Emory, Vanderbilt, and perhaps other schools. A plethora of theological education opportunities now exist. All have been affected as a result of the controversy and have particular points of view —not to say biases—and their students will be educated or indoctrinated in a variety of ways.

Along with the problems presented by changing requirements for church membership, calling ministers, and deciding on theological and political persuasions, churches are now challenged to determine how they want to "do missions." Formerly, most Southern Baptists supported mission and educational causes through the Cooperative Program (CP). The definition of the term is now debated in a half dozen states. Further, many churches object to some of the uses of CP money and refuse to contribute. Some are designating funds and want them called CP funds to affirm their support of missionaries or schools. Increasingly, congregations will re-evaluate their methods of mission giving and missions participation. Indeed, the SBC controversy affects most all Southern Baptists.

The Larger Christian Community

When one moves beyond the local congregation of Baptists, the relationships with the larger community of Christians have been seriously altered as well. Whereas Southern Baptists were formerly considered conservative or even fundamental by other Christians, they came to be labeled by those unfamiliar with the nature of the problems as fundamentalists. Millions did not deserve that designation, but the affiliation of the leadership with the forces of right-wing religion and politics won the designation for all. At best, the problems of the convention and its constituents have been poorly understood by others.

Some fellow Christians thought that the leadership was "dragging the denomination kicking and screaming" back into the nineteenth century. Many felt that a century of progress in higher and theological education was compromised in a matter of a decade. Schools that had risen to the top echelons of excellence in theological education were now criticized or investigated by accrediting agencies. A system of denominational organization and polity that was the envy of many around the world suddenly turned autocratic. Democracy seemed to be abandoned in favor of politics and control. Power appeared to the public to be the basic reason for the conflict.

In the secular world, the witness of the denomination was seriously compromised. Some persons saw Southern Baptists as fractious, backward, and selfish. Others questioned why the largest non-Catholic denomination in America suddenly turned to devour itself. The issues announced by the fundamentalist leaders seemed to unbelievers to be much ado about very little. The name Southern Baptist began to imply mean-spirited, argumentative, and sometimes ignorant people who had lost touch with a modern world.

For others, the name became synonymous with right-wing political causes. This identification became so pronounced that one knowledgeable historian remarked:

> Southern Baptists are a mirror image of the white South. The Southern Baptist conflict is a model of the changes in the white South. It is now difficult to distinguish between Southern Baptist leadership and the right wing of the Republican Party.[1]

The 1994 election campaign in which the Republican Party won such a resounding victory substantiated the professor's comments. Southern Baptists were prominent in many places in the local elections. National leaders apparently made no efforts to cover their sentiments or activities

---

[1]Wayne Flint, Auburn University, personal conversation.

in behalf of Republican candidates. Aggressive criticism of the Democratic president and other officials represented departure from the practices of former officials.

Of perhaps more importance is the fact that in many places, churches have discovered that the goodwill accumulated over generations has dissipated. Non-Christians are not interested in what Baptists are saying. The conduct of many persons involved in the conflict has convinced the unbelieving public, "Behold how they hate one another." Naturally, most people are not interested in a religion filled with disrespect, anger, and hatred.

Formerly, in much of the public mind, Southern Baptists were characterized as conservative, Bible believers, not creedalists, recognizers of the priesthood of all believers, and a people with a worthy purpose. They were seen as supporters of soul and religious freedom for all persons and worthy adversaries concerning the use of public tax money for religious purposes. Too often now, we are seen as fractious, power hungry, politically taking advantage of our tax-free status, and setters of rules of conduct that amount to a rigid creed. This creed has more to do with the preconceptions of the leadership than with the interpretations of scripture that are more praised than practiced.

The Washington establishment that has looked to Baptists for support on church-state problems is confused. National politicians are receiving mixed signals from different groups. One faction holds to traditional separation stances; another clamors for tax money for Baptist schools, government interference in matters of public prayer, and secular help for religious objects. One group advocates a free church in a free state; the other says we want a partnership with government in the pursuit of the better life. One segment believes that government should leave religion alone; the other maintains that government should help religion accomplish its purposes.

Ambitious politicians are using the fundamentalist movement to accomplish their own goals. The fundamentalists see themselves as leaders of a new age. Whatever they are, they are far from the bloody battlefields of their forebears where freedom from religious tyranny was won.

In the process, the problems for the ministry have multiplied manyfold. In the pluralistic and secular society, the difficulties are multitudinous. Ministers are in a quandry to find or hold to a clear sense of self-identity. They must contemplate their proper relationship to their peers, denomination, church, and school and their proper role in the SBC problems.

Consider that the present generation of ministers, under forty-five years of age, professionally has never known a denomination that was at peace. Here is a generation that "knows not Joseph." These ministers have never known the exhilaration of being swept up in a mission that had as its goal the sharing of the gospel with a whole world.

Many of those who should be role models for young ministers are either involved in endless, mindless controversy or have been brutally relegated to the never-never land of expulsion. Every convention meeting the young ministers have ever attended was either torn by strife, or the tension over issues was just under the surface. Seldom has there been a meeting of the national body in the last fifteen years that did not revolve around some divisive issue.

Perhaps one of the most disturbing aspects of the matter is that a minister very often, if not always, must choose sides at some point. Many different attitudes or actions may make the choice for him/her: which meetings to attend, which attitudes to adopt, whether to criticize one side or the other, where his/her church gives its money, who to choose as friends, which school to support, who to have lunch with, how to vote in the association or state or national meetings, and so forth.

Inevitably, if a minister is active beyond the local congregation he/she will be labeled, and the future will be limited or determined by the label. The opportunity for fellowship and friendship will be limited to those who share that label or to the few who as yet have no label. In these matters, one is talking about the possibilities of personal development and growth, denominational service, and satisfying professional relationships. Conflict or at best personal coolness develops between the ministers, depending on which side they choose or others have chosen for them.

A lengthy conversation with two young doctoral graduates of Southern Seminary gave personality to these problems. One said, "My generation of theological students doesn't want to be pastors. . . . I don't know any role models. . . . Religious educators are split into about four groups. I can fellowship with one or two groups, but we can't seem to get them together." The other student said, "What we are missing is the fellowship with older mentors. . . . There is no sense of oneness."

At a Smyth and Helwys display at a state convention a bright, young, recent seminary graduate commented, "There seems to be a line around our area. The conservatives won't even walk around it." Next to that display, the "conservative Baptists" had a booth with color tapes promoting "conservative candidates" for the state presidency.

Academic institutions, boasting academic freedom and excellence in education, shun anyone remotely controversial. Former trustees, faculty, academic officers including former presidents, and any other persons who have become the object of criticism by the fundamentalists are quietly abandoned. Few, if any, are invited even to ceremonial occasions on campus.

Virulent attacks on schools and administrations have made it difficult for the academic community to hear any view differing from the party line. Faculty must be chosen from the non-controversial, and prominent visitors are carefully chosen. One speaker of doubtful reputation (specifically, a moderate) can arouse vitriolic criticism by fundamentalist powers that be. Yet, some persons wonder that colleges and universities have fled their ties to the state conventions.

As the trust in the system has broken down, the isolation of many persons by old friends, the cutting of ties to institutions, and the uncertainty about who believes what has grown. Awkward relationships have multiplied simply because one is not certain whether differences are personal or can be accepted simply as differences. Such problems are not limited simply to clergy but affect all professional church-related persons and a multitude of the laity, especially those who have made the greatest contributions to the denomination. For persons to believe that the controversy does not affect them is to confess a lack of knowledge of the problems.

Atmosphere of Confrontation

Another serious consideration from the conflict is a change of attitude. Southern Baptists have labored together out of a sense of brotherliness and cooperation for common purposes. We have now moved from cooperation to confrontation. Although we have never been "a silent people," we have usually rallied around common objectives after our arguments. Now we are in a situation that by its ferment and distrust makes every issue a life-and-death one in the minds of many.

In Alabama, arguments about higher education, the freedom of colleges, and other such matters have produced a major conflict. Instead of working out the problems between trustees and state leadership, a special meeting of the board of directors split over whether to move the meeting of the convention to prevent one college from having an advantage. The problem may be severe, but the reactions have exacerbated the difficulty.

In Virginia, a group representing both sides of the argument formed to work toward solutions that would allow continued cooperation. The president of the Baptist General Association of Virginia later announced to the general board that the effort had failed. The interim executive of the newly-formed Southern Baptist Conservatives disputed the president's conclusion. The president said in part: "Events beyond the council's control made its task virtually impossible." He attributed the problems to events in the SBC, the refusal of conservatives to accept a proposed giving option, the election of an interim director of the conservatives, and the alternative evangelism conference about three weeks after the state's annual conference.[2]

The Texas events described in chapter nine set the stage for future confrontations over many issues. Fundamentalists met after the state convention to formulate plans for future action, including the possibility of a new convention organization. Seasoned observers do not think this will occur, but it illustrates the atmosphere between combatants.

The confrontations of the national body have now penetrated a large number (perhaps a majority) of the state bodies. Regional local associations of churches all over the country have experienced much of the same conflict. As the struggle continues, the atmosphere of confrontation has invaded large numbers of churches.

Seemingly, the movers and shakers of the fundamentalist movement have thought only of the next move to accomplish their goal. One wonders if any of them have given serious thought to the ultimate end of the present course. Some leaders seem to feel that the storm will blow over and the course will be smooth. Evidently, by now this is not the case.

The mad dash to conformity has not produced uniformity. On the contrary, the result has been unimaginable fragmentation. Fundamentalism has set "parameters" of thought that inhibit thoughtful exploration of concepts, theological questioning, and publication of anything not clearly

---

[2]Baptist Press, 27 October 1994.

within the party line. No Baptist faculty member, denominational employee, or loyal party member dares to question the orthodox dogma. Denominational and professional suicide is the penalty, and the witnesses are many.

The last fifteen years have been filled with squelched ideas, unproposed ventures of faith, unreleased trial balloons of hope, and unexpressed suggestions of possible solutions. The whole landscape of Baptist zion is now limited to the incomplete or erroneous understanding of the leaders. Their brooding presence looms over the SBC, and their threatening stance intimidates the timid. Distrust breeds distrust, hate multiplies hatred, and love begets love. The bitter seeds of confrontation are yielding a bountiful harvest throughout the Baptist zion.

Some persons talk of forgetting the problems and "going forward." This view avoids the true issues and does not deal with the substance. Every announcement of inclusiveness that ends in the hypocrisy of exclusiveness simply adds to the hurt and distrust within the Baptist family. Its effect on unbelievers is perhaps the saddest addendum of all.

The Cooperative Baptist Fellowship

One of the most traumatic results of the conflict has been the necessity for numerous Baptists to seek other ways of expressing their faith and living out their corporate Christian experience. By the late 1980s, it was increasingly evident that the rift in the SBC was growing and that little would be done by fundamentalists to salvage what unity was left in the denomination. The often-repeated line of a newly elected president, "I will be president of all Southern Baptists" was a press conference line. Several presidents declared that they would be inclusive; yet, no one was.

Closed-door caucuses, executive sessions, terminations, wasted money, and disrupted educational and missionary efforts increased and cast a longer and longer shadow on what many people thought the denomination was about. No amount of protest or argument seemed to have any effect on the leadership. In the mind of the moderates, SBC leadership was pressing toward total control and absolute mastery.

After the final defeat of a moderate candidate for the presidency in New Orleans in 1990, it was obvious that many individuals and churches would be seeking new ways of corporate cooperation. Daniel Vestal, pastor of Dunwoody Church in Atlanta, the defeated candidate, responded to requests from many moderate Baptists to call a consultation of their kind to consider the future course of action. (Many of the details of this effort and others are recorded in *The Struggle for the Soul of the SBC.)*

Many of the older leaders of the former SBC were gravely concerned about the future of thousands of missionaries and the six seminaries. Many felt that they had given themselves to the Baptist cause in good faith and had been commissioned by the denomination and churches in good faith. The responsibility for the care of these people and institutions seemed to rest more heavily on the shoulders of the moderates than the fundamentalists if one considered the financial support of the past.

Fundamentalist leaders had seldom been enthusiastic in their financial support of denominational causes. In fact, several leaders and their churches had supported non-convention efforts far better than SBC causes. On the other hand, many of the moderates had a good record of support for denominational causes. Their concern late in the conflict was that the educational and missionary causes not be starved. They would seek some means of carrying out their concerns that would bypass the rigid control of the fundamentalists.

Others would take alternative courses. Duke McCall, in a document sent to about forty former leaders, asked:

> Having lost a billion dollars worth of property and funds, and having no programs administered by compatible people, what will moderate churches support? They will mount their horses and ride off in all directions.[3]

Prior to the meeting of the first Consultation of the group that became the Cooperative Baptist Fellowship (CBF), McCall proposed an alternative funding mechanism that would allow the churches to contribute to SBC and other causes of their choice. His pre-convocation suggestion was the organization of an alternative funding effort to be called Baptist Cooperative Missions Program (BCMP). He had projected such a possibility in the 1980s but received little response until his May 1990 announcement.[4]

---

[3]*The Struggle for the Soul of the SBC*, ed. Walter B. Shurden (Macon GA: Mercer University Press, 1993) 243.
[4]Ibid.

Now the issues were focused, and decision time was at hand. Would some method of cooperative work be devised, or would the churches "mount their horses and ride off in all directions"? McCall and I had been presidents of two of the seminaries. We, along with many others, had many friends on the various mission fields and seminary faculties, so some of these issues were quite personal.

About the time McCall's paper was circulated, I prepared a paper called "A Suggestion for Alternative Methods of Finance for SBC Causes." I sent the paper to Jimmy Allen, the leader of Baptists Committed. I noticed on arrival at the convocation that the paper had been duplicated and included in the information packet given to the attendees. Two days later I discovered that the section on "Suggestions about a Plan" was omitted. That section was a list of ways the churches could support the causes of their choice through several different existing methods. This could be accomplished by designations of various kinds. One suggestion was that a board chosen by the convocation could be set up to direct the handling of funds and channel them to the appropriate place. Obviously, someone did not like my ideas of using existing mechanisms to designate funds to SBC and other causes.

By the time of the meeting of the consultation on 23-25 August 1990, McCall's plan was formulated, and a group of former leaders and a few others had been invited to a meeting to consider formalizing it. The organization was formed, but the nominee for president refused to serve. Since 1 was well known as a sacrificial lamb with more intestinal fortitude than sense, I was elected as president of the corporation and chairman of the board. The group intended from the beginning to turn the corporation over to whatever organization came out of the consultation.

Criticism of the effort surfaced immediately. As McCall said,

> the directors represented "the good ole boys network." The charge was legitimate. First, younger men and women had other agendas than creating a workable organization. . . . Second, the old friends who had worked together and trusted each other were the only ones willing to serve initially on the board of a new corporation with such political and economic risks in behalf of goals not yet commonly accepted.[5]

-----

[5]Ibid, 245.

I cannot avoid the temptation to comment that if the good ole boys had not acted, the organization would not have been able for a considerable period of time to properly handle funds and have tax-exempt status. Six weeks after the meeting of the Consultation, BCMP was in operation. In a very short time, the Internal Revenue Service recognized the organization and extended tax-exempt status.

It was obvious from the beginning that the older leadership of the group would not be popular in this context. Most of us upon turning the BCMP over to the CBF withdrew from active participation. Several persons were used in one capacity or another because experience and credibility were needed in formulating and executing policy. Carolyn Weatherford Crumpler, Cecil Sherman, and finally Keith Parks were recognized after a time as leaders. But, "the old order changeth, yielding place to the new"—and properly.

The Baptist Cooperative Mission Program operated for only one full year before legally yielding to the CBF. During 1991, 59 percent of funds received were for SBC agencies, 17 percent for specifically CBF causes, and the remainder for state Baptist convention institutions or other Baptist causes. In the initial year of the CBF and the temporary funding mechanism, the churches (391) and individuals sent about $4.5 million for various causes, mostly SBC. The numbers have grown rapidly since. By the end of October 1994, the CBF had received about $9.2 million from churches and individuals, up 12 percent over the same period in 1993. The number of churches contributing rose to 1,325 in the first nine months of 1994 compared to 1,210 in all of 1993.[6]

Funding through the CBF grew rapidly for various Baptist causes and, within a year or two, fundamentalist attacks began in earnest. The SBC forces asserted that the CBF was a new denomination. Various definitions of a denomination were offered and, according to the SBC leadership, the CBF qualified. Most of the churches that affiliated with it had no intention of leaving the Southern Baptist Convention, however. Various pastors who participated in it soon discovered that their churches were not as far along as they were in determining who they were as Baptists and what direction should be followed.

After a number of abortive attempts, the SBC leaders decided the best way to rid themselves of the dissidents was to refuse to accept

---

[6]Associated Baptist Press, 1 December 1994.

money from the churches and individuals given through the CBF. As indicated earlier in this volume, in June 1994 the Southern Baptist Convention voted to direct the agencies to refuse such funds.

This radical departure from Baptist polity has had serious reverberations in many places. True Baptists were scandalized that the SBC was in effect telling the churches and individuals how they must give to be acceptable. This stance was unheard of and a departure from historic positions held by Baptists. It also raised the possibility of a serious shortfall in funding the agencies. Increasing numbers of moderates were losing their concern about the agencies.

The action said in effect that any possibility of future solutions was now permanently closed. The CBF had to rethink its position and method of handling the funds, a reworking of relationships on several fronts. Churches and individuals now must either return to the SBC method of funding missions and education, or abandon their support of these causes, or designate funds directly to them (which is a part of the SBC methodology). All of this because the SBC leadership has called the CBF-channeled funds "tainted money."[7] The inevitable response from others is "It is tainted because it taint theirs!"

To this point, the CBF has been slow to define itself and its positions in the family of Christians. Some of the adherents want no definition, no statement of faith, and no structural organization. Such a body will not long endure as its environs become the suburbs of indecisiveness. Other followers want a new denomination, having declared themselves to be no longer Southern Baptists. Still others want only to be left alone to pursue their own ways in a loosely knit group doing education and missions. Any of these courses seems filled with theological and organizational chug-holes offering considerable hazard.

Southern Baptist leadership seems intent on forcing CBF adherents out. The moderates have been invited out of the SBC by such persons as Morris Chapman, president of the executive committee of the SBC; Ed Young, a former president; and Herschel Hobbs, a former president, often claimed by the fundamentalists—although he denies having taken sides.

The only effective method of excluding the moderates is to exclude the churches of which they are members. This is a difficult process and raises another set of issues, however. Some convention leaders have

---

[7]Ibid., 28 June 1994.

pronounced outlandish accusations that falsely place the CBF among the heathens. Various persons have accused the organization and its adherents of favoring homosexuality, pornography, abortion as a means of birth control, and various other sins. These are the present preoccupations of the fundamentalists and fit the political right-wing agenda.

David Wilkinson, communications coordinator of the CBF, made several pertinent comments dealing with some of these issues:

> During its first three years, the Fellowship organizationally has been very nebulous. It is more a spirit, more a movement than an organization, though it is taking on organizational character.
>
> The Fellowship carries a price for pastors in terms of career advancement. When a pastor is identified as pro-CBF, that definitely has implications for the network of moving from one church to another and particularly from a smaller congregation to a larger one. . . .
>
> And particularly recently, there are reports of influential SBC leaders meddling in local churches that are leaning toward the Fellowship by encouraging individual members to oppose the effort.
>
> Unfortunately, many of the false issues that were raised about former SBC (moderate) leadership are still being used today to try to intimidate churches and individuals from endorsing the CBF. "They don't believe the Bible." An openness toward the Fellowship is interpreted as "Your pastor is trying to take your church out of the SBC."
>
> I think there are literally thousands of pastors and other church leaders out there that are very disillusioned with the SBC, whose response will be simply to withdraw. They will focus on their church and their community. What is potentially lost is the larger part in the Baptist vision and in Baptist cooperation, which I think is a tragedy. I think this a potential fallout from the SBC wars, regardless if there was a CBF or not.
>
> I think one of the challenges for the Fellowship is to articulate the vision that captures the imagination of Baptists who are disaffected and feel disenfranchised by the SBC. It's one thing to be put out of the SBC; it's another to find a home elsewhere.[8]

These comments are strangely reminiscent of Duke McCall's, "They will mount their horses and gallop madly in all directions."

---

[8]Associated Baptist Press, 10 August 1994.

My friend Fred Hofheinz, a former priest of the Catholic Church, reminded me that one should take the long look. He commented that the present trauma, though lasting through fifteen years, is a minor blip on God's time chart. "A thousand years are as a day." Fred is right if one can look at God's time chart. My own problem is that I am on the scene only for that short day, and this affair has cast shadows over about a fifth of my life. The hope that a functioning organization consumed by the "commission" could be handed on to our spiritual descendants is a dream that has turned into a nightmare. The chill lingers.

Chapter 11

Life in the System Purely Personal

In February 1976, I wrote an article entitled "Not the Accent—The Message." It was published in *Facts and Trends*, a Sunday School Board publication that was mailed to pastors and other denominational workers. The article contained some striking impressions gleaned from my six weeks of travel in the fall and early winter. It said in part:

In Macon, Georgia, the meeting was in historic Mabel White Baptist Church for Mobilization Night. In Illinois, it was the state convention with a full agenda of the Lord's business and an enthusiastic crowd. In Michigan, Metro Reach kicked off with a great rally of those interested in doing something about the multitudes. In Ohio, the convention gathered for business with a great spirit. In Tucumcari, New Mexicans honored their man of the year and launched a new era with a new executive leader. In Alabama, Samford University is filled with students and is off to another good session.

In North Carolina, the alumni from seven colleges gathered in one meeting for perhaps an historic first to consider the problems of Christian education. In Indiana, a young convention planned to come to grips with a new push in missions and evangelism along with the other states in the great North Central Thrust. In Kentucky, a strong, stable old convention met to talk about the year and plan a better one. In Tennessee, a fine country church, Powell's Chapel, marked a century of service; and in South Carolina, Centenary Baptist Church celebrated its bicentennial a year before the nation.

In all these places and with these people, the accents are varied. The crisp northern talk of the Wilsons in Michigan was different from the soft southern drawl of Rev. W. H. Roberts of Centenary. The backgrounds of the Ohioans is not like that of the Georgians. The Spanish and Indian influences in New Mexico are different from those in the mountains of Kentucky.

The most vivid impressions of these six weeks, however, are not of differences but of similarities. Everywhere the talk is of churches, the lost, responsibility, missions, the Bible, the conventions, the fellowship of believers, and evangelism. The minds of the brethren seem to be on the Lord's business. How can we best do what God has called us to do? There is little confusion about what needs to be done. There is widespread concern that we do not miss any golden opportunity. . . . Our people seem to be trying to do their part in helping God do whatever it is He wants done.

By October 1980, I was writing about the newly-revived arguments concerning prayer in public schools. In November 1980, I felt it necessary to reprint my inaugural address at the Sunday School Board about the Bible in which I said:

> I have signed the Baptist Faith and Message statement because I believe it. I will not substitute it for the Bible. With clear instructions from the convention through our trustees, I see our task at the board to be teaching of the word, not debating about it; helping "bring men to God through Jesus Christ," rather than controversy; helping men toward maturity in the faith more than arguing a point of view.

By December 1980, the water was hot enough for me to publish an article about the artificial separations in the denomination: " 'Them and Us'—An Ungrammatical Meditation." By early 1981, the choice of only fundamentalists for service on the boards of the agencies was creating problems. I published an open letter to the Committee on Boards asking that it return one-term trustees, send us another cross-section of Baptist life—people who loved God, the church, and God's word—and "please do not send us people hungry for power or who will want to use the institution for selfish purposes."

In March 1981, I discussed the power structure in the SBC and expressed my belief "that if the power structure—the pastors—know the truth and the real issues, they will come out in the right place." My claims on prophethood suffered a severe blow with that one! Either many of them did not know the truth or issues, or I was dead wrong.

I wrote about the bottom line of a creed in an April 1981 article. I warned:

> If a creed is applied to organized Baptist life, it will soon be applied to you. This course will decimate the denomination; it will cause untold

problems in the churches; lovers of soul liberty will once again flee to freedom; and huge numbers of devout Bible-believing people will seek other fellowships.

By May 1981, the creedal problems were coalescing around the nature of the Bible. I and a host of others were concerned that the issues would unnecessarily divide us. I was troubled that we were getting ourselves into a situation that many people did not understand or care about. Educational methodology was threatened; narrow creedalism looked askance at inquiry and the desire to look at all available evidence. Many leaders demanded that the convention declare itself in terms that would ultimately threaten the educational processes and deny freedom of conscience.

I was compelled to say in an article in *Facts and Trends*:

> Freedom is dangerous, as our Baptist forebears on both sides of the ocean will testify. I rejoice in this treasure. Shall we let good words about the best book become the judge of conscience and procedure, or shall we rely on the Book? We should think long before we take good statements of what we believe (about the Bible) and make them the creed by which we dismantle the rest of what we believe (about soul competence and freedom of conscience).

With the approach of the 1981 convention meeting, my cogitation was labeled: "Now, I'm Scared." In part, I said:

> My fear, however, is that the continuing effort to adopt an increasingly narrow creedal statement by which we measure orthodoxy will cause an irreversible rupture of fellowship. When we test the nature of being a Baptist by the tenets of scripture, we are on safe ground. When the test of orthodoxy becomes the words of men (almost any words of almost any men) about the Bible, we will have painted ourselves in a corner from which we cannot escape. (I believe in the total reliability of scripture.) I do not believe that the forcing of an act of faith on anyone for any purpose for fear of the loss of job, or ordination, or a place on a board, or an office in an association or state convention is baptistic.

Those were the days! This litany of old articles is relayed for the purpose of demonstrating the rapid changes underway in the denomination and the concerns that were voiced as early as 1980. The problems that seemed to be looming were in fact there, and their possible results were in almost all cases understated.

One of the reasons for our vulnerability was our freedom. It was both our greatest strength and greatest weakness. No one had tried to build into the system protection from ourselves. We really believed no one was wicked enough to try to control the convention for any purpose. We were naive and careless. Yet, the SBC was based on a marvelous system of freedoms, not extended by any authority save God's. This freedom, discovered by our forebears and paid for in their blood, was an inherent right. The system gave everyone the right to participate according to their ability and dedication. Many persons did not achieve their goals, but their failure often was not the result of the system.

The local congregation of believers was subject only to itself. To be sure, the church did not always function according to the ideal, but the ideal was the goal; and no one forbade the church to attempt anything that was legal. Individuals exercised their freedom in the context of the congregation as they or their peers chose.

The regional association of churches had only one power related to the churches: determination of its own membership. Sometimes the associations did this with a vengeance, but it was the action of the church's peers, not an ecclesiastical machine. Here was a basic unit of cooperation and fellowship.

The state convention almost always had some issue of contention or disagreement over the election of the president of the convention. The arguments became heated on occasion, but usually after the meeting, the delegates went about their business and looked forward to the next convention. Here was a larger base of cooperation and fellowship.

In the state meetings there was a regular stream of talented, stimulating, and dedicated people who spoke on the various interests of the time. They were sometimes proud and even arrogant, but in the main they were inspirational, challenging, and often interesting. At the state meetings, pastors and laity heard about the work and methods of others. They heard of new victories and testimonies of the goodness of God in other places. They rejoiced and were strengthened. They met in alumni meetings of the colleges and seminaries, met old friends and made new ones, and generally had a good time.

The meetings of the Southern Baptist Convention were a sort of vacation time for pastors and their spouses and other ministers and leaders.

The convention was old friends time, alumni time, and a time of great music and preaching. The reports of the agencies contained the heart of the denomination's activities, although many of the report sessions were poorly attended and often ignored. The report material was in the book of reports and available to all. Debates were limited by too little time. True deliberation was impossible due to such large numbers of people present. Yet, trust in the leadership and each other allowed the work to continue. The mission board reports for many years were the highlight of the meetings. One had to go early to the meeting place to obtain a seat.

Presidential elections were exciting, and someone often had an issue to inject that was important or sounded important. All of the messengers had a favorite candidate, but they accepted whomever was elected before 1979 since that person would conduct the business of the convention, not his own agenda.

The SBC was a crazy patchwork organization, evolving over a hundred years. It came to include good business methodology, careful handling of funds, good accountability, and efficiency that was often criticized by the clergy and lauded by the laity. Many persons understood the basic functioning of the denomination, though some were often vocal about something they did not understand until they were elected to a leadership position.

The system worked. The polity acknowledged all of the people, even if it did not use them all. It recognized the right of any person to do or not to do and tried to enlist all Southern Baptists in the purposes of the denomination. Acceptance of decisions often depended upon the degree of participation by the constituents. Many of those later identified as fundamentalists were sometimes critical of the system, and some were left out of leadership because of their criticism and unwillingness to "pay their dues" like others did.

It was a great system, full of humanity and its foibles. Egos sometimes got in the way. Ignorance hindered the progress. Hurt feelings were a part of the price paid for service. Selfishness sometimes hobbled the aspirations for kingdom good. Sometimes, we forgot the meaning and focused on a slogan.

We were inadequate and sometimes ignorant. At times we focused on the narrow. We were dragged along by the enlightened and held back by lethargy and ignorance. We could not or did not reach everyone, did not teach all, and left some out. The work and teaching were too often elementary, but we took each other where we were and tried to go forward. Periodically, the Sunday School Board was criticized by theologians for not educating the general constituency in the finer points of theology and biblical study. The criticism was justified, but the board answered to a people that ranged in education from post-graduate level to abysmally uninformed.

Yet, the ideals of the denomination were always there. It pursued a common goal: the purposes of God. To Southern Baptists, these included evangelism, worship, missions to an unbelieving world, equipping the people for the work of the ministry, and ministry to whomever needed it.

We wandered all over the theological and ecclesiastical map on occasion and argued over many things. We hurt each other, mostly unintentionally, but we usually made up. We chased all kinds of theological and philosophical rabbits and once in a great while caught one, though sometimes we did not know what to do with it when we caught it.

Finally, after our sins and wanderings, the denomination usually came back to its objectives and ideals. Individually, most often we were trying. We usually thought the other guy was trying too. Somehow we hung together believing we were walking in the way of the Lord, imperfectly but trying. We were keenly aware that we held "this treasure in earthen vessels," but mostly we were ordinary human beings imperfectly struggling to do what we thought was right.

The Trustees

When the system of electing trustees of the agencies began to change, many persons without considerable experience with the organizations did not foresee the inevitable result. When the criterion for election became "They were with us in the struggle" and "They are inerrantists," an unusual number seemed to be recommended by their combativeness.

In the earlier version of the SBC, the trustees from a practical view were in fact the determiners of policy and directors of the agencies. The institutions took on the character of the presidents and the trustees. Some trustees accepted the administrative leadership and its direction without much dissent. Few took the course now followed by the fundamentalist establishment. The trustees of the new era seem to have taken the institutions out of the hands of the administration and practice micromanagement, much to the detriment of the agencies. This course of conduct opens the way to any personal peeve becoming an issue of controversy. Many unnecessary arguments have been very detrimental to the organizations because of individual agendas.

Many of the modern trustees seem to operate on the theory that since they are in the office, they can individually give instructions to anyone on any subject. This violation of the basic principles of administration causes severe problems. Some of the new trustees believe they have a right to individually instruct the president as to the course of action. (According to many reports, this behavior was a major problem at Southwestern Seminary.) Administrations cannot respond to the individual's instructions since another individual will have an opposite opinion. James Sullivan used to comment that he acted only on the official votes of his trustees. Any other course leads to disaster.

Before I went to California, I had the privilege of serving on the Foreign Mission Board and the board of trustees of New Orleans Baptist Seminary, Oklahoma Baptist University, and the state boards in Oklahoma and Alabama. Those years of training as a trustee and in the nature of administration were of immeasurable help to me when I began to work for trustees.

In the Southern Baptist General Convention of California and at Oklahoma Baptist University, New Orleans Baptist Theological Seminary, and the Baptist Sunday School Board, I had a wide variety of trustees. In most instances, the trustees were elected before the SBC controversy became so prominent. They represented many points of view, personal persuasions, and varied backgrounds and held a variety of opinions. The vast majority of them came to the boards with a view to learning the ropes and helping the institution if they could. The trustees were elected for various reasons: to pay tribute to them for service rendered, for outstanding abilities, for wide experience, for particular expertise, or because a member of the committee liked them.

They brought to the board a wide range of ability and dedication. Frequently the laity were knowledgeable in many areas. Laypersons had good judgment about situations of which the clergy were not familiar. Investments, contracts, engineering, legalities, finances, planning, and a myriad of other responsibilities required trustee attention. Most often, I had the help I needed, or one of the trustees knew where I could obtain it. The ministers brought to the board their understanding of theological, church, and denominational affairs. Some of them were experts at evaluating the response of the constituents to a given situation. Many were familiar with areas of work other than the church. Some had a particularly sensitive response to personnel problems.

My trustees usually gave me the credit for knowing more than they did about the condition of the organization. They knew that I was there, deeply involved, day and night. Frequently they trusted my judgment. Often they would give me the benefit of any doubt. Any information they wanted, good or bad, was available to them. No information was deliberately hidden from them. They asked questions; and if the answer was adequate, we moved on. If they did not like the answer, they asked for more information or time before deciding an issue. Sometimes they said no to a recommendation, in which case we started over. They were the legally responsible body.

Without the trustees, I could not function. Without me, or someone like me, they could not carry out their duties. In response to the fundamentalist criticism that the older trustees were "rubber stamps," some were I guess. More often, if the recommendation made sense from a competent administration, they voted aye. We were very careful in our preparation for trustee meetings, attempting to present only the necessary and sound recommendations. If the trustees felt we were making a mistake, they postponed the matter until a better suggestion was presented or the problems were solved.

My relationships with trustees were on the whole very good. They were usually cordial. One fundamentalist wrote a few years ago to new trustees: "You have to watch those chief executive officers. They will make a friend out of you if you aren't careful." For once, he was right. I tried to make friends of trustees since we were in a very important venture together. We were dependent on each other, and more importantly the future of the enterprise depended on us. I found that friends usually can accomplish more than enemies or adversaries.

I also found that most trustees were competent partners in an agency that did not belong to us, but to the Baptist people and the Lord. Our job was not to carry out the desires of individuals or groups, but to do the best we could to help the cause to prosper. The agency had been founded for a good purpose, and we were responsible to see that it fulfilled the stated purpose.

Some of the finest people I have ever known served on the boards of trustees to whom I reported. I was not responsible for selecting them and did not choose them. I worked with whomever the denomination elected. It was a good system, and it worked for me and the institutions I headed. Some of the trustees became lifelong friends. Some of us maintained contact through the years with great personal joy. Only a few trustees with whom I worked did not seem to be interested primarily in the health of the institution, but they were not able or did not want to interfere seriously with the work. If a trustee left the bounds of reason, usually other trustees would manage the problem.

One news report in Nashville suggested that my early retirement (for health reasons) was the result of the denominational conflict, specifically that the trustees and I were on a different page. Although by the time of my retirement, the board had a few new trustees who were said to be of the new variety, they gave me no problems. The fact is I had radical surgery for stomach cancer, only the beginning of a series of physical problems. I was in the hospital six times in the last two years of my tenure and underwent three more surgeries during that time, plus another surgery the week after my retirement. The doctors thought I would get no better as long as I bore the heavy responsibilities and suggested that I should retire. I felt that the situation at the board would grow only more difficult and demanded the services of someone who was healthy and could bear the stress. In August 1982, I asked to retire on 31 January 1984, thus allowing adequate time to find a successor.

It seems worthwhile to tell again a short story about trustees. One day on a plane, I sat by an executive who had vast experience with trustees in the business world. He asked me how many trustees I had, and I answered more than eighty. He was aghast. He commented that General Motors had maybe fifteen. How could we do business with eighty? I thought about his question and finally answered, "They are people of good will." In retrospect, that seems to be the secret of the successes of the trustees and the secret of many modern failures.

Agency Relationships

From the early days of my ministry, I was interested in the larger denominational body. I missed one meeting of the SBC between 1946 and 1987 due to my wife's illness. State convention meetings were a way of life for me. During my days of denominational service, I sometimes attended as many as five in one year.

In the course of those interests and meetings, inevitably I met a long list of persons who served the denomination in one capacity or another. My first SBC meeting in Miami in 1946 made a lasting impression on me. Pat Neff, Baylor University president and the convention president, was an hour late for the opening session. (He forgot Miami was on Eastern time.) More importantly, I was exposed to exciting and interesting information about what the emerging convention was about. I was just home from the war. The devastation of the Philippines and Japan, together with the memory of the dead and dying, was fresh in my mind.

The convention was alive with birthing new plans to try to meet the needs of war-torn lands including our late enemies. I returned home with a profound conviction that the world needed what the Lord could do, and the SBC was talking about that. Shortly I would know about the European problems and see some of them first-hand.

Certainly I had ambitions. I had no idea that I could ever be involved in the leadership of such efforts, but I could do something. I wanted to know some of the people who had such ideas and the courage to propose them. In time, I began to meet some of them. Some names still stand out as significant in my life or more particularly in my thought processes.

I easily remember the gray-maned John Jeter Hurt Sr., M. E. Dodd, L. R. Scarborough, W. W. Hamilton, John R. Sampey, George W, Truett, John Buchanan, Louie Newton, and a host of others. Those people were the platform personalities and leaders in various ways during my beginning days of ministry. As time went by, R. G. Lee, Ramsey Pollard, J. D. Gray, Theron Rankin, Ellis Fuller, Perry Webb, J. W. Storer, and many others gradually moved into the spotlight.

Some of the leaders could preach, and others could lecture. Some of them could plan, lead, analyze, or promote. They had a wide range of skills and personalities. They were sometimes argumentative or out of sorts. They were to me—a small town boy—what we now call role models, and I wanted to know and do what they did. Quite possibly the public persona and the private person were different, but that was not of primary concern to me.

Here were men who dreamed dreams and saw visions. They were trying to do something worthwhile in the world. They were thinking at least about the task of the Lord. In retrospect, I am certain that they had personal ambitions and sometimes were arrogant or lost the vision in the fog of circumstance. Yet, I remember that the denominational leadership of those days made me want to rise above circumstance and limitation to do something important.

As a pastor, I tried to listen and learn. Though I learned that he used a lot of canned phrases, R. G. Lee made me want to be a word-smith. Ramsey Pollard made me want to be kind to preachers. J. D. Gray led me to want to help anyone who needed help. Ellis Fuller had a marvelous ability to put the deep things of the faith in terms anyone could understand. I would drive across the state to hear him preach. Theron Rankin helped me see the world from a different perspective. In my college days, L. R. Scarborough—who preached long enough every time for two or three sermons—made me want to win people to faith in Christ. Some leaders inspired me, some challenged me, some stretched my mind, and some made me want to be a better person.

The idea that I could serve in some of the capacities of my role models was a challenge to me. I wanted in. My motives were probably wrong and my performance imperfect, but I wanted in. It had little to do with power. Those denominational wheels had a most remarkable opportunity to observe, know, and serve. As the years went by, I served on state convention and university boards. There I became familiar with the structure, issues, and opportunities of the denomination. The state leaders were generally people of integrity and leadership ability.

I was most involved in Oklahoma where T. B. Lackey came to the office now called executive director just as I was beginning to get involved. He had an outstanding term of service to the denomination. Most of his decisions were sound, and he constantly cared for the welfare of the convention. One matter he and I did not see eye-to-eye on was the matter of organizing Baptist hospitals in every small town that needed one. I thought it was a trip to frustration with the rapidly changing medical scene and growing influence of the government in hospital affairs. Baptists could not tolerate governmental control of religious facilities. He won the argument, of course, and we remained friends. The state convention finally had to turn the hospitals over to an independent board.

When I became president of Oklahoma Baptist University, Lackey and I worked together closely as friends and colleagues. He had a limited educational background, but was one of the most effective state leaders I ever knew. With him while I was a pastor and later as colleagues, I learned the ropes of denominational administration. I discovered that state leaders were ordinary folk like me who had a difficult job.

In California, I began relating professionally to national agencies. They were a diverse group of operations and leaders. We argued with the Sunday School Board about "state strategy" and endlessly negotiated with the Home Mission Board about funds for the endless list of things we needed to do. We related to the executive committee of the SBC informally, but kept up to date with what was going on. The California convention was a "new kid on the block" of state bodies, but many people had a real interest in that vast mission field. It was larger geographically and in population than many countries.

Also in California, I struggled with an underfunded college, a program of child care that belonged to another era, and a foundation that had threatened to go bankrupt on a number of occasions. I had no authority over any of those agencies except in emergencies. We had to work together in various ways and carefully divide the limited funds available. My knowledge of relationships of various denominational agencies grew rapidly.

Trust was a key factor. When it broke down, the enterprise faltered. When it was strong, we could proceed with the work. Cooperative relationships were crucial. There was no room for intimidation, threat, or coercion. Sometimes we felt that the national agencies pushed us around, and perhaps they did. More often, I am now sure, they were trying to balance the needs of the world against their inadequate resources. We sent to them what we could of the Cooperative Program funds. We promoted their programs along with ours.

I left state convention work with the deep conviction that without it the national body could not function effectively. National agencies depended on the state to promote, collect, and distribute the basic mission monies. I also believed that the integral relationships between the states, churches, and national bodies were about as effective as it could be in a free church setting. A system based on ecclesiastical authority would never function with Baptists.

When I moved to the university setting, the relationship factor was larger still. We were totally dependent on the state convention and its constituents. It was a denominational college with all of the rewards and entanglements. One of my first major decisions was to determine what that denominational relationship would be. The university had been involved in a public brawl over its direction. The president and the chancellor had contested the control and direction of the school. Friends of the president were of the opinion that the school should drift or run away from denominational control. Friends of the chancellor believed that the school belonged to the state convention and should strengthen its ties to the denomination.

The year was 1966, but the argument sounds like 1994. I decided that the school indeed belonged to the convention and its future depended on that support. Few people recognized that the decision even pended. After my administration began, there was little discussion of the issue. It was clear to me that we were a denominational school, so we proceeded in that direction. Many persons in these times may question my decision, but I do not, though the Oklahoma convention is controlled by fundamentalists. Among other things, I learned that for Baptists relationships based on trust and cooperation were superior to any exercise of authority.

As a college president, I was exposed to a whole new world. I learned from college professors that preacher estimates were not good enough, that precision was much to be preferred. I was impressed with the demand of faculty members for absolute honesty and integrity. I discovered that they were not the larger equivalent of a church staff.

The association with the many publics of the university was both enlightening and instructive. The larger educational community was an interesting study. The relationships to secular politics were stimulating and sometimes alarming. During one election campaign, the governor asked me to go to the capitol and tell him what he should do to win Baptist votes. I was of little value to him since I was leery of lending any influence to a political campaign. He was probably sizing me up for other reasons that I did not understand at the time. I was publicly apolitical and remained that way throughout my entire ministry.

Whether it was because of my lack of political involvement or in spite of it, the govenor appointed me to the Oklahoma education commission that was responsible for formulating plans for education in the state for the rest of the century. I was named chairman of the education committee by my peers and was hard at work on the project when New Orleans Seminary asked me to become president. This was no church-state conflict; I was a private Christian citizen serving the cause of education without religious strictures.

During the 1960s, the educational establishment was pushed in all directions by the social unrest of the day. The politicians wanted the schools involved, the dissidents recruited faculty and students for their endless causes, and the constituency wanted the support of the schools if the schools were on the right side.

During one heated period of attempts to enlist the support of the university in some cause or other, I asked David Boren, then a professor of political science at the university, to speak to the community on the topic "Don't Politicize the University." He did so in ringing terms. He advised that we were an educational community and should stick to our knitting. Boren moved on to become a two-term governor of Oklahoma, a U.S. senator, and now is the president of the University of Oklahoma. My advice to David is "Don't politicize the university!"

These comments are recorded in an effort to show that in the world of constant change, things change little. Only voluntary cooperation and mutual trust would work. Do not miss the point about authority and cooperation. The cooperation had to exist between the university and its constituents. The matter of authority was different within the university community. My authority was almost total because the trustees seemed to trust me and I trusted them. We worked together to set policy, and they left it to me to handle the administration. No other system would have worked, since most every Baptist had an opinion on almost every subject.

When I became president of New Orleans Seminary, the school had been through hard times. Trust and cooperation from alumni and constituents of the school were low. The faculty morale was poor and financial support left much to be desired. Shortly after I moved to New Orleans, the six seminary presidents held their annual meeting. It was immediately obvious that the problems of the school had cast their shadow over the domains of the other five presidents. After a long lecture by one president about the sins of my predecessor, we stayed past midnight discussing the formula. The formula for distribution of funds between the seminaries was enrollment driven, and my school enrollment was down, along with its other problems.

The presidents council had a rule that all decisions must be unanimous before any action was taken on the formula or other matters. This led to long sessions of negotiations, sometimes bickering, and now and again hurt feelings. The larger schools, Southern and Southwestern, had more pull and more endowment than New Orleans; we were third in the pecking order.

In spite of all the competition and difference of perspective, we presented a united front to the SBC and its executive committee. We had some heated discussions with that committee and its executive, but they did not interfere with our business nor use threats or money as weapons. We came out of those years as friends and colleagues. Cooperation through differences and conflict was essential to the functioning of all the schools. We were Baptists to the core, independent and sometimes selfish, but theological education in the SBC prospered as never before.

Seminary education was close to my sense of identity and call, but too soon the Sunday School Board summoned and I went. This hybrid organization is the most complex of all Baptist ventures. It is basically an educational and publishing venture. It receives no mission contributions and must make its own way through the design, development, manufacture and sale of almost anything a church needs. In those days, the board was totally dependent on the goodwill of the people and was considered to be a center of ministry in the providing of material, development of programs, and furnishing support for its programs with the states and churches.

In addition to these basic functions, the board related to many facets of the denominational enterprise. Executives and program leaders were in constant discussion with the Foreign Mission Board, the Home Mission Board, Woman's Missionary Union, the commissions, the Baptist World Alliance, and the seminaries.

Because of the nature of the Sunday School Board and the many expertly trained employees, opportunities to do good were numerous. Educational leaders served the Baptist World Alliance and the Foreign Mission Board all over the world, often at the board's expense. A program was developed in which the board furnished a liaison professor to each of the seminaries. Large gifts of endowment from profits were made to two of the seminaries. The board published at no cost to the recipients a concordance of the New Testament in Estonian, the first in more than a hundred years. Mini-libraries were sent to more than 6,000 ministers all over the world who did not have the basic books they needed in ministry. The list could go on, but suffice it to say that this organization was dedicated to ministry in many shapes and sizes.

The Baptist constituents in this country and many other places were blessed by the attitude of family and sharing. No attempt was made to exercise any control over those who shared in the ministry of the board.

Cooperative relationships were negotiated with all state conventions, and funds were supplied according to a formula to assist them in their work. Cooperation and trust were again the basis for functioning. This is not to say that everyone agreed with our efforts or that things always went smoothly. As the problems arose, we either retreated from the matter of difficulty, negotiated the solution, or proceeded with caution. Again the enterprise was full of humanity and its foibles. Sometimes selfishness, incompetence, and bad attitudes surfaced. Still the work continued, imperfectly but massive and effective.

The Fellowship of the Saints

Through those years, the denomination in many ways became the larger church for me and many others. No matter where one went, there was a group of like-minded believers. Sometimes they were humble country or ghetto folk. Sometimes they were university or seminary faculty members and administrators. They were sometimes in the suburban churches, and sometimes they prayed in cathedrals seating thousands. They came from many backgrounds. They were rich and poor and mostly in-between. They were highly skilled or grossly unprepared for the context of their lives. They were at first mostly white, but that changed rather rapidly after the 1960s.

In one church in California, we counted thirteen nationalities in the choir. As the years raced into yesterday, the gospel came to be preached in more than a hundred languages in the U.S., and I insisted that literature should be prepared for the people in their own languages. What a fellowship! We were different but the same. We looked different, but somehow it mattered less and less as the family of Baptists grew and the word was proclaimed. As I traveled over the nation and many foreign lands, the family of believers was to me a great joy.

Once I stood in a plane aisle halfway across Africa talking to a Nigerian Ph.D. from Southern Seminary. It seemed that, though we were different, we were brothers and consumed with the same mission in life. Perhaps I understood the problems of administration better than he, but he understood the living of Christ in impossible circumstances far better than I would ever know.

Out of the dim past photos reappear. Beside the sea, I was the first American a certain Japanese man saw as the war ended. He was a

Christian, and the war was over. I remember a small association in North Carolina where some of the brethren were unhappy with the BSSB. We talked awhile, they complained, and I explained. I preached, and they responded as Christian brethren. We parted friends. At a reunion of retired seminary presidents and the incumbents, we told old yarns and laughed at ourselves and rejoiced that they were our kind.

I spent a pleasant semester at Louisiana College with friend and president Robert Lynn and his wife, Bonnie. Old friends and new made the meeting of a new generation of students and faculty very enjoyable. Their interest in Baptist history and polity made the preparations and lectures a joy. The invitations to visit many schools and teach in several places—though I could not accept all of them—and the gathering of the saints in many places recalled wonderful days of fellowship. I represented the Baptist family in many places in the world where God's people rolled out the carpet—sometimes red—to an American visiting fireman. I preached at many places. I remember the Sunday morning in Berlin when a lady said after the service, "You believe the same gospel we do!"

They and I were not perfect. We believe the church is not a museum to display the saints but a hospital for limping souls. But it was glorious to find the people of God everywhere. As a Southern Baptist, sometimes envied and sometimes hated, the world of Baptists was my home—and the same for everyone else who would come to the water of life.

I had no long list of rules for saying the right words. There was seldom a Sanhedrin to sit in judgment of my sociology, psychology, philosophy, and theology in the vast majority of places I frequented. We were fellow believers who sometimes did not understand each other or even sometimes did not like each other, but we were family. No one was empowered to excommunicate any one of us, and only very rarely did anyone try.

I learned compassion from the missionaries, love of learning from the faculties, organizational administration from a long line of practitioners in the field, denominational loyalty from SBC leaders, a strong desire to preach effectively from a hundred preachers I had the privilege of hearing, and a little smidgen of humility from a succession of hard knocks and failures. The people of God who have blessed my life is too long to even hint at, but I pause to say thanks to God for them all.

The fellowship of the saints was one of life's greatest blessings. All of this came because of my association with the Southern Baptist

Convention. The purpose of the denomination was clearly to "bring men and women to God through Jesus Christ." We constantly tried to remind ourselves of the goal. We sometimes discussed what held the convention together. Some persons said theology, some the foreign mission enterprise, and others evangelism. They were all correct. The real cosmic glue was the lordship of Jesus Christ leading willing but imperfect minds toward his purpose in our lives.

We had no inquisitions, few mandates, and little financial intimidation. Trustees were not selected for "being with us in the struggle" but for struggling with us in the cause that was larger than all of us. There was no politicization of the convention for secular purposes. Occasionally someone suggests that the invitation to the President of the U.S. to address the convention was as political then as it is now. In former days, elections and political agendas were not discussed. The president's appearance did not signal convention political involvement.

We did emphasize the Cooperative Program and perhaps too much. There came to be some competition between the states and between churches to see who could give the most. The problem did not bring us to fratricide—some envy perhaps, but not total disruption of the process. The envy or pride in mission giving, in retrospect, seems a small sin, but we will let God judge our shortcomings.

If confession is good for the soul, I will own up to a few facts. Life was no bowl of cherries and certainly not always pleasant. The work was hard. I rose at 5:45 A.M. for years, ate a hasty breakfast in the cafeteria, and was in the office by 7:00 A.M. If there was a night meeting, the day frequently did not end until nearly midnight and sometimes later. Travel was incessant and filled with second-hand smoke, often poor hotels, fatty foods, and total exhaustion. Until after my cancer surgery, there was no such thing as a regular day off.

I was often on the spot about something or the other. Once an administrator criticized me for having breakfast after the faculty prayer meeting. This reminds me of James Sullivan's story of riding up the elevator with an employee at about eleven in the morning. The girl commented that she wished she could come to work at eleven. He did not tell her that he had been up all night trying to get back to Nashville for a meeting.

We who worked together did get mad, criticize one another, argue, and generally act like human beings, but it was a great life. I would not have missed it for anything. I feel sorry for a whole generation who will never know the joy of fellowship with like-minded people who invite everyone into the task.

Some Basic Concerns

We now have a whole new generation of Baptist people, particularly the ministers, who have never known the kind of denomination described in this chapter. Some persons made choices based on the old-fashioned way of dissenting when necessary and then mending the fences and going on with the work. When they tried to "come home," the welcome mat was not there. Good-natured arguments were allowed only within the sanctuary of the elect. Anyone who disagreed with the fundamentalist power brokers or on some doctrinal issue were shut out, often permanently. For the multitude, one decision was often life-determining. Dissent and argument were to them a part of being a Baptist. Suddenly the rules changed. The directional choice was made for them by their exclusion.

Some ministers in mid-career and some just in the beginning of their ministry are being lost in the cracks. They received poor advice about their decisions, or no one was available to properly evaluate the situation. Even with the best of advice, few alternatives were available to them and often their churches. Herein is contained the reason for many defections to other fellowships, other schools, and other mission endeavors. One of the greatest hazards is that anticipated by some churches that incorporated the Baptist Cooperative Missions Program. Many churches are turning away from the cooperative efforts and seeking ministry within themselves or local situations.

After the decisions of the Texas, North Carolina, Virginia, and Georgia conventions in the fall of 1994, this situation will probably grow and intensify. The fundamentalist leadership probably does not realize what it has done. The warning bells of decreasing funds will likely be the only alarm they will heed. Some believe that the frantic rhetoric about the Cooperative Program will rally the troops. Perhaps it will work short term. Whether it will be effective when the embryonic conflicts within the fundamentalist camp become full grown is another question.

The deliberate trashing of vast numbers of clergy and laity by the fundamentalists is a crucial error for them and the work of Christ. To decree that about 45 percent of the ministers and laity cannot have any official say in the affairs of the denomination is a major error and an offense to God and the churches. Thousands of ministers and unknown numbers of lay persons have been deliberately cut off from cooperative support of the denomination they helped build. No denomination can afford such profligate waste of human abilities.

When one thinks of those persons eliminated from effective leadership in the national body, the list reads like a "Who's Who" of the SBC: Randall Lolley, Al Shackleford, Dan Martin, Lloyd Elder, Keith Parks, Russell Dilday, Roy Honeycutt, Molly Marshall, most of the faculty of Southeastern Seminary, too much of the faculty of Southern Seminary, nearly 200 of the top people of the Sunday School Board, and a number of administrators at the Foreign Mission Board and the Home Mission Board. Probably no one will ever know how many employees of the institutions and agencies have quietly departed for greener fields where service was available in more harmonious circumstances.

Of course, many of these persons will continue their service of God in other relationships. Yet, the opportunity for ministry beyond the local congregation is forever closed to many ministers who have chosen to remain in their Southern Baptist churches. Experience, wisdom, energy, and intellectual acumen are needlessly shunted because dedicated people are unwilling to give up their convictions about a score of things. This reckless waste has deprived the denomination of much-needed wisdom in the agencies. The searching sadness illustrated in the letter in chapter eight from the the young pastor is a small sample of the great problem. His name is legion.

The deliberate elimination of women from many places of service concerning the issue of "authority" over men is an exercise in discrimination that is as yet unknown in its impact. The opposition to Woman's Missionary Union by fundamentalists is strange and foreboding. One of Baptists' most effective missionary activities is threatened by the prejudice of leadership. The only discernible cause is the lack of control by fundamentalists over WMU.

The nurturing system that was of immeasurable help to my generation of preachers is now changed. The role models are too often sharp-edged and sometimes just confrontational. As the young pastor said, in nearly every speech you hear the "agenda." The young ministers now are required to choose from the dichotomy that pervades all aspects of Baptist life. The choice may be binding for life. The too-often monolithic leadership they see at public meetings displays unbaptistic conduct. They learn early that their aspirations for participation depend on towing the line of the current sociological or theological fad. Unless they choose to go somewhere other than the denominationally blessed gatherings, they will hear one tune only. What this will produce in the next generation of leaders remains to be seen.

A multitude of people, myself included, feel disconnected from that which was very meaningful and enriching to life. My people now seem to be scattered. Yes, I am mindful of the oft-repeated idea that we are not the Diaspora or the remnant, but the truth is that we are not quite sure about whom to relax around. We no longer see like-minded people en masse as we did for a lifetime. A hesitancy emerges between many of us. We do not want to offend unnecessarily and walk on eggshells sometimes. Others who were friends for a generation no longer speak or greet one another cordially. Many brethren in associations and state conventions no longer joyously greet one anther. Tension hangs like the sword of Damocles over many if not most Baptist meetings. State conventions labor to maintain fellowship while according to churches their rights as the body of Christ. Fundamentalism must answer to God for what it has done to people.

Weapons of Warfare

The emphasis on scripture and its inerrant character has been a major point of argument for the fundamentalists. A basic problem with such an argument is that following the dictates of scripture is much harder than arguing about its nature. Consider the words of 2 Corinthians 10:3, 4:

> We live as human beings, but we do not wage war according to human standards, for the weapons of our warfare are not merely human, but they have divine power to destroy strongholds.

The passage continues with a discussion of what God's power can do and magnifies the work of God.

A major problem with the fundamentalist movement is the abandonment of scriptural and spiritual methodology for solutions to differences. This goes hand-in-hand with the scriptural admonitions concerning the attitude of brother to brother. Scripture never instructs Christians to persecute other Christians because of a difference of opinion. Following the admonition of scripture on the subject, fundamentalism usually has carefully avoided using the civil courts in the controversy. This is as it should be. Why then adopt the methods of the world in the use of power and intimidation to settle religious differences? Political maneuvering seems as out of place in determining missions giving as suing one another in a court of law.

The power of exclusion for honest opinions hardly seems to fit the New Testament pattern. One could understand it for blasphemy, gross immorality, denial of Christ, departure from Baptist doctrine, denial of the authority of scripture, or some other genuinely unchristian conduct. To use power to exclude all who disagree with the current regime is to use the way of the world for supposedly Christian purposes. The Sermon on the Mount seems to have been rewritten: "Blessed are the meek (those with the votes and power and the best political organization) for they shall inherit the earth."

I am reminded of one pundit who, after observing the conduct of a religious dignitary, commented, "How could it be that the 'humble life of a Jewish peasant should have force to make a New York bishop so bigoted?' " One wonders about the issue of motivation in the SBC conflict. None of us, I am afraid, can claim purity in this matter. The words of the essayist Montaigne return to haunt us:

> There is fear and intolerance in pride. The less promise and potency in the self, the more imperative is the need for pride. The core of pride is self-rejection.

What Is a Baptist?

The systematic abandoning of various traditionally Baptist positions on a variety of issues is a measure of how radically the SBC has changed. I will discuss a few of those about which there can be little argument as to where the SBC once stood and where it is now.

Priesthood of the Believer

This matter goes to the heart of the free exercise of religion. If any person claims the right to make religious decisions for another, be he pastor or some other, that person claims a right that belongs only to the individual and God. Pastoral authority in the church is a basic violation of this principle.

Freedom of the Churches

When the denomination can exclude churches for exercising their autonomy, the problem of ecclesiastical authority rises. The SBC told the churches how they could give their mission funds, excluded two churches for their actions related to homosexuality, and opened the door to exclude others for whatever reason. Associations have withdrawn some churches from membership for ordaining women deacons, and at least one other has split over the issue. While any Baptist body has the right to determine its own membership, great care is required when the matter invades the sanctuary of the church.

Freedom of the Ministry

The professional reputation of a minister depends heavily on the choice he or she makes about the controversy. That person's future is sometimes controlled by political maneuvering behind the scenes by denominational leaders. In Virginia, it is said that some retired military man compiled a list of "approved ministers." In many states, there has been a flood of calls from well-known fundamentalists to church pastoral search committees urging the election of someone approved by the hierarchy.

Creedalism

The list of beliefs and actions now required to be a "loyal Southern Baptist" is long and growing: the Baptist Faith and Message; the Peace Committee report (that part of it spelling out theological beliefs, not that part spelling out Christian conduct for the fundamentalists); the right attitudes toward abortion (not that held by the SBC before 1979), homosexuality, and pornography; the right ideas about women, school prayer, the sacred how, and the Cooperative Program and how one gives to it; the right attitude toward the people who support the Cooperative Baptist Fellowship; and on and on.

Exclusion

As stated earlier, about 45 percent of Southern Baptists have been eliminated from any national service because they do not agree with the direction of the convention or follow the party line. If all dissidents had been eliminated through the years, there would be no convention.

Secular Politics

The public generally has the view that the SBC is in the hands of the right wing of the political spectrum and possibly in the hands of that segment of the Republican Party. Never in our history has the denomination been so closely identified with secular politics. Modern leaders do not seem to understand the historical implications of their choices.

Church and State

The SBC from the beginning contended for a free church in a free state with no government interference or participation in religious affairs. Now, the denomination encourages legislation to secure tax money for religious schools, a constitutional amendment to mandate school prayer (in most states already permissible), the elimination of the more strenuous Lemon test for such issues in the Supreme Court, and the support of government for a variety of religious activities.

Mission of the Church

For generations, Baptist churches followed their own consciences in participating in the educational and mission activities. Many of the present ministers led their churches in giving very small sums to the denominational enterprises. Some of these leaders give a fraction of the national average. The present denominational atmosphere says: "If you are going to participate in our affairs, you must give according to the dictates of the denomination." The same criteria applied to some of the super-churches would cause chaos. Whether the national leadership ever admits it or not, the pressure on the church and pastor to conform is very strong.

*****

Whereas fundamentalism has given its own meaning to the Baptist ideals, the traditional beliefs, as stated by Walter Shurden, follow:

> Bible freedom, for example, focuses on the lordship of Jesus Christ as revealed in the scriptures and is the Baptist understanding of religious authority. Soul freedom focuses on the primacy of the individual and reflects the Baptist approach to salvation, with implications for other areas as well. Church freedom highlights the prominence of the believing community and the Baptist way of being and doing church. Religious freedom is the Baptist approach to religious liberty and focuses on the relationship of religion to the state.[1]

A Personal Confession

When Sam Pace—whom I had known in Oklahoma—was chairman of the SBC executive committee, I saw him at the national meeting. I commented to him that his group was excluding a lot of good people. He responded, "Well, now you see how we felt when we were left out." Sam missed my point. I was not complaining about who was in power or who was left out of power. My problem was the systematic exclusion of many persons who simply wanted to remain a part of the denomination and cooperate with its programs.

As I try to sum up what the controversy is all about, several things come to mind. The problem for me personally is not one of control. I have had my share of that somewhat over-rated commodity. The difficulty about controlling something big and important is that the responsibility

---

[1]*The Baptist Identity: Four Fragile Freedoms,* 5.

always comes back to your desk. The nights are long and dark, and the days are hectic and sometimes frenetic.

The controversy is not about power. When one exercises power and is responsible to a democratic organization, one is likely to discover a wide variety of opinions as to how it should be exercised. Evil creeps out of the darkness urging special privilege for some and less for others. If power corrupts, and it tends to do so, then for a Baptist to exercise it, extra special care is essential lest spiritual corruption become the order of the day.

To hold power over many of the Lord's servants is a fearful and dangerous matter. One in power is apt to hear only a part of the problem—sometimes a small part—but must make decisions affecting the career of someone God called. No matter how "small" the position, the responsibility is for a human being who has aspirations, hopes, dreams, family, and a livelihood to provide. When power must be exercised concerning persons, the burden is greater than the glory.

Power enables the directing of the Lord's work. It can be used for good and God, or it can be abused for personal advantage and gain. One may feel good about his name getting in the newspaper and having leadership attributed to him, but if he is sensitive to his call and his God, power rests heavily on his conscience.

The conflict for me is certainly not about prestige. Present day leadership will discover soon, as my generation did, that the words of the unknown "poet" are true:

> Fame is a fleeting fitful flame
> That shines awhile on John Jones' name,
> And then puts John right on the spot;
> The flame shines on, but John does not!

The fifteen minutes of fame, now so well-articulated, is soon spent; and the currency thought so precious, even as Jesus said, turns to dust.

This conflict is not for me a problem of orthodoxy. I do not feel that anyone has dug up much heresy. For me, this has been a struggle of conscience—the issue of right and wrong. It is about a terrifying decision to alienate hosts of friends and create a host of enemies. It is about the decimation of many of the faith's most effective institutions. It is battle about acting with integrity and honor. It is about the critical wounding of the integrity of our witness to a lost world. We could not have done anything that would damage it as badly as what we have done. Instead of "behold how they love one another" it is "if they can't get along among their 'born again' kind, we want no part of it."

I am and have been a Bible-believing, old-time Southern Baptist. I am and will be a member of a Southern Baptist Church, although I know that the denomination I knew, served, and loved will be no more. The church remains the bride of Christ. Thousands of churches continue to do his work. After all, this is where the work has always been done. Whatever hope there is for the fading new denomination will be found in the integrity and vitality of the churches.

Make no mistake. God is not dead, and God's work will certainly go on. The tragedy to me is that the denomination seems to be diverging from divine purposes; and if it is, it will be bypassed for more cooperative and useful people. At the moment of highest privilege and greatest potential, Southern Baptists chose the ways of triviality. After the sleepless nights, alienation, abuse, rejection, and years of pain and sorrow: "Here I stand; God help me, I can do no other."

Index